THE LIMINAL LANDS

THE
LIMINAL
LANDS

*One Woman's Journey
in Search of Soul*

Robyn Sheldon

SOPHIA

ISBN: 978-1-9160033-0-9

First published 2018

Printed and bound in the EU

Front cover image from a painting by Peter Van Straten.
Cover design: Anne Hoefinghoff.
Interior illustrations: the author.

About the author

Robyn Sheldon is an artist, midwife, mother and Soul Integration facilitator who helps individuals to connect to their innermost resources. She has more than twenty-five years of in-depth experience in meditation practice which provides the inspiration for her writing and illustrations.

Her Soul Integration work includes connecting parents to the consciousness of their unborn babies. This is captured in her book, *The Mama Bamba Way*, in which she describes her approach to creating sacred and meaningful births to thousands of parents across the world.

DEDICATION

In honour of the soul-knowing that runs through us all as
a constant source of inspiration and surprise.

To get out of this unending cycle, we must allow ourselves to be drawn into sacred space, into liminality. All transformation takes place here. We must allow ourselves to be drawn out of 'business as usual' and remain patiently on the 'threshold' (limen, in Latin) where we are betwixt and between the familiar and the completely unknown. There alone is our old world left behind, while we are not yet sure of the new existence. That is a good space where genuine newness can begin. Get there often and stay as long as you can by whatever means possible. It's the realm where God can best get at us because our false certitudes are finally out of the way. This is the sacred space where the old world is able to fall apart, and a bigger world is revealed. If we don't encounter liminal space in our lives, we start idealizing normalcy. The threshold is God's waiting room. Here we are taught openness and patience as we come to expect an appointment with the divine Doctor.

RICHARD ROHR
Author and Theologian

CONTENTS

FOREWORD

by BABA MANDAZA KANDEMWA

The world over needs lasting and binding Peace.
Our world is praying for Peace.
What is missing in the human world is Love and Peace within ourselves.
Peace is within ourselves, so is War.

Reading through this book, the reader will discover that there are many ways of bringing Peace, Love and Compassion. The author has been, for a long time, guided by Spirits, and directed to write a healing story based on her personal experiences through her spiritual journey.

This story can also help you overcome your fears.

Read it, for your own healing.

Baba Mandaza Kandemwa
International Peacemaker
Svikiro: carrier of many earth and water spirits
Mhondoro: one who is in constant prayer on behalf of others

.

FOREWORD

by KITTISARO & THANISSARA

This is a truly unique and exceptional book. It offers guidance and companionship for those weaving mysticism into the earthy challenges of everyday life. Robyn's personal journey through the terrain of her home countries of Botswana and South Africa is captivating, while at the same time introducing us to a range of awakening experiences and spiritual trainings. Through her own initiation as a medium, Robyn reveals the age-old, yet often lost, art of direct communication with Spirit Beings. All of this is grounded in a very real life of being a wife, mother of three sons, exceptional midwife, trainer of doulas, author and courageous heart in the face of numerous challenges. This is a nourishing read for the soul, awakening each of us into new possibilities, some perhaps never imagined possible until shown through the transmission of this book.

Kittisaro & Thanissara
Dharmagiri Sacred Mountain Retreat, KwaZulu Natal.
Authors of *Listening to the Heart, A Contemplative Guide to Engaged Buddhism*

PROLOGUE

Let the words in this book emerge out of the tips of your fingers, just as buds unfurl from the bough tips of the apple tree. Yield to them seeping through you as your journey unfolds. The tree does not question the sunshine flowing through her dappled leaves, nor the sap from Mother Earth rising from her sturdy roots. Quietly, surely, Spring follows Winter, and apple blossoms follow buds.—Melchizedek

This book is my story of the journey that Melchizedek and Mother Mary took me on. It is the story of Becoming Real.

In an elitist, cold-blooded boarding school in the early nineteen-seventies, I was a shy, goody-goody teenager who wasn't allowed to wear make-up. I didn't know any sexy, rebellious surfing boys, and I didn't care to know any wealthy, groomed-for-daddy's-business pretentious boys. I wasn't an academic. I was on the B-team for sports. I wasn't funny, warm, or confident. It was not a good fit.

I lived on a farm, which was both my sanity and my downfall. None of the farm girls were particularly popular, but because I was shy, I was also invisible, so invisible that perhaps I was the only one who noticed it. While hanging around at the periphery of groups of giggling girls, listening to their stories about parties and music and make-up, part of me longed to be like them. I recognised that I could never really belong in their world and possibly I didn't want to; nevertheless, I didn't want their rejection either—I wanted to be popular and admired. Yet the 1950s Peter Pan collars my mother added to my homemade dresses in the early 1970s and my one-piece bathing-suit tan—when everybody else had bikini tans—conspired against me. At home, I doused my tummy under my swim suit in cooking oil and lay broiling for hours in the sun, in the hope that I would tan through it, but despite the sunstroke and high fever that ensued, my tummy remained embarrassingly white. I pretended to know all the latest hits on Springbok radio's Top Ten every Saturday afternoon, but in actuality I was a pop music dunce and owned only one album, bought not because I liked the music, but because I thought Shawn Phillips looked both suave and spiritual with his long hair and black cape on the album cover. I searched my dictionary for 'hore' or 'hoar' or 'hor' to find out what it meant, but my search came to nothing. Since everyone else clearly knew what this slightly illicit word meant, I smiled knowingly and vaguely when they mentioned it.

My tummy was constantly constricted with low-grade anxiety at being exposed for a fraud, and it read every nuance in the atmosphere.

Back home on the farm over the school holidays, my horse had a foal. I had watched her conception. I was present for her birth. I watched her umbilical cord dry up and drop off and her spindly legs grow stronger. Her name was Zhoma.

Zhoma belonged to the raw, primal power of Africa. Her name meant *Bushman harp* in the Nharo language of the San hunter-gatherers living in the Kalahari Desert of Botswana. I must have known in my bones that one day I would be living among Nharo people when I named her, but I found the name in a small booklet of San poetry that belonged to Mum. Zhoma was as African as the people who created the soul-stirring music of her namesake harp. She was descended from Egyptian ancestry, her genetic inheritance coming straight off the windblown expanse of the Sahara. The haunting sound of her bushman harp was a Siren call wafting between our worlds and calling us close. My filly was slate grey, dish-faced, with a floating, sensitive gait. She was not familiar with humans, wary of me, skittish. I admired the way she mouthed grass gently to taste the flavour before cropping it. Even while grazing, she was constantly alert, ears twitching, and in a split second she could leap away from harm before becoming ensnared. Her beauty was in her wild, capricious nature, so attuned to the earth she tapped with her delicate hooves, so aware of me watching her. When I was home, I would watch her for days, weeks, and months. I watched her change from a slip of

a filly, discarding her silky grey skin as she became a yearling, and then grow into the pure white, rump-round musculature of her full feminine power. I watched her as the wind ruffled her mane and tousled my hair, as the sun burned my skin and dried my cheeks out. And as the cold seeped through my tailbone into my hips because the ground was frost-covered, still I watched.

If I captured her, she would lose the wildness I yearned for, the wildness that was the opposite of being cooped up in boarding school. So I watched and waited through the seasons until she trusted me as much as she trusted her mother. I lingered close to the edge of sleep to draw her in, with drowsy half-closed eyes, waiting for her warm smell and the subtle sounds of twigs cracking to sense her approach. If I opened my eyes in the early days, she fled.

She snorted at me, and I huffed back gently. She retreated; I waited. I sat on grassy hummocks and chewed blades of grass, listening to the doves and the piet-my-vrous cooing in the trees. Over time she got used to the smell of me, nudged me, sniffed me all over, and I gently bent my forehead towards hers, dipped my head slightly and rubbed my cheek along her muzzle. More time passed, and eventually my face was buried in her neck, inhaling the warm, grassy smell of her and her love of life. When she allowed me to mount her without a bridle, saddle, or halter, I did so from this same sleepy place of lying half over her, my leg gradually sliding over her bareback. It was a gentle act of sensuality, more like lovemaking than domination or ownership. But she was quivering, highly strung, and snorted in fear before remembering that she trusted me. Every now and again in the weeks that followed, I would be sitting on her back in the field as she grazed, and she would leap off in wild fright. Except for the fact that my perineum and thighs had melted into her, each time it felt like she would throw me. Instead, her energy flowed through mine; my body felt her intention; it knew before she shied or bucked or twisted direction where she would move next. We were as resonant as the murmuration of a flock of swallows coordinating their twirling high in the sky. And in her galloping, as she recognized the synchrony, her snorting, white-eyed fear would relax; she'd slow down to a trot and then pause, lowering her head and continuing to graze as if she had always been part of me.

We fell unhindered into the natural flow of life.

And then I returned to boarding school and to what was supposed to be the real world where my teenage awkwardness and my environment were misaligned, leaving me anxiously out of place but without the emotional skills to either recognise or voice this. After my final year, I cut my ties to school. Four years ago, at age 56, I was coaxed back to a forty-year reunion with my classmates. They all seemed to remember their school years, and one another, myself included, very fondly, and I felt like a traitor for having possibly fabricated my history. Memory is like that. I hope they were right.

I do remember very clearly, though, that it was Zhoma who first taught me the art of attunement. I didn't know it as a gawky adolescent, but she was my introduction to resonating with Mother Mary, Melchizedek, and the Universal life force that connects us all. I only met Mother Mary and Melchizedek after I had moved to Botswana, given birth to three kids, and Zhoma had long since died. But in them, I recognised the same connection I had had with Zhoma. I needed to watch and wait until I fell into their resonance with synchronized breathing and a delicate aligning of my senses to theirs, which led me to a deeper, more trustworthy truth.

EARLY DAYS

I had precious little awareness of the Mystery in the first half of my life. The monstrous snakes of my fears were my only experience of fantastical worlds as a young child because my life was unremarkable and mundane. As with so many children, I was a bundle of unmanageable feelings which I had to learn to push down because they were unacceptable out in the adult world, and I desperately wanted to be accepted. I unwittingly buried other dimensional realms alongside my unacceptable emotions, so while I longed to see fairies like in the fairy tales, I could only pretend that I did. I think my five-year-old friends, Jean and Shelagh, also pretended that they did, although, for all I know, they may have been telling the truth. I told my toddler brother about the pale blue and white shimmering fairy, tiny and dancing about us in the paddling pool, but I was uneasy in case he could actually see it, when I most definitely could not.

Some people are clairvoyant and fully immersed in the ethereal realms from birth or early childhood. They are the healers who always felt different, who denied their gift during adolescence, and who went through a spiritual crisis of some sort in their twenties or thirties, to regain it. They seemed like special people, and they were not me.

As a child, I buried the land of fairies and imagination in places deeper than my waking world could reach, and only the snakes escaped into my night-time world where they lived under my bed. They were terrifying creatures, at least as wide as me, with gaping mouths and black eyes. They didn't bite, but they could swallow me whole. There were at least three of them, and I couldn't get out of bed at night in case they devoured me. I called out to wake my parents, sometimes thirteen times a night, to come and tuck me in and tell me about 'nice things'. My dad was especially patient with my night terrors. Only once in my life did my exhausted parents take me into their bed at about 4.30 in the morning. It was blissfully safe; I wanted to live there forever.

Besides the serpents, I was ten years old before I had my first remembered experience of the mysterious world. Dad had left me sitting in the back of the wide, cream-coloured Holden station wagon with red seats as he strode into the All Saints Anglican church in Somerset West to find Reverend Johnson. He wasn't angry; he strode or bounded everywhere. Dad wasn't a churchgoer either; he had gone to pick up some architectural drawings for Mum, who was doing some renovations for Reverend Johnson's home. But he was taking a long time. I was hot and bored, and my mind was rerunning disagreeable thoughts about Reverend Johnson's son Andrew, who was in my class at school. Andrew was good-looking in a clean, shiny-black-hair-slicked-to-one-side, red-lipped kind of way, his school shirts neatly tucked into his shorts. He liked me, and it was my duty, therefore, to ignore him and be mean to him sometimes. Boys, unless they appreciated me for being a tomboy, were humiliating creatures who carried huge potential to embarrass me. I hoped he didn't come outside when Dad came back.

The car was parked next to the church's great beige face-brick steeple tower. There was a large, untidy, flowering apple tree arching over the car, which was parked half in the shade, half in the sun. The masses of apple blossoms caught the light.

The next moment something unexpected happened which felt to me as ordinary as the sweaty red seat of the car. An apple blossom made contact with me. If the silent communication had words, they would have gone something like this:

Apple Blossom: Hi.

The apple blossom was gorgeous, silky, radiant.

Me: Huh! Wow, you're beautiful!

It was the first time I had consciously noticed beauty, the first time I had really noticed it, in an awe-inducing, breath-catching, eye-blinking way.

AB: I am God

These ideas had seeped into it from the church steeple.

Me: No, you're not, that's ridiculous! You're an apple blossom.

AB: And I'm you.

Me: I'm me. You're an apple blossom.

Silence.

Me: You're beautiful.

Silence.

The apple blossom hummed wafts of apple blossom beauty into my heart.

Dad came back with the drawings tucked under his arm and drove apple-blossom-me back home.

High school, as I've mentioned, was a fraught affair. I was painfully shy, skinny, with no waist and no breasts, and at fifteen and a half, I was the last in the class to menstruate. I didn't know any boys, because for some reason my brother's friends didn't count. The years of ignoring Andrew Johnson were long past. When I did meet real boys, I was dumbstruck with stupid, hazy terror. Instead of being witty and pretty, wearing miniskirts and make-up, my parents sent me to parties wearing white socks and Alice bands. Apart from being good at art, I generally considered myself wholly inadequate. I had Zhoma back home, but when I was at school, she was so far away as to hardly count. Mystical life was nothing more than a dream of escaping my adolescent traumas by entering a convent like Julie Andrews and becoming beautiful and spiritual in a wimple.

When I was in my final year of school, my class walked from the art room, in a crocodile, to view a visiting Henry Moore sculpture exhibition at the National Gallery in the Company Gardens in Cape Town. 'Crocodile' meant that you lined up two by two, wearing school hats and blazers (pale blue dresses no more than two inches above the knees when kneeling), and walked in a long line from school to the cathedral, or from school to the museum or the planetarium, looking more like a pale blue songololo or millipede than a crocodile.

The curator of the museum told us that we couldn't fully comprehend Henry Moore by simply looking at the sculptures; we needed to touch them with our eyes closed. She wore red lipstick and a svelte French hairstyle and with this instruction, just as Mother Mary changed my direction twenty years later, she altered the direction of my young life for the next short while at least, from horse vet to sculptor, quick as a blink.

Closing my eyes disconnected me from What Other People Thought of Me. The smooth, cool stone beneath my fingers entranced me, and the rough texture of the granite pieces felt ancient and wise. Time slowed down into a blind fumbling with something Godlike in the beauty of the moment. I became the stone in the way that the apple blossom had become me, in the way that Zhoma and I had become one being. We returned to school, and I, who had remained dry-eyed through the trauma of my humiliating party gear and my total inability to talk to boys, locked myself in the toilet and cried. I decided to study art at university because one day I wanted to be Henry Moore.

11

GROWING UP IN APARTHEID SOUTH AFRICA

Are you brave enough to come into the light? Where your illusions shatter, where your masks crack off, where the petrified wood in your heart of darkness bleeds its sorrows out of your wounded self, where you are soft and pure and filled with joy, where you become strong and flexible inside, that you may bear the power of God in your core?
—Melchizedek

I experienced a childhood of privilege and grace, yet there were still a lot of masks to crack off, and a lot of petrified, inherited, ancestral wood hidden away in my darkest heart. My father was the manager of an apple farm. The father of my best friend Jean, Uncle Bernard, was the other manager. Uncle Bernard managed the business side of things, while my dad grew the apples, and Uncle George and Auntie Kay did the admin. Auntie Kay took care of lots of scraps of paper while Uncle George gazed through bifocals at large ledgers where he wrote long columns of tidy figures in pencil. They were all white, as were Charles, who ran the farm shop, and Uncle Daan, the mechanic, who fixed the tractors, the lorries, and the farm vehicles. Apartheid[1] was blooming more healthily than the apple blossoms, so on the next tier down were the coloured folk, who worked in the pack-sheds and cold-stores and drove the tractors. They lived with their families in cottages near the stables, and the farm school catered for the coloured kids. And then one rank lower in terms of privilege and pay-slips were the black men. They lived in dormitories and were migrant labourers from the Transkei. They came in buses for the fruit-picking seasons and then were bussed back home to their families at the end of the pruning season. We never gave much thought to the inequalities as kids; it was simply the way things were.

Despite my mum and dad highly disapproving of apartheid, it was still the order of things. I had always thought it was only the Afrikaans-speaking people, who voted for the Nationalist Party, who were racist;

---

1   Apartheid was a system of institutionalized racial segregation and discrimination that existed in South Africa between 1948 and 1991. It was based on white supremacy and the repression of the black (African, Coloured and Indian) majority of the population for the benefit of the whites.

cultural conditionings are much easier to recognise in other cultures than in one's own. A discreet form of racism grew and bloomed in my blood the way apartheid bloomed in the country. It manifested itself by not listening to the stories of people on the other side of the racial divide. Like undiagnosed cancer, I never even knew it was there. In any case, I was more interested in animals than in people, white, black, or coloured, in those days.

Besides the apples, peaches, and pears, we had cows and horses and sheep until my dad sold the sheep because he said all they ever did was cluster in circles discussing new ways to die. My brothers and I all went to boarding school quite young because we lived so far away from the whites-only schools. We were stoical about it though. We were stoical as a family. We had Presbyterian blood flowing through our once-up-on-a-time Scottish veins, and it was stoical blood. As kids, we were taught not to cry or whinge (well, frankly my mother failed dismally at teaching me not to whinge, but she certainly inflicted a good deal of irritation on me while trying) or get angry or speak badly of others or be bored—boredom was not allowed in our house. We had a strict code of values (blindly excluding racial equality), and we were expected to behave ourselves. My older brother, Ian, got A's at school and studied medicine and anaesthetics at University. My younger brother, Ken, lagged behind Ian at school and only married in his early forties, but he was just a slow starter; these days he has a PhD and a professorship in oceans economy, which I think is all about protecting the oceans from the megalo-corporate rape machine. I sort of dawdled along with my head in the clouds, and with the exception of Art and English, obtained D's and C's at school.

Outwardly, despite the racial inequities and boarding school, everything in my South African upbringing was seemingly buoyant—playing happy families in the fresh farm air of the Vyeboom Mountains, playing *skop-die-blik*[2] and giddy-yup with my dad on the lawn when he got home from farming each day. Dad would wake me at 5.30 every morning until I eventually left home. He would go to work, and I would muck out the stables, groom the horses and ride them. It was a beautiful time of day when my head was always at its clearest, and my heart was wide open. All our skeletons, ancestral, colonial, and individual, were packed

2   'Kick the can.'

away very neatly, thank you. But years later, after Mother Mary and Melchizedek arrived in my life, they too tumbled out onto the carpet. Blood and bones became exposed. Unbeknown to me in my youth, my body carried the epigenetic memory of my mother arriving home, age 19, after playing tennis in the heat of a Johannesburg summer, to find her father in a semi-coma, half drunk, half dead, in the back of their Buick, with the exhaust gas pumping heavy carbon monoxide fumes into stale, alcohol-sodden air. She dragged him upstairs and put him to bed. Alone in the house, she didn't know what to do next. She took a shower to wash the tennis sweat and alcoholic exhaust fumes off her body. When she emerged, dripping wet, naked, she found he had dragged himself back downstairs into the car and finished himself off. I grew from embryo through foetus to tiny baby in the unprocessed memories of her dead father in the back of the Buick seeping into her amniotic fluid. I did not notice my spine forming itself around that memory and encasing itself in carbon-monoxide-flavoured cerebrospinal fluid. I did not know that my menstrual blood gushed the memory out of me, in month after month of menstrual grief. Nor that my breasts leaked it into the mouths of my hungry babes. But we were not spared. I was not separate.

Mum was a perfect person. Perfectionism is a hard act, but she played it well—almost to perfection. She was nice too, and generally kind to people, although I could irritate the hell out of her in my late teens, and often her jaw would tighten even when I walked into a room. I was ridiculously forgetful, I lost all my possessions, I never remembered to do my homework, I dreamed about a different life elsewhere while stepping heedlessly on other people's feelings. I was a bog-standard teenager without the skill to rebel against my upbringing, so I simply breathed dissatisfaction out of my pores.

Mum's perfection extended beyond being a highly intelligent architect, ceramicist, horse-woman, and farmer's wife. She was also thoughtful to neighbours and her friends. Her anger was deeply buried along with her unresolved grief about her dad, and it was mostly directed towards herself or, in muffled undertones, towards me. I never once heard Mum and Dad fight, so as a child, I assumed they didn't. But I suppose they occasionally produced needle-like wisps of resentment and bitterness that whispered through their dark bedroom air, looking for entry into impenetrable hearts almost impervious to hurt. Mum almost never cried. The first time I ever saw her cry, I was 18 and sitting on her bed while she was at her sewing machine, mending a seam on a dress that I had sewed incorrectly. Her jaw was clamped in irritation at my late adolescent self-absorption.

My dress seam was proving difficult to repair. "God damn it,' she frowned and set her shoulders.

I was weeping silently on the bed, feeling sorry for myself because it felt like I never got approval for anything. 'Didn't you ever irritate your mother when you were my age?' I sniffled. She was silent. I looked at her and watched in amazement as the most unexpected tears flowed silently down her cheeks. In some very simple way, I had broken through and touched her heart. It stretched back out and touched mine, whisper-soft. Her tears flowed between us and bound us in a sisterhood that lasted until her death less than ten years later.

That first year, my first year of University, where I was studying to become Henry Moore, I met Charlie, and instantly became fickle and distracted from that larger purpose, so that instead of changing lives by creating awe-inspiring sculptures, I ended up, five years later, marrying him and moving to a cattle farm in Botswana. Charlie had warm, brown eyes that were on a constant search for mischief. With my background of being proper, I was immediately drawn to the part of him that was able to flaunt social conventions in a carefree manner. He played the piano beautifully, mostly in the popular student pub called 'The Pig and Whistle', where people would buy him drinks. Initially, he was everything my mother disapproved of. He drank too much—and that triggered very deep fear for her; he seldom attended lectures, and he was not concerned what other people thought of him. But he was also warm and he loved me, and because he loved people generally, and cared about them, he was almost always forgiven and loved in return, even when his behaviour was particularly outrageous. The vast majority of people on campus knew Charlie, from the professors who mostly thought him an irresponsible reprobate, to the students who were inspired by the amount of fun he could generate, to the cleaning women at the University who described him as an 'emotion', to the political activists who considered him a go-to place to unwind from their dangerous lives, to the traffic wardens who, instead of giving him traffic fines for always parking his beach buggy in illegal places, took him to their homes for supper.

At the same time as I was not becoming Henry Moore and was having the best amount of fun that I could pack into my slightly unproductive days, the Universe gave me a little blessing that would serve me well later in my life. Although I studied art, my minor was comparative religion because somebody had told me it was the easiest course to pass without studying. It was one of those life gifts that landed in my lap seemingly by coincidence, and I loved it best of all my classes. The mystical aspects of different religions enthralled me, especially how similar they were in all the various traditions, from indigenous tribal cultures to God-worshipping Christians to Islamic mystics. I didn't give the course the attention it deserved, since I was too distracted by late nights, hangovers, and making up for all those years cloistered away in boarding school, but I was delighted by some of my lecturers' ideas. I remember one of them describing how we were each like a wave in the ocean that rose up as a distinct form for its lifetime, and then dissolved back into the sea to which it belonged, after it had run its course. I found the idea utterly satisfying, and a part of me recognised that this was a world where I felt completely at home. Then I turned my attention back to day-to-day concerns, minimal effort towards graduation and eventually towards marrying Charlie and starting a new life in Botswana.

We married on the lawn at home, a perfect white wedding, and then packed our ten-ton cattle truck with all my stuff; including quarry tiles for the floors of our cottage on the farm in the Kalahari, an old second-hand piano I had bought Charlie as a wedding present, a small, antique yellowwood dining table which was a wedding present from my parents, Zhoma, who was tied up on the back of the truck, and Tank, my long-haired city cat, who sat up front with us in the cab.

For the second time in my life, Mum began to cry as we left, gulping sobs that she was trying very hard to suppress. We drove away, but they cut into my heart so deeply that I wept for two solid days of the four it took us to drive to our new life that was less than perfect but filled with Botswana heat and the warmth of a whole lot of love.

Growing up on a farm in the Western Cape had meant that the wounds of apartheid, along with my grandfather's sorrow, and my mother's unexpressed grief, were hidden; they had been easy to dilute in the vast expanse of clear air that filled the valley, then flowed over the snow-capped mountains and beyond. Those sorrows were absorbed and

16

transmuted in Zhoma's thick winter coat that smelled of belonging. But the hefty, unrecognised guilt of apartheid became glaringly obvious when it dropped like rocks off my shoulders as Charlie and I drove through the border and out of South Africa.

LIFE WITH CHARLIE

After Charlie and I drove truck through the creaky, iron gate of Ghanzi Ranching Company, our farm in the Kalahari semi-desert, I settled into the wildness of the Botswana bush, with its freedom from the pressures of apartheid, and its massive, wide-open skies, where the stars were undiminished by smog, light pollution, humidity, or low altitude. These stars woke up an ancient longing to be as free and expansive as the Universe. We often slept out in the bush, with the sounds of jackals, owls, and nightjars, or if we were driving down South, in the central Kalahari, where we built a great fire next to our bedroll, to keep lions at bay. My heart would fill to bursting with the smell of wood smoke, the crisp, winter air that dropped below freezing at night, the sounds of lions growling in the distance, the enormous sky above me while I curled up next to Charlie under a great pile of blankets.

As long as the truck didn't break down—a frequent occurrence on those roads—it would take us two days to drive the 750 kilometres down south to the town of Lobatse, or beyond that, to the city of Gaborone. The tar road had yet to be built up the western side of the country, and in long sections, the ruts in the desert sand were more than forty centimetres deep on the Kalahari roads. Everybody drove trucks, mostly Ford 250's or J5 Bedfords because their spoor size fitted best into the sandy tracks. We carried our own diesel and water in great 200-litre drums, with enough food in case of breakdowns.

Charlie had moved to the farm two years before me, and we lived there together for a further three years before relocating closer to Gaborone. Once a year we would choose between trucking or trekking a large herd of cattle to the abattoir in Lobatse. It took thirty-eight days to walk approximately 400 head of cattle from our farm to the abattoir. If we hired trucks to transport the cattle, it took two to three days but was very expensive. There were big *boma* or wooden kraals to pen the cattle at watering points on the trek each night, which had been built by the many farmers who walked their cattle to Lobatse each year. But each night of the trek, we would still have to build big fires to keep the lions and hyenas at bay.

Farm staff on horses or on foot would herd the cattle during the day. The cattle walked at a grazing pace for approximately twenty kilometres a day, with the occasional day off, and we followed in a Ford 250 with supplies.

It all sounds idyllic when I think back to those times. I forget how busy my mind was back then, even in the midst of the unhurried, ambling cattle, with their slow, infrequent moos, the laughter of the San cattle herders, and the *tong, tong, tong* of the cattle bells in the clean desert air. I brought my university mind along with me on those treks; it was forever analysing, planning and judging everything—although mostly it focused on judging myself—as good or bad. No matter the beauty of the moment, I seldom escaped my busy mind. I didn't know that my external reality was coloured by the way I viewed it. I didn't know that I needed to embrace both my little self and the larger self that was beyond me, to be whole. All that would come later. I simply remember that sometimes I would be sitting under those extraordinary desert stars, loved by my husband, pregnant with my first baby, wishing fervently that I was more alluring, or more amusing, or more loved and admired and respected by the world at large.

During my pregnancy with Rory, we bought a small, four-seater Piper Cherokee aircraft. We had discovered that it was cheaper to fly than to drive trucks through the thick, desert sand. Charlie loved flying, and the plane quickly became our primary mode of transport. At Easter time, when Rory was five months old, we flew into the Central Kalahari National Park to visit our friends, Doug and Jane, who were doing research on wild dogs in Deception Valley, which was in fact only a slight depression in the flat Botswana landscape. We hadn't managed to alert Doug and Jane of our plans on our two-way radio, and when we arrived at their camp, we discovered that they had flown to Maun to get supplies and see friends over the long weekend. It was too late to fly home, as our dirt landing strip did not have night-lights, so we spent the night in their tent.

Early the next morning, Charlie, and I, with Rory strapped to my tummy, went for a walk. We wandered among herds of grazing impalas, wildebeest, eland, and zebra, all seemingly unconcerned by our presence.

Turning homeward, behind the camp in the far distance we noticed a lion and two lionesses; all three were watching us intently. Despite the other game, and even though they were beyond the tented camp, they focused on us as if we were prey or playthings. The lion padded forward from the rise and headed down into the depression to cut us off. The lionesses broke away and disappeared behind the ridge. We could no longer see them but could feel their intention to ambush us from behind and drive us towards the lion. The hair stood up on the back of my neck.

Fumbling, I untied Rory from my belly as we began jogging back towards the tents. Charlie grabbed him from me, flew out of his slip-slops, and sprinted off. I followed as fast as my legs could pump through the Kalahari sand. I could see the lion lolloping along ahead of me. He was moving languidly across our path, still beyond the tented camp. His gaze was unwavering. His lollop was faster than my sprint. As we got closer to the tents, he was screened off behind the Kalahari scrub. It was almost more frightening not knowing where he was.

Charlie bundled Rory into the tent, grabbed a spade and came hurtling back to save me from the lions. I was still about a hundred metres from the tents. "I don't care if they fucking kill me,' I wheezed through lungs that ached for the whole of the following week from the overexertion.

We decided to spend the remainder of our Easter break back at our cattle farm, where there were jackals and occasionally a leopard, but no lions.

On the way home, high in the impossibly blue autumn sky, I was washed through by wave after wave of gratitude for my precious baby and his dad. We were alive. Life was priceless. The lions had brought it all into the sharpest focus.

Arriving home, we taxied the plane down the landing strip to park under the shade-cloth hangar that adjoined our cottage, where we could hop out of the plane as if it were a car in a lean-to next to a suburban house.

The farm staff ran out to meet us. 'Come and look, quick, quick,' they clicked, in an excited mixture of Bushman Nharo and Afrikaans. In our garden of desert sand, all the way around our house, were lion's footprints. At the same time as the lions were stalking us as possible prey in Deception Valley, another lion was padding around our home.

The Fates had dropped by in lion guise. Twice, to make sure we noticed. It was as though the lion footprints padded up my spine and knocked gently at the base of my neck saying, 'Let us in, let us in; we are the shamans of your interior world.'

A DEATH AND A BIRTH

Big moments, like the birth of Rory, or the encounter with the lions, were often moments of intensity that woke me up. Even the intensity of pain or tragedy could create this sense of alert wakefulness in me. I had never, for example, seen a sky as blue as the one on the grief-filled morning that I heard of my mother's unexpected death. Mum died of asthma at 51, when I was pregnant with Maf, my second child. It was a huge shock. After my difficult teenage relationship with her, and despite living far apart, I relied heavily on her for advice and female friendship via weekly letters, and then weekly phone calls after we had moved from the farm, via a year in Gaborone, the capital of Botswana, to settle on a small holding outside the city.

I stayed with Dad for a month after Mum died and then gave birth to Maf at a hospital in Cape Town. Early the next morning, lying in bed in the hospital, I heard the public phone ringing down the hall. I padded barefoot down the grey, linoleum-lined corridor, smelling of hospital disinfectant, to the phone at the far end. The early morning sun was streaming in through the window. I lifted the handset, the ringing stopped, and I heard Mum on the other end of the line. 'Hello, Robby.'

'Hi, Mum.'

'Is he lovely?' she asked, her voice warm and happy.

'Yes, he's beautiful,' I told her.

'That's all I wanted to know.' I put the phone gently back on the hook and woke up in bed again.

I had always expected that it would be Dad who died first, but he soldiered through life with remarkable tenacity. I hero-worshipped my dad as a young teenager. He was a strong, silent farmer. I thought he looked and behaved like Clint Eastwood in *The Good, The Bad, and the Ugly*. He even had the same bandy legs. When I was 15, he developed emphysema. The lugubrious pulmonary specialist warned us that we should start to say our goodbyes, as he gloomily predicted that Dad wouldn't make it through the winter. Instead, Dad took to running five kilometres on the farm every day to cough up enough emphysema phlegm to make a slip-n-slide of his running route. He lived another forty years, through a heart attack, a stroke, prostate cancer, and osteoporosis from all the cortisone the doctors had prescribed for him. He remarried a wonderful woman named Bob, remaining strong and silent for most of the rest of his life, and then his gruffness thawed in his final years. Observing him soften and accept help from others melted something in my own heart.

Whether caused by tragedy, synchronicity, or by prodding from the Liminal Lands or the more mystical and hidden aspects of my existence, those moments of an undiluted experience of being alive were points in my life when the fogginess of my daily humdrum existence cleared. The sensation was one of being relaxed and simultaneously alert, of breathing deeply and appreciating each sensation in my body with gratitude and a smile of welcome. Every time I found my way back to this true home within me, I experienced a sense of awe and wonder at the miracle of being alive, and I was determined to remain there. It felt like where I belonged. Yet it was remarkable how often I forgot this pledge to myself. I spent much of my life setting it up for a better time at some later date. It went like this: I would lie in bed thinking about getting up because I wanted to brush the night fuzz off my teeth. I would brush my teeth while thinking about meditation and about how little time I had before I needed to leave home. I would be meditating while thinking about my day at work. I would be working so that I could be appreciated or pay the rent or make a difference in the world. Then my task became one of returning, without beating myself up, to the spacious centre that allowed me to be imperfect, that allowed Mum to die, and that allowed me to breathe more deeply and surrender into life.

MEDITATION

I first attempted meditation at age 26. I sat cross-legged in a quiet corner of my garden between the sand and the weeds and the aloes, under a small under-watered syringa tree, staring at a white wall that had brown

21

smudges of dirt on it. I felt self-conscious and wondered what Rose, our housekeeper in colonial Botswana, thought of me. But I didn't discuss it with her because I was embarrassed, and besides I lost interest in the wall quickly. It was a passing phase where I was more interested in being a meditator than in the actual meditation. I was also interested in the fruits of meditation, which I imagined as the ability to be undisturbed by the challenges of life, someone who exuded an air of peacefulness and joy. I was unaware that the best approach to meditation was to first sprout the seeds, then grow the plants, then produce the blossoms, get used to the flies, and wait while the fruit slowly, very, very slowly, ripened.

After those first unsuccessful attempts, we moved house to a small-holding in Mokolodi where I had more space to find a quiet, undisturbed spot to pursue meditation. It got off to a rocky start, though, because I was still focused on parenting, running a craft centre and partying a lot. It left little time for enlightenment. However, my old lecturer's metaphor of the wave being part of the sea kept prodding at me for deeper investigation. I eventually returned to meditation and found that it filled a deep longing.

I bought a Zen meditation instruction book called *Hara*. It described a technique of focusing your attention on your belly, two finger-breadths beneath your belly button. This area of the body is called the *tan tien* in China or *hara* in Japan. It is the centre that martial artists focus on when they are breaking bricks in half or subjugating opponents with a glance. It was supposedly grounding and strengthening to place your focus there in meditation.

I walked up to the little dam on the smallholding each morning after my two older boys had gone to school and Nix, my toddler, was having his early morning sleep. Rose pattered around the house, making beds and sweeping up dust and dog hairs, with half an ear open for him in case he woke up. I sat for twenty minutes a day under a paperbark acacia tree after first brushing away the thorns that lay beneath its branches. I read that in the Zen tradition you were supposed to keep your eyes half open when you meditated. After a few weeks of doing *hara* meditation, the technique awakened something called *kundalini*[3] energy in my belly,

---

3   *Kundalini* is a form of subtle energy (Shakti) that lies dormant in the belly. With spiritual practice, it uncoils, moves down into the genitalia and then up through

which didn't move very far before it slammed into a whole heap of stuck emotional sludge that belonged both to my own past and the past of my rather prudish ancestors, all lodged in my lower spine.

Apparently, most people accessed *kundalini* energy under the guidance of a teacher, which was a good idea. I knew none of that since I had never heard of *kundalini* or, as it is sometimes called, Shakti energy. I lived in Botswana, and to my knowledge at the time, I was at least 200 kilometres from any meditation teacher. It was also before the days of the Internet, email and instant correspondence. This was not a good thing. Because I had no idea what I was doing, fairly soon the *kundalini* was crashing through my lumbar spine, an area of my body that had spent far too long in shame-induced lockdown. Ninety percent of my life force began draining out of that area of my energy field. Which was exhausting.

However, simultaneously a very beautiful violet light built in front of my half-open eyes during the meditations. I loved the violet light; it made me feel secretly special, and so even though I walked home from the dam feeling more and more exhausted each day, I kept on with the meditation because of the violet light. Eventually, I checked in with a meditation teacher in Cape Town by sending her a letter. It took three weeks to get a reply. She advised me to stop meditating for a while. It was the worst possible advice as I then had a leaking hole in my *hara* and no violet light to replenish myself with. I spiralled downhill fast, into a grey depression of chronic fatigue that overwhelmed me and caused chaos for my family for months.

I tried to explain to the doctors that my lack of energy happened as a result of meditation. A *kundalini* snake that was coiled in my belly

the spine until it eventually reaches the crown of the head. *Kundalini* energy can move quietly and imperceptibly or with violent power that can 'blow' tightly closed circuits in the energy centres in its path. It feels either like an internal tingling sensation, or like a strong and powerful almost muscular contraction happening in the spine rather than the muscles. Actually, it feels like an orgasm that happens in the spine rather than in the genitalia. Many practitioners of *kundalini* yoga describe it as residing near the base of the spine, but in my experience, it slumbers in the *hara*, which is situated two centimetres below the navel, and is the sexual centre of the body. From there it moves downwards into the perineum, before ascending through the subtle nerve channel of the spine. *Kundalini* energy is the *prana* or life force that can be experienced as a vital power surging up the spine in waves, where it clears the energy field of old stuck debris. As it wakes each energy centre up in the body, it supposedly transforms them.

was thrashing about there and knocking repeatedly through my spine. They raised their eyebrows and gave me pills for depression that felt like they were going to kill off some deep part of my soul. I took them for a short while, but the inner urgency that that was not the trajectory I was supposed to be following was too strong, and I stopped. I do believe such pills can be lifesavers for people, and I recognize in retrospect that my symptoms must have looked very like depression. However, my exhaustion was too strongly linked to the *kundalini* work to be cured in any way that wasn't also energetic in nature. I was confused and scared and didn't know if I would remain ill forever, or whether I would ever find anyone who would understand what had happened to me.

Charlie took me on a holiday to recover. I was exhausted, but grateful for the space to lie prone on the sleeper couch on the train listening to the clickety clack, clickety clack of elderly train wheels on tired iron tracks. I was too worn out to move, too disinterested to take in the Kenyan savannah beyond the dusty windows, antelope grazing nearby, giraffes, and a herd of zebras in the distance. They all looked grey to me. I felt like I had lost my connection to myself, to Charlie who was reading a spy novel on the opposite couch, to my children who were being looked after by my parents, to the women who worked in the craft centre I ran back home in Mokolodi, who had needed way more attention than I had the capacity to give them while I was so unwell, to any kind of higher power or to the animals in the veld beyond. It took an effort to brush the hair off my face.

Charlie offered me a slice of mango, but I shook my head; food tasted like sawdust and stuck to the roof of my mouth. I didn't seem to have the will to make enough saliva to get the food past the great big rock in my throat. This rock didn't feel like unshed tears as lumps in my throat often did; everything in me felt bone dry, and there was not enough liquid in me for tears. The conductor rattled on the door with his metal key. Did we want to reserve places in the dining car for lunch? I couldn't have cared less.

We did go to lunch, though. Charlie needed to eat and get out of the carriage. In the corridor, there was a sign above the toilet that read, 'Strictly Europeans.' Kenya got her independence in 1963, and this was 1989, but strangely, nobody had thought to remove it yet. I wasn't sure who was more run-down, the train or me? At least it still had forward momentum.

I felt a bit badly for Charlie, who was taking me on this special holiday, but it was a vague awareness that I couldn't quite grasp hold of. I was more aware of the trembling in my fingertips and the gaping hole through which my energy was escaping from my belly. The hole was more of a feeling than something I could see. It was an exhaustion that seemed to start in my pelvic area, and from there it infiltrated the rest of my body and my bones, like a weary cloak of ennui, that even today I associate with a feeling of deep sadness. It was the unrecognised sadness of my ancestors, of my ultra-perfect childhood, and perhaps also an undefined sadness that arose out of unconsciously longing for Melchizedek and Mother Mary, before I even had any idea that they existed as anything more than paper-thin Biblical figures.

The exhaustion and disinterest persisted for weeks, then months, then half a year. Charlie took the kids to school, packed their lunches, fetched and carried them; I stared out the windows blankly.

Time passed in a blur of exhaustion, but six months after my first encounter with the *kundalini* snake and the beautiful violet light, my eccentric English aunt with healing hands picked me up from my parent's home where I had been sent to rest. She packed me into her rent-a-wreck Citi Golf and took me away with her to De Mond, a family-owned river cottage three hours from Cape Town, where we always slept outside, and the heavy broad-backed grunters with their big eyes flapped their fishy tails on the water late at night, disturbing the reflection of the stars. To this day, I'm still unsure how this happened, but one twenty-minute hands-on healing session filled with her unbounded enthusiasm for life was all it took for my body to heal its energy leak. I wish I could have understood what actually happened so that I would be equipped to help other people in similar circumstances. But the best I could do in my attempt to comprehend it was to rationalise that perhaps she had believed in me so wholeheartedly that she dissolved the tiredness that had held my *hara* hostage. Whatever it was, she hauled me out of a deep hole that I had fallen into, where I had no energy, no belief in myself, no sense of connection to the life-force that Zhoma had taught me about all those years ago. I had been operating with ten percent of my energy for six months, and miraculously, I was back to 100 percent vitality, just like that. It was like a light switch had been flipped on. I dismissed the months of weariness with a gentle shake. I reconnected back to my life force and emerged out of what had felt like a long, dry, dark night of the soul.

Colour came back into my everyday life. I felt the stirring of my longing for my children tearing at my heart; the moisture was starting to come back into me again; I laughed in the salty, muddy water of the estuary, which washed away not only the grey mist but also dissolved the heavy, dark lump in my throat that had extended beyond my oesophagus and felt like a dead albatross around my neck.

TEACHERS

A few months after my aunt healed me at the river cottage overlooking the estuary where the fish didn't know that their seawater brethren were being sucked into trawlers and swallowed up to feed humanity's insatiable appetite for sushi and fish-fingers, this cottage where the mudflats fed mud-prawns and waders and spoonbills and herons and kingfishers, where the swallows nested under the eaves—a few months after this time of peace and laughter and restoration, I decided to return once more to meditation, albeit with a guiding teacher this time; many teachers, in fact.

I accepted meditation teachings from whoever was willing to impart them. Over the next few years, there was the Zen teacher perfectly attired in pristine grey robes, the exceedingly tall Sri Lankan lay teacher dressed in brilliant white, the orange-robed Theravadan monk, the nun and the monk from a Thai tradition, who disrobed to get married and were expelled from their respective monasteries, the Westerner in sandals and corduroys, the Vietnamese Zen Master in brown robes, the Tibetan Geshe dressed in maroon and golden yellow, the dreadlocked Jamaican guru, and the skinny Irishman with wispy hair and an unassuming smile. If I travelled anywhere outside Botswana, either with my young family on back-packing trips to Asia or South America or on more frequent trips within Southern Africa, I first found out whether there were meditation teachers nearby. Instead of settling with one teacher, I floated from one to the other, available to whoever was visiting South Africa, whoever I could persuade to come to Gaborone in Botswana to give teachings. Although I arranged retreats in Botswana, I kept my meditation practice relatively quiet and led a separate non-meditative life out in the world at large. Back home, I read volumes of books on meditation. Dipping into and out of every tradition was not the best way to deepen my practice, but I did get to experience most of the different types of meditation techniques, and I soon realised that different techniques suited different personality types, and that not every technique was suitable for every person. In fact, I realised that sitting meditation was not a technique that was suitable for everyone. And even though it was meditation that caused the *kundalini* all-fall-down event, I only really started learning meditation after my aunt had healed me at the river cottage

Before I found myself flitting from teacher to teacher, before I met my main teachers, Kittisaro and Thanissara and their inner deity and spiritual friend, Kwan Yin, before Melchizedek and Mother Mary, in the years before computers, back in the 1980s, I recognised that the yearning that had been slowly growing within me, for something I didn't quite understand, was a yearning that I needed to commit to with a full and open heart.

So when Wendy, a young friend who used to work at the Buddhist Retreat Centre near Ixopo, which is situated at the foothills of the Drakensberg mountains in South Africa, encouraged me to go on a week-long meditation retreat there, I figured this might be my chance for enlightenment. Perhaps there I might find all the answers to questions I hadn't even formulated yet. I arranged nine days, including traveling time, away from my family. My justification was that once I became enlightened, I would be much nicer to live with, a better mother and wife. However, I could only get there at a time when the formal retreat on offer was two days in length, so for the five days before that I planned to meditate on my own, without a teacher. Undeterred by my previous *kundalini* experience, I set up a punishing schedule and sat in silence. No instruction, no guidance, just sitting and walking meditation from pre-dawn until I went to sleep at night, in silence for the whole period, albeit surrounded by residents of the centre who were chatting about upcoming retreats, maintenance issues, gardening schedules, and local Ixopo news. Because of my upcoming enlightenment, I didn't have time for such distractions.

By day three, things were beginning to get grim. My body was sore, I was bored and grumpy, the rest of the week was stretching out uncomfortably ahead of me, and distressing feelings were stirring inside of me.

At lunchtime on day four, June, the caretaker of the beautiful gardens, asked me if I was okay. 'Yes, I'm fine.' My response was curt because I was in silence and she wasn't supposed to be breaking it with me. 'FINE' is an acronym for Fucked up, Insecure, Neurotic and Emotional, but I didn't find that out until about three in the afternoon when all hell broke loose inside of me. It started with me feeling a bit tearful during my walking meditation after lunch. I was observing my footsteps one at a time, down the steep path leading from the dining room to the river. There are ancient fern trees and cycads in the gorge, and the narrow path winds over swollen tree roots. It was shady, cool and smelled of the black wattle being cut across the valley. I only noticed the tears that I was trying very hard to suppress. They were not enlightening; they were depressing, and I wanted them to go away. They spilled out all the same, fat drops that soon became a river. I slouched back to the meditation cushion in the meditation hall, brushing them away as I tried my best to appear calm and serene. I was alone in the zendo, but I was afraid that someone would hear me crying. That would have prodded my humiliation button too strongly, and the tears were coming faster, stronger, and louder. There was no containing them. I wasn't sure why I was crying, although it had something to do with my mum who by then had been dead for five years. I think it was to do with our early relationship and me feeling as under-appreciated as children often do. I think I wanted to feel worthy and special, but I didn't. The tears were getting more strident and were refusing to be discreet. I was getting too anxious that someone might see me crying, so I gave up on my set meditation schedule, which was very hard for me to forgive myself for because The Buddha would simply have sat through this howling storm, and wimps don't get enlightened. I walked back to my small room with the uncomfortable, slatted bed in the female section of the sleeping quarters. Alone there, the sobs built into an unstoppable crescendo of raw, wracking, gasping gulps and howls. It was a tear-fest, a waterfall of incessant wailing. I lay curled up in foetal position and whimpered and wept for an hour, then two, then three and a half. Eventually, exhausted, and because I didn't know how to make the tears stop, I broke my silence to go and find Mervyn, who ran the centre. I was embarrassed by my vulnerability. He told me that it is normal for emotions to come up on retreat, to take it easy on myself, to have a good sleep. I had missed supper, so he gave me a boiled egg.

The rest of the retreat was uneventful. On the last two days, I joined the formal retreat. I didn't get enlightened and was very disappointed in myself.

The tears softened something of how hard I was on myself, however, although it took twenty years before I could look back on that week with enormous appreciation for the value of it. And even today, decades later, Melchizedek my inner guide, who arrived to point me in a clearer direction in my life, still needs sometimes to remind me to soften.

 Soften your shoulders, now your jaw, now your shoulder blades. Soften your breathing, your stomach, your belly. He touches each place gently. *Soften your wrist, your pain, your eyes and your heart. Soften that you may slip through the cracks of your brittle, little self.*

It was through his direction towards softening that I began to gradually tap into the quiet, tremendously humble power in the Still Point at the centre of my being.

THE PERFECTIONIST

In the Buddhist tradition, the purpose of meditation is to develop an understanding of the true nature of the mind, or the awakened self; that which is indefinable and non-conceptual. But my initial purpose for meditating was to fulfil my mother's longing for perfection. This had poured from her subconscious mind into mine in my early years, like brandy and cream into a sponge cake, trifling with my self-worth and creating something that looked pretty enough, but was really a mushy mess.

However, despite all my misguided attempts to acquire perfection, the meditation itself had another agenda, and so long as I practised consistently, it worked its magic on me. I didn't drop the longing to be perfect for many more years, because it was an underlying theme for me, a sneaky shadow requiring both mindfulness and deep investigation to expose. But at least part of being a perfectionist meant that I did apply myself with dogged determination.

I learned through trial and error and guidance from my teachers that creating a daily meditation practice that became a ritual as normal as teeth-brushing brought me the best results long-term. It worked better for me to set aside a short period daily that was sustainable than to create a rigorous schedule that didn't last. Somewhere between twenty minutes and an hour plus was good, depending on my level of commitment. Then I began to realise that the usefulness of meditation was greatly enhanced if I could extend that kind of awareness into eating breakfast, paying traffic fines, and dealing with looming deadlines. I slowly learned to infuse the quality of being that I discovered through sitting meditations into my everyday life. I also found that it helped me enormously to attend meditation retreats to get direction from teachers who had walked the path before me and had experiential understanding of the techniques and effects of meditation. Meditation retreats also gave me the opportunity to find other practitioners who could support me in my practice and make it more light-hearted.

At the retreats, I learned how to find a comfortable seated posture, although it took me a long while to realize that most of the pain arising from sitting cross-legged for long periods of time came from resisting the tension that was already held in my body. Sitting in a chair didn't make the tension any better or worse. What did help was to keep my spine upright with my head balanced in the centre, loosen my jaw, soften and drop my shoulders and open my shoulder blades, let my arms hang easily at my sides, and place my hands on my knees or in my lap. Sitting like a soldier created back pain and tension, while slumping also caused my back to ache. I had to adjust to find an easy posture that was well balanced. Then I would close my eyes, or if I were at Zen retreats where that wasn't allowed in case people dozed off, I would focus them softly on the floor or the wall in front of me.

About two years after that first retreat at Ixopo, I was sitting on my cushion in a small shrine room I had built in the eaves of our thatched house, and I realised as a simple truth that when my mind and my emotions quieted down, the underlying ground of my being was not only utterly benevolent, it was infinitely spacious. It felt like love.

It was a once-off occurrence in the beginning, and only slowly took on a quality of being ever-present. Often, when I was starting to meditate, instead of becoming still and spacious, the most noticeable result was an increased awareness of how noisy my mind was. Sometimes, instead of meditation making me feel peaceful, it made me more anxious, on edge or irritated. My mind would be distracted, demanding, full of stories, judgements, boredom or discomfort. However, when I let go of judging those states as good or bad, they fell away, revealing peacefulness beneath them. I remember too, how my mind used to run like an old-fashioned long-playing record on a turntable speeded up to seventy-eight revolutions per minute (rpm) so that it only sounded like garble. It tracked around and around on grooves that repeated refrains of 'I'll drop the kids at school in seven minutes, then five minutes to the pharmacy, and don't forget to buy plasters as well, then maybe time to rush to the bookstore, three minutes max, and get to my meeting by 9:25. Or perhaps I could dash into the supermarket instead of the bookstore, but then when would I go to the bookstore? Maybe after my meeting, but would I still have to put fuel in the car?'

Meditation slowly changed that. It slowed me down to thirty-three rpm so that I could begin appreciating life and could choose what was garble and what was music.

Grit was required on my meditation journey. It was easy to keep going when the experiences were wonderful, but I was tested at times too. When there was no experience of bliss and grace, my task became one of faithfully persisting. When I felt mired in the darkness of difficult life circumstances, there often didn't seem to be an end in sight, and then trudging through was the only option. An anonymous poet described people who knew how to deal with the gritty aspects of life effectively. 'It's easy enough to be pleasant,' he wrote, 'when life flows along like a song, but the man worthwhile is the man with a smile, when everything goes dead wrong.'

For me to focus on the goal of arriving at a blissful place was counterproductive. I had to remain in the dark and the difficulty. I could not force my way out. I could only keep on trucking. This slogging brought its own transformation, its own tempering of my soul. It was a release and relinquishing of a different sort. Sometimes it just felt awful.

PRAYER

I learned many different techniques of meditation over the years. Some of them were engrossing, some were so boring I could have chewed my arm off to create an interesting distraction, and all of them were hard work. My judgement of the ones I disliked was Robyn's judgement. I knew other people who swore by the boring techniques. If I were enlightened, I would have found all the techniques delightful, but the enlightened self didn't need to meditate.

Having tried many different techniques, the ones that worked best for me were the ones I used constantly. The more attention I gave to the technique, the better it worked. Of course.

And the one I used most of all was prayer. For me, prayer was a powerful combination of focussed awareness and gratitude, compassion, trust, and imagination. It included developing insight into what was most valuable for me to pray for. Because I integrated so many other meditation techniques into the praying, it became fluid and one-pointed, slow and sure, sensory and still. My prayers were mostly prayers of gratitude. Prayer was something I felt in my body. I needed to be very present as I prayed, and then I surrendered the intention of the prayer to the Universe to manifest in its own way for the highest good of all concerned.

The prayers of gratitude were a heartfelt outpouring of love, for myself (in due course), for the multitude of things that make up the Universe, and for the blessed Oneness out of which all things arise and to which they all eventually return.

Prayers of gratitude were 'a breathing in and a breathing out' of the world's essence. They brought me into alignment with my true heart. The felt sense of prayers of gratitude was soft. Prayers of gratitude created a home into which my anger, my fear, and the horrors of the world could tumble and be kept safe for a moment or a lifetime, that they might dissolve their tension and soak back into the heart of the Earth for healing.

Prayers of gratitude were unhurried. This did not require that they be slow, but they had to be sure. They could be slow as a breath that was certain and deep, or sure and swift as a sunbird darting between flowers. Whether they were like a flow or a flicker, they were never rushed. Their time, their cycle, was something that I aligned to through delicate tuning. It was like twiddling the knobs of a radio to receive a good signal. Through listening with care and adjusting my awareness and my heart space, prayers of gratitude taught me that it was possible for us to move into a receptive state that harmonised with the surrounding energy so that we could begin broadcasting a peaceful resonance into the space around us. Once aligned, our prayers could flow out on the clear, pure stream of love emerging from grateful hearts. Like the Voyager spacecraft could send signals back to earth from a computer with less hard drive than a cell phone, this stream could flow from our tiny human hearts further out into the Universe than we had the antennae to perceive.

I did occasionally pray for outcomes, sometimes for the world and sometimes for myself. But prayer was more about giving thanks. The person who taught me the value of gratitude was my father. As an unbending patriarch of too few words and fewer hugs, he had been a moral, highly ethical man who was awkward with emotions. Even though he was really good with kids and could play rough and tumble with us for hours on end, my mum told me once that he only felt comfortable picking me up for the first time when I was fifteen months old because babies were women's work. This same dad, near death, having never easily received help from anyone in his adult life, became physically feeble and bedridden. Receiving help made him soft and grateful. 'Thank you,' he would say, 'for coming to visit me.' 'Thank you for the tea.' 'Thank you for rubbing my feet.' 'What a beautiful day. Thank you for the day.' My upright father began exuding sweetness and softness through his gratitude. It lifted him closer to the angels who began to surround him, and it taught me that they are only ever as close as we allow them to be.

Even though I never had to deal with overwhelming challenges in my life, sometimes I had asked the Universe to improve my difficult circumstances in one way or another. I can't say that those requests were tremendously successful. What I did finally learn as a result of not getting all my demands met was that there was something deeply satisfying in recognising, during the hard times, that difficult experiences were not bad and pleasant ones were not necessarily good. If I looked back at the more trying times—being bedridden with the *kundalini* energy blowout, Mum's death, and later in my life, divorce, recreating a new life in South Africa, or my kids living so far away—each one of them mirrored back to me, in perfect synchronicity, exactly what I most needed to learn. The *kundalini* blow-out taught me that I was more than my limited version of myself had believed. Mum's death taught me to trust that she was still there in my heart. My divorce taught me to stand in my truth. Recreating my new life in South Africa taught me the value of resilience, self-worth, and becoming empowered. My kids living so far away taught me to let go of clinging. When the going got tough, my best response was to trust that it was perfect in that moment. And it was meditation and eventually my connection through meditation to Melchizedek and Mother Mary that helped me to remember that.

THE LIMINAL LANDS

.

Today, aged 60, resting on the couch in my son's house, reading a book, I can hear Pame, my Peruvian daughter-in-law, chatting melodiously in Spanish to my two grandchildren down the hall. Their conversation is interspersed with smatterings of 'mi amor', 'mi vida', and 'mi corazon', like gentle plops of rain nurturing all our soul seeds. The harmony of it reminds me of Zhoma, my childhood horse, and of my relationship with Mother Mary, and with Melchizedek.

I wholeheartedly believe that our only hope for resolving the planetary crisis we humans have created is to find our way back to the soft pulse of life that resonates with the songs of the earth. And before that happens in corporate boardrooms or parliamentary caucuses, it must first happen in our individual hearts. For me, that happened through tuning into the frequencies of Mother Mary and Melchizedek because they blasted my heart wide open.

Mother Mary and Melchizedek resonate with an exceptionally high level of consciousness that I experienced within myself as a tranquil euphoria through which the world looked different. When I aligned with the sacred quality of their energy, resolutions to my problems arose spontaneously. It changed who I was in my world.

Mother Mary is electric blue, and when I first met her, she was radiating a serenity that left me breathless in wonder. She entered my life in 1994. I had driven from Botswana to South Africa for four days of Soul Integration sessions. The sessions were an introduction to the inner dimensions of my being; they taught me to open up to my own unconscious shadows and driving forces. At the time I was still living under the pretence that if I made my life look good for everyone outside, I would be just fine on the inside. Since childhood, I had been hiding my pain and improper feelings in places where even I couldn't find them.

I had recently sold my craft centre for the princely sum of 5,000 rand, which I then blew on one four-day set of sessions. It was a rash but inspired decision that led to my eventually training as a facilitator of Soul Integration work, something that I still do today. Mother Mary arrived in the last hour of the last day of my first set of sessions. She wasn't there as a solid physical person; she came to me in the session as something like a vision or an imagined experience that was hyper-real and felt very authentic. I was lying on a massage table, eyes closed, guided by a facilitator from Nevada named Francesca. She taught me how to use a process of active imagination to feel into the quality of my own Higher Self. This is the aspect of me that is unconditionally loving and deeply wise. My Higher Self would then show me either what I needed to clear out, or alternatively, imprint into my life. During those four days, my Higher Self often took me to 'past lives'.[4] On the fourth day, Mother Mary arrived in a 'past life', as me! A softly shining white light surrounded her, while she herself was azure. The observer-me in the session could see her blue light shining particularly strongly down her spine. Now, of course, I knew very well that she wasn't me, so I kept trying to persuade myself that I was, in a past life, a nun that looked like her. With that, her energy dissipated. Then the Robyn-me, the one who in 1994 was attending the sessions, got really sad, searched for her again, and there she was, tranquil and emitting this intense, glowing blue light with a white halo about it. She was showing up as my inner knowing, as my potential, as Super-Me, in fact. Again, I lost faith in myself, as obviously I knew I was not really her and that I definitely didn't live her life back when BC was about to shift over to AD, and she disappeared once more. Eventually I surrendered and allowed that perhaps it was okay to experience how it was to be her after all. I (as Observer-Me) asked Mother Mary (as Super-Me) how she healed people. She answered so tenderly and peacefully by saying, 'I don't heal them.' Confused, I asked her what she did with people who came to her for healing. She replied, 'I listen to their pain.'

Mother Mary re-aligned me to an inner longing that I had lost since the days of Zhoma. It was a longing to live attuned to her energy, which was similar to being attuned to my life force itself. Zhoma introduced me to this energy, Mother Mary reminded me of it, and Melchizedek, whom I met seven years after Mother Mary, became the familiar figure who integrated it into my conscious, constant awareness.

My first encounter with Melchizedek occurred at a numerologically

4   Our subconscious works outside of time and space and speaks a highly symbolic language, so while clients tap into 'past lives' that are often so authentic that we might all wonder where that information came from, they could equally be 'simultaneous lives', or simply symbolic stories from the collective unconscious that represent themes we are carrying in this lifetime.

auspicious house number, seventy-seven, Seventh Avenue, Johannesburg. It was 2001, I was 44 years old and had been practising Buddhist meditation daily for thirteen years. Since meeting Mother Mary in the Soul Integration sessions, I had trained in the work of facilitating sessions in Amsterdam.

By the time Melchizedek arrived, I had built up a client base who demonstrated over and over, with all their skeletons that came clattering out onto my carpet, that there was no such thing as a perfect person. Yet in those days, I still wished to be perfect myself. As I've mentioned, it was a trait I had inherited from my mum. That perfection part of me didn't realise it at the time, but in meeting Melchizedek, it had just embarked on a suicide drive. Mother Mary was gentler than Melchizedek, but she, too, guided me to follow life paths that challenged me in various ways. The thing about working with beings resonating at the level of consciousness that Mother Mary and Melchizedek inhabit is that they lovingly guide you to follow the scent of your particular effluvia until you find the source of your imperfections, and they do this not to make you perfect but to have you embrace your imperfections. *See*, they show you, with a wave of their imaginary light filled hands, *this is you, Beloved*.

When I met Melchizedek for the first time, I was visiting friends. I was lying in bed at 7 in the morning, enjoying the early light filtering through a skylight onto my bed. As I lay quietly, half-awake, I felt something press on the left side of my ribs, gently at first, then more firmly. The feeling was not threatening, only new, yet strangely familiar at the same time, like someone touching me with his or her hands. As I observed the sensation, the 'hands' pressed right through my ribs, and the energy behind them filled my body with golden light. I was caught in such a place of stillness that I was transfixed, hardly breathing. It was as if the knowledge contained within this golden light was being encoded in the cells of my body. I understood instinctively that to move would be to break the connection with this glorious light, which was simultaneously loving, trustworthy, and gently containing. After a short while, the golden energy subsided, and I began to breathe deeply again. My body felt different, glowing, at peace.

It sounds weird but meeting this God-like being was as normal and ordinary to me as oats for breakfast. It felt like it was quite simply meant to be. What wasn't normal was that it made my everyday reality seem round-the-bend rollercoaster crazy. Seeing the world through his eyes meant that I no longer accepted everything in my everyday world. I began to question things more. Up until then I was a wife and the mother of three boys, living on a beautiful small-holding in Botswana. It was filled with acacia trees; there were purple hills in the distance and the smell of 'mangana' blossoms in the springtime. Having trained as an artist and having run a craft centre for eight years, then a Soul Integration therapy practice for the next seven, I had been leading what looked from the outside to be a perfectly 'castles in the air' existence. We laughed a lot, probably partied too much, loved our enthralling children, and lived in a country that was stable, racially harmonious, and relatively wealthy. But the dragons were beginning to rumble in the caverns of my subconscious, and the underlying truth of the parts of my life that were really not okay was beginning to spew outwards. Yet I couldn't mention this, or anything about Mother Mary or Melchizedek, to the people I lived and worked among. I didn't have the language or the confidence to show my family, my colleagues, and friends how different I was becoming. My kids were still small and trusting of me, but the rest of them would have thought my new ideas were bizarre.

When Melchizedek first appeared, I was in the habit of keeping even my meditation practice relatively secret, since it was so out of the norm among my peers. At the time, I was going through a Zen phase of trying to be mindful of the present moment and undistracted by imaginative wanderings. The instruction I had been given by my meditation teachers, to focus on the material reality of the here and now and ignore my imagination, collapsed and crumbled under Melchizedek's gaze. I was pretending to my friends that I was interested in the same things as they were and pretending to my Buddhist teachers that I was meditating with my eyes open while counting my breath. But inwardly, I was drawn to Melchizedek like a bird is drawn to its migratory path, with an instinctual urge that would not be deflected. I became immersed in his liminal world of feelings and heart opening. For the first few years, he remained unnamed and undefined: a feeling, a masculine, light-filled energy that entered my body and heart at random moments and blasted me clean with pure, crystalline energy. I couldn't consciously call on it or direct it yet. One day I heard the name 'Melchizedek' mentioned in conversation and with a lightning bolt of recognition I knew that I belonged to him;

he was the golden light. It was very simple and very clear.

Even though by the time I met him, I had quietly considered my-self a Buddhist for many years, Melchizedek, I discovered, is a biblical figure in the book of Genesis in the Old Testament. However, when his hands touched me, his open, golden force field radiated outwards into the vast and endless expanse of the Beloved, which belonged to no one spiritual or religious tradition but rather embodied a Heavenly realm and integrated it into the Earth plane.

I recognised through Melchizedek that we were each magnificently unique and that each one of us was as pulled toward discovering our inner truth, as we might be attracted to some 'unlooked-for treasure.' Not everybody actually wants to go on a gold-seeking quest, but the vast majority of us wouldn't mind waking up to it in our bedroom.

Melchizedek's vision saw further than the remotest galaxies and universes, beyond time and space, deeper than the hidden recesses in my soul. His light could beam into the depths of my mind. As darkness fled before the sun rising over the horizon, the world was laid bare in Melchizedek's light. I was caught with my pants down, immobile in the glare of it. I could not turn my back on that beam. Yet I could not tolerate it for long. It burned, his light, and it dissolved the solidity of my known world.

He explained who he was to me:

> *I Am as I Am.*
> *What you see of me or of others is a reflection of you.*

How I saw it in the beginning before I recognized that he and I were One was that I was his student; he was my mentor. He loved me in a way that was completely unconditional. I felt it in the marrow and the bones of my body. In the first few years, he had a body, although it was a light-body, not a physical one. I felt it as an energy touching me or moving through me. I was blanketed in his warm and golden love. Of course, a celestial being would love unconditionally, would love me unconditionally. But sometimes it was hard for me to comprehend.

Eventually he became me. Or I dissolved into him, and by that time he was no longer male; he had become vast and formless. In that space, names—his, mine, or others—were no longer relevant.

A NEW CONSCIOUSNESS

The insights that arose from the guidance of Melchizedek and Mother Mary changed how I lived my life because they changed who I was on a fundamental level. Change wasn't easy, though, especially when I resisted working through the obstacles they presented to me for my soul's growth. I wanted Melchizedek there. I wanted Mother Mary there. But I struggled against the changes they created like a wild horse baulks at taming, by digging my heels in, spooking, bolting, and slamming on the brakes. All my struggling was just fear of the unknown. They were immensely patient, wise and loving. Eventually, even more than Zhoma had, they merged with me so completely that I could no longer tell where they stopped, and I started, or where they ended, and I began.

Although they are both recorded historical figures who have been loved and worshipped, the Melchizedek and Mother Mary that I befriended and loved so deeply were not only actual beings of light, they were also more insightful and compassionate parts of myself. They taught me to engage with the joy and the suffering in our world from a wiser perspective than my limited comprehension had previously allowed. It was from them that I learned the wisdom of Oneness.

Seen through their eyes, one of the reasons we are here in the midst of the chaos we humans have created on our beautiful Earth is to give birth to a new form of consciousness that recognizes the Oneness within the multi-layered, multi-hued, multi-crazy, multi-separated dissonance of everyday life.

This is a consciousness shift that holds the vision of transforming our existing ideologies into something grander and altogether different. Out of this birthing, peace could arise on Earth. It is a magnificent vision of harmony, ecological awareness, care, and love, which could potentially metamorphose the shattered, exhausted, and violent existence in which most of us dwell.

I had seen the concept of giving birth to a new form of consciousness expressed by different groups, ranging from religious fundamentalists waiting for the New Jerusalem to arrive to pragmatic environmentalists who recognised that without a change in consciousness we were as good as dead as a species.

I believed that too.

And yet most people I knew were opting for 'epidurals' to cope with this 'labour and birth' by 'numbing' themselves to the reality of what was happening in the world. They did so either through the comfort of plush living while complaining about their hired help nicking their sugar, or by tuning out with fast food and TV soaps, or maybe by checking out of their humdrum lives through taking ecstasy tablets and going clubbing.

I concede that at times the vision seemed (and still sometimes seems) impossible. How could we achieve such a reconstruction of our world, particularly when the old-world order only seemed to be strengthening its grip on the Earth, when there was a real possibility that she would be strangled, and all of us would die as a result of our destructive behaviour?

There may be too many people caught in the virtual reality of violent video games, the unconscious grasping for more consumerism, and the thoughtless web of blaming others for experiences and events that are not optimum. There may be too many people whose 'optimum' is diametrically opposed to mine. But giving birth to a new form of consciousness is a bright vision that can potentially, sneakily, infiltrate the prevailing collective consciousness, subtly changing the direction of its focus.

We are living in the Liminal Lands, teetering between choosing a global way of life that is bringing us critically close to extinction as a species or discovering a more luminous way of being, where our choices are made from the centre of our compassionate hearts.

We have not yet left the old way behind. And we have yet to make the courageous shift to a higher vibrational frequency that could make wiser and more heartfelt decisions. Melchizedek and Mother Mary have a particular vibrational frequency or energy signature that feels like unconditional love. It is expansive and inclusive. I call it a higher frequency, although I feel it in my body all the way down to my toes. A lower frequency is denser and more constricted, and I associate those frequencies with feelings like hopelessness, despair, shame and guilt. When I feel them, I experience being very small inside, so small that I can't even relate to my surroundings, and they tend to cause me to exclude everybody and everything.

Even though I call these loving frequencies 'higher', early on in our relationship Melchizedek insisted that:

If you wish to move out of the chaos and into harmony,

peace and goodwill, then you must be firmly grounded in the drudgery and density of your earthly experience while simultaneously embodying the uplifting spiritual state of one who resides in the heavens. This is why we need you, my love, and countless others too, to do the work. You are perfectly created to bridge these dimensions, thus lifting yourself and the collective consciousness inch by inch, slow, muddy footstep by footstep upwards, until you glance back at the pure, golden footprints that trail behind you, and you can see how far you have come.

A LONGING TO WRITE

Humanity is fumbling for an ancient longing at the centre of her aching heart. She is like the blind mother labouring to birth her precious child whom she has forgotten she knows in every cell of her body. She is like the young woman searching for her lover who has gone missing in action. She is like the moon howling to her soul in the dead of night, pleading to see the beauty of the stars. I am the thrum of your steady heart. I am your midwife, your lover, your moon pointing to the stars. Follow me through veil after veil of illusion in your dark labours as you un-earth your true consciousness from within the blood and the bones of your beautiful body.

Mother Mary and Melchizedek each had distinct roles in my life. Mother Mary pointed me in new directions, which I followed, sometimes obediently, and sometimes with fierce resistance. Melchizedek felt like my home, or like bliss; he was the Gateway to pure Presence, and unbeknown to me in our early relationship, he was always there. I felt him come and go and longed for the connection but didn't know how to create it yet. When I was aware of him, I marinated in his fire: a whirling dervish on a rotisserie, spinning, swirling and reeling giddily under his gaze. I had yet to learn how to intuit or perceive his 'voice'. On my journey, I initially had to learn the 'feeling' of him. At first, he felt like a beautiful light-being, then I gradually learned to tap into the words that emerged out of my sense of him.

Both of them together drew me towards this book. In fact, the book itself drew me towards it. As a book-to-be, it called me even though I didn't know what it looked like, just like a baby-to-be sings out to its parents with its pure soul song before conception. 'I'm here,' it chanted, 'remember me, remember me.' When I considered aborting the book because writing it was a lot of work and the topic felt too difficult, my body ached for it as it ached during a threatened miscarriage for my middle son, Matthew, when he was in my womb. The idea of not giving birth to it felt wrong to me, and if I failed to follow its song, my soul would grieve. There is a wildness in each of us that feels like freedom. It comes from following our hearts. It felt to me that the reason Melchizedek wanted me to write was to teach me to follow the yearning of my soul. Perhaps my longing would touch other people's longings, stirring soul to soul, because that is what heart calling does.

 Your soul calls to you, Beloved, he explained, *through the dull ache in your heart when you are distracted. It whispers to you through the soft and tender unfurling of your inner truth. Search for your most secret longing. If it is free from harm, then follow it to the ends of the earth, and into the next dimension of being.*

The longing to write my journey into a book grew slowly out of many years of feeling into Melchizedek's and Mother Mary's energy. I wanted to share what they were showing me, and I wanted to teach spiritual truths, as my Buddhist meditation teachers had taught me. But I didn't know how to do that without talking about Melchizedek and Mother Mary. In the Buddhist tradition, we are not encouraged to share our meditation experiences because they are so individual and because of the very real danger of creating spiritual competitiveness or unrealistic expectations. What was right for me might not be right for anyone else. Besides, Melchizedek didn't speak to me in a voice as clear as a crisp winter day in the Cape. I was not psychic. One of the reasons I was good at my work in the subconscious realms with the Soul Integration sessions was that I understood my clients' insecurities about their ability to see, hear, or intuit their own inner knowing since I, too, had struggled to trust my own. Over years, I slowly learned to attune to my guides, as I might tune into a far-away radio signal by adjusting my frequencies in barely perceptible increments. I searched for the calling of my heart in the quiet, shadowy places, where I had to feel my way forward with moth breath. I extended antennae out before me from my Solar Plexus, touch-tapping the atmosphere around to discern its hollows and hummocks and to perceive where my yearnings synchronized with the flow of humanity's life force. I unfurled these whispery whiskers upwards into my heart area to explore my secret longings.

If I were going to teach anything even vaguely significant, it would have to come from the place of Mystery and Truth. Melchizedek and Mother Mary were going to have to show me how to write this book and how to become a teacher. It was a long and winding road I took to learn enough about the Mystery from them that it would be worthwhile passing it on.

THE BLACK MADONNA

Mother Mary was the archetype that had grown out of the prayers of a multitude longing for reprieve from the suffering of earthly form. And yet she was not here to take away my earthly experience; she was here to guide me to live it more deeply.

She was quieter than Melchizedek, more hidden. But she was equally powerful, and her impact seeped into my life. In those early days it was harder for me to summon her at will, so she was more a figure of extraordinary grace than a daily presence. It was only after I moved into more of my own power that Mother Mary became a valuable and powerful force. In time, I would simply turn my attention to either her or Melchizedek and would be filled with their energy—quiet, serene, and heart-opening for Mother Mary; powerful, wise, and very pure for Melchizedek.

Mother Mary was more Yin; Melchizedek more Yang. Yin is quiet, womb-like, and darkly fertile. Yang is light and active and a powerful force of becoming in the outside world. The Mother Mary that I experienced was tranquil, peaceful, and less directive. She seldom spoke to me, unless I asked her questions, and I didn't ask her much. I felt her presence, and it was beautiful to be close to her, so overall, I didn't expect her to speak to me as well. Beneath her purity as the archetypal

Mother, she held a less-known aspect of herself that was untamed, a dark womb of juicy fertility, a divine Cosmic mystery. The Divine Mother looked innocent and pure, but she had a hidden side that I identified as the Black Madonna[5], which could be deep and wild and wise; and this one loved me with a ferocity that burnt holes in my skin. She belonged to the earth, to the tempest, to nature in its unrestrained magnificence. She might have felt like the opposite of the serene Mother of Christ, but she was simply the other side of the same coin. Mother Mary in her different guises taught me about love as a way of being. I felt her love as a smiling, maternal energy that was quietly undemonstrative and yet utterly accepting of me. And I felt the love of the Black Madonna as a tigress. The tigress Madonna emerged unbidden as on the night when I was alone at home with my three small children and heard what I thought were burglars at the front door. The tigress took over, tore the door open to confront them and to protect her babies, only for me to discover that instead of burglars, the clamour at the door was being created by the border collie, desperately trying to escape from distant, rumbling thunder.

Mostly, Mother Mary felt like dappled light through a grove of trees, or a field of barley swaying in the breeze, absorbing the sun through its kernels and water through its roots. She was like a patient rock, spaciously enduring millennia. She was like the sea that may be churning its experience as heaving waves, but deep beneath the surface is a vast expanse of ocean flowing with the ease and grace of the life force that feeds its soul.

There was a quality to her understanding and ability to listen that was as present and as serene as the natural world, which no matter how wild it became, was accepting of the cycles of coming and going.

From the Void space of her womb, souls were called to Earth, her children: you and me. Beneath her quiet purity, her soul force was passionate, dark and delicious, whereas Melchizedek's spiritual strength

5   "The Black Madonna" is the fiercely passionate aspect of the Madonna archetype, who manifests as protector and destroyer. She is described by Clarissa Pinkola Estes PhD, author of Women who Run with the Wolves, as 'she who stands at the juncture between two worlds and protects us as we enter the dark places'.

was untainted by earthy distractions. Mother Mary was more present in the dark, quiet time between midnight and dawn, when we were asleep, and our dreams roamed around, looking for entry. She wove my dreams into my body, threading heart to soul, and viscera to tangled brain stem.

It was difficult for me initially to find ways to incorporate Mother Mary and Melchizedek into my traditional Buddhist meditation practice. However, out of all the different teachers and books and meditation retreats, I encountered over the years, I finally found two teachers who became long-term guides and friends, who were supportive of this new path my meditation was taking. Kittisaro and Thanissara were the nun and monk who disrobed to get married. They run a retreat centre in South Africa and teach internationally. I loved their wise yet humble advice, and I loved that they were so accepting of Melchizedek because they worked with their own spiritual guide or deity, Kwan Yin. They had a deep respect for 'Bhakti' or devotional practice. 'Kwan Yin' in China or 'Avalokiteshvara' in Tibet, when translated into English means the same thing: *The One Who Listens to the Sounds of the World with Ease.* He (Avalokiteshvara) and she (Kwan Yin) have a thousand hands and eyes to see and respond to the world. He/she is as well-loved in the East as Jesus and Mother Mary are in the West. The collective energy created by the reverence and the numerous prayers to the *One Who Listens to the Sounds of the World with Ease* is a nourishing well of compassion that anyone can tap into for their own benefit and the benefit of the world.

Mother Mary, just like Kwan Yin, listened to the sounds of the world at ease. Her auditory skills were so finely attuned that internal and external sounds blended into one harmonic impression for her to decipher. She had a stillness about her, a stillness so deep that it allowed her to receive the sounds of the world with her ears and her heart, that heart which is also the heart of Melchizedek. That heart that has at its centre a pinprick of heart that is me.

Kittisaro and Thanissara recognised the similarity between Mother Mary and Kwan Yin, and they encouraged me to work with these beings of light as they worked with Kwan Yin.

If Mother Mary was the listener, Melchizedek was the seer, and I was the kinaesthetic one, burrowing through the soil of Earth, which was sometimes moist and deliciously crumbly, sometimes caked and dry, where the smells were intense, be they of flower petals or excrement., I was so squished into the bones and blood, into the mitochondria and spider-web meridians of my physical body that I often felt crushed by the heavy boots we humans use to walk all over the earth and one another.

But oh, the view from down here was beautiful! I was the one who was blessed with the colours reflecting off the mountains that were filled with the songs of eagles, owls and cicadas. I could see Melchizedek's light and Mother Mary's finely tuned resonance from my vantage point. They delighted in the panorama viewed though my eyes.

My yearning to reconnect through Mother Mary to the Divine Feminine was related to my longing to live my divinity in the world. Gandhi, Mandela, Jesus, and Mother Mary represented exquisite embodiments of the Divine Feminine. They stood powerfully in their truth yet could listen with deep equanimity and care. They all represented the Great Mother in the quality of compassion that they manifested, and her qualities were sure and unswerving.

I could experience Mother Mary's Divine Feminine essence through my individual explorations of intuiting and 'feeling' into what my soul's purposes was. When I cleared the sticky emotions and churning thought patterns that arise out of the emotional residue from my body, I made space for the gestation of her sensitive, graceful wisdom. The calling to embody the Divine Feminine is the soul work of our time and it required an awareness of how I responded to the world on a deep and often unconscious level.

When I had self-serving agendas, caught up in a maelstrom of fear, resentment, judgement, or low self-esteem, Mother Mary simply watched me patiently. If I fine-tuned my awareness to her frequency, her gentle smile brought me home to myself like a boat being tugged into a harbour. There was nowhere better to be than home, and it was only me that cast my little self adrift.

Mother Mary and Melchizedek were like lighthouses in my interior lands, where my ego force met my life force as a turbulent counter current. This place of meeting was where the Soul-Self divided itself into the myriad experiences of my life on Earth.

I needed Mother Mary's and Melchizedek's guidance because sometimes my three-dimensional reality started wobbling and tossed up so many challenges that my life felt impossible to negotiate. Mother Mary smiled at this. *You are still searching for your perfect life*, she said, *and this is your perfect life right here.* Something about the way she said it made it abundantly clear to me that it was perfect because it was mine; everything I disliked in my life was only a mirror created to perfectly reflect whatever it was that I needed to let go of to find my Soul-Self. The soft breeze of her presence blew through me, and I could feel my resistance melting away.

Her advice reminded me of something Buddhist teacher Ajahn Cha used to say: 'If it wasn't meant to be like this, it wouldn't be like this.'

Or as my son Nix liked to say when he was quoting lyrics from the Wood Brothers, 'It is what it is, and it isn't what it ain't.'

My journey of becoming real needed Mother Mary as the Great Mother, the One who loved and listened. It needed Melchizedek as the Golden One who knew. And it also needed me as a scribe, who was bound to the earth through my heavy boots, my laptop, and the plus 1.75 glasses on my 60-year-old nose.

THE REALMS OF IN-BETWEEN

Like the snakes under my bed at age three, Mother Mary and Melchizedek belonged to the Liminal Lands. Liminal means 'between.' These were the lands of the fey people, populated by dragons, daemons, angels, and the dark, shadowy underworld of my subconscious. These were the in-between realms, which were barely perceptible, a mere whisper and hint of a secret idea. The liminal lands were in-between this earthly land and Awakening, which, in fact, included the Liminal Lands and this earthly experience as an expression of Itself.

The Liminal Lands are a threshold between sleep and waking, between life and death, or between the breakdown of an old order and the establishment of a new one. Whenever a liminal state exists, it allows for fluid boundaries and creates malleable situations. Out of this dissolution of being neither here nor there, or in both places at once, new institutions and customs can emerge. It is the necessary 'gap' that we need to fall into in order to create a new paradigm that is less hierarchical, one that is more aligned to being in tune with the earth. Tibetan Buddhists refer to the liminal state as the Bardo. Traditionally the Bardo states refer to the time between one life and the next.

In the Tibetan Buddhist worldview, at death our souls leave our bodies, and attached to this pure whisper of a soul are all of our unresolved issues—our attachments to those we love in a needy kind of way, aversion to people who have caused us difficulties or caused our loved ones harm. All those issues accompany the soul as baggage, sometimes quite heavy baggage. We travel with our unresolved baggage through the Bardo states. The Bardo is the in-between land, the Liminal Land that we traverse after death while searching for our resting place.

First, we apparently encounter the Absolute, the experience of emptiness and fullness, everythingness and nothingness, accompanied by a light so bright and harsh in its unrelenting truth that almost everybody turns away from it. Then we move through all the heavens from the highest heaven to the lower heavens, which are more like playgrounds of luxury. Beyond these realms we are confronted with purgatory and the hell realms. And we settle wherever our baggage feels most comfortable. If my baggage includes killing someone, I settle in the realm of murderers because that is where I resonate best.

According to the Tibetan Bardo teachings, after a period that is forty-nine days on Earth but is outside of time and space, so I have no idea how long a period feels like there, we choose to return to Earth to experience another cycle of life in an attempt to resolve some of the attachments and aversions that are weighing our souls down.

Coming back to the liminal spaces in our everyday lives, they represent the transition between realms, one foot in dream space and one in waking consciousness, or one foot in our present way of life which is destructive to the planet and one in the hopeful resonance of a more integrated consciousness where solutions to the looming crises can reveal themselves. This space of liminal awareness is the pivot point. The new form of conscious-awareness we are awakening on Earth arises from this point. It is a consciousness of inter-being.

The feeling I tap into through liminal space is one of being poised, hesitant, vulnerable, and simultaneously bursting with potential. Liminal spaces are this and that, here and there, both and neither; they are in-between. They present the opportunity for massive transformation, and yet they are as delicate as newly unfurled butterfly wings. They make demands of a different sort of all of us, requiring that we stop our daily distractions, notice their luminous, transparent quality, and breathe anew.

The Liminal Lands are vast territories that include both the astral lands where my hidden emotional gunk is stored and the many dimensions ranging all the way from the hell realms to the Heavenly realms and way beyond. Everything that is not resolved in my life, either through clinging or aversion, locks me into the astral planes of the Liminal Lands, even while I am in my body on Earth.

The magic of these Lands lies in the startling realization that whatever I concealed in the hidden lockers deep down in the starless depths of my consciousness created my reality on the surface of my everyday life. When I unlocked these closets so that the murky detritus behind all my polite and civilized masks could be released from my aura, then the lands became clearer, naturally expansive and heavenly. And the stickiness, the unresolved karma, the ancestral jealousies and disgruntled grudges gradually fell away to reveal what lay beneath. The underlying quality of being in these lands was unconditional love, but my emotional debris tended to mask this.

My outer world was simply a great mirror reflecting the personal and the collective patterns stored in my Liminal Lands. And while my friend and I might have been sitting in the same restaurant eating identical plates of fish and chips, or drinking identical power green smoothies, our Liminal Lands would have reflected entirely different worlds to each of us. My power green smoothie did not taste or smell or look like hers, even if we shared the same glass, because mine might have tasted of a hangover, or a troubling interview coming up in half an hour, and hers might have tasted of sunshine. My reality was not the same as hers because it was coloured by my perceptions.

In the Liminal Lands, I was both the very large and expansive experience of my soul-self with a glittering, gleaming connection to wisdom and intuition and love, and I was simultaneously my previously unhealed wounds, with all my ancestral history and all of my life experiences.

After my first encounter with Melchizedek, I wanted to find out how to live in a place of bliss, surrounded at all times by his golden light so that I would be free of suffering. Then, as an aside, if he could also heal the world or at least help it along a bit, that would be a great bonus. I had yet to learn that healing the world from the outside, instead of beginning with transforming the obstacles in my mind or heart, was never going to get anywhere. My environment and I were intertwined, but it was a stretch for me to recognise that to change the world, I needed to change myself at a deep level.

Along with many of my friends, I recognized that we were trembling as a species. And we were still looking for solutions by trying to understand how we could blame others for what had gone wrong rather than through finding the root cause of why we had *all* gone so horribly wrong. It was like we were trying to build a massive wall out of shadows to shelter us from a hurricane.

Melchizedek showed me a new way of looking at the problem. As we were poised at a defining moment of being either on the brink of wiping ourselves out or collectively transforming to a higher level of consciousness, Melchizedek disclosed that we were momentarily hovering in liminal space. It was as if life had become transparent. This offered us all the potential for more clarity since we could see through the density at last, yet at the same time my external world had become more ephemeral and had lost some of the reliable solidity of material existence.

I still perceived the world as solid, but the solidity was not reliable any longer. It was not solid because our ecological crisis made it fragile and vulnerable. But it had also lost its solidity as I awakened to the understanding that my external environment was only a mirror for my internal experience, both on a personal and a collective level. The feeling of hovering on the brink of possibilities that could either be transformative or very destructive came from the recognition that it wasn't happening to us; it was happening as a result of us. We were responsible for our world.

The recognition that we could change who we were, that we could raise or lower our vibrational frequency, that we could change our environment through our intentions, Melchizedek said, made our world lissome, supple, and graceful. It also made it scarier. More unknown. More astonishing in its possibilities.

We have moved into liminal space.

SKINLESS
The Liminal Lands didn't make it easier to be here. When I resided in liminal space, I was more transparent. I had thinner skin. Sometimes I had no skin at all.

I had wanted Melchizedek and Mother Mary to make things better for me; I wanted them to wrap my wounds in Band-Aids and fill my everyday life with happiness. I wanted them to provide me with a perfect man to love and a perfect life to live—a happily ever after, as in the movies. I had yet to learn that that was not the way of archetypal beings of light. Their presence not only gently cracked the pot of my life to let the light shine through, it shattered it and left me leaking light and dark out all over the place, with no skin, raw and dripping blood on the carpet. Melchizedek explained it to me,

What begins as a small leak through the cracks of your armouring gradually expands into a widely flowing river until you dissolve entirely, and there is nothing left of you, but the vast ocean of pure awareness.

Skinlessness was a temporary state that lasted about seven years, from when I first met Melchizedek to a few years after I had left Botswana and moved back to Cape Town. I had to build a new way of being in relation to the world. But first I had to deconstruct the old way. In Kalk Bay, where they had been rebuilding the road for five years, they had to pull up the tarmac, dig deep down, replace all the rotting sewage pipes and broken electricity fixtures beneath the road, and then finally build a new road on top of the old one. There was nowhere to divert the traffic, however, so for months and years we all had to queue for hours to get through one lane of traffic for both directions.

That felt like me: under reconstruction while the rubble of my old self lay scattered. The skin of my new self had not yet grown; I had no idea if it ever would grow again, and the inner noxious network and outworn DNA were slowly replaced, one cell at a time. Would the new me protect the Earth or myself better? I had no idea, but presumably, the new fibre optic cables of my neurological pathways would be better at communication, better at pulling love through my system, better at broadcasting it to the world.

During this time, Melchizedek embraced me with his golden presence, and I felt his resonant voice speaking inside of me.

Your earth is in a crisis so deep that it requires you to turn inside out with your vulnerable soul-self exposed and raw that you may come to understand how to protect yourself in order to protect her.

'Flayed' was how it felt with my soul-self exposed. 'Skinless', I had to slowly learn to protect myself from within, rather than wearing armour to ward off the world. Turning myself inside out turned my world upside down.

The things that happened to my exterior world may well have happened anyway, but up to then my life, which was only pretend perfect, rambled along, and I made do with it the way it was. Then Melchizedek arrived, and I lost my skin, and life became a lot less easy than it had been before. It wasn't that Melchizedek caused the external changes in my world, but they did occur at the same time as I lost my armour.

After twenty-five years of marriage, Charlie and I got divorced. I had been so clear that I did not want my spiritual searching to disrupt my relationship. But somehow my marriage warped and broke apart anyway. I couldn't pin down any single reason for this happening, and I would prefer him to have taken the blame. Isn't it supposed to always be their fault? But I couldn't deny my part in it when I finally became aware of my jaw-clenching passive aggression, nor my irritable shoulder tension that monumentally failed to control him. It took years of grief and spilled love for us all to recover from the ache that each one of us in the family went through. None of us were exempt, and it felt like I didn't have the emotional wisdom to protect any of us from the truth of painfully separating, even though we all tried so hard to take care of each other through the turbulence.

Then Africa spat my children out. Spat them as far as she could spit, leaving them yearning for her, but far, far away. She spewed them to different ends of the earth, trailing my scarred heartstrings after them.

Then I left Botswana, which in those days was easy-going and friendly. Botswana is hot, dusty, and lazy. When I lived there, the inequities were still hidden, the corruption was minor, friends were family, and we all relied on one another for support through the hard times. We were Batswana and expatriate, multi-hued and multi-cultural. Every Friday evening, we gathered to celebrate Shabbat, although not one of us was Jewish or particularly religious. It was a celebration of 'family', a time to listen to how the week was and a time to be grateful for one another. Apparently, it is different these days, but that information comes second-hand as I moved back to South Africa after Charlie and I split because there was more work there and because my dad was ill, and I wanted to be closer to him.

Without skin, I couldn't avoid the trauma of South Africa—where the simultaneous miracle and disaster of living on Earth were inseparably entwined. The unequal distribution of wealth followed me to work, where a woman giving birth didn't even have a cloth to wrap her baby in to take back to her tin shanty where there was no tea, no sugar, no food, in that order of importance, and where her disempowered partner took his frustration at the system out on her by regularly beating her to pulp.

I gave a hitch-hiker a lift. He was a fireman, hurrying home from fighting fires in the mountains after he had received an emergency call on his cell phone. He had heard that his shack had burned down. The blaze began at his neighbour's gas cooker; it had gutted five cabins constructed of wood, corrugated iron, and plastic bags, including his own, because they were built too close together. All gone.

LISTENING TO MELCHIZEDEK

There was a slow progression in my encounters with Melchizedek. Early on, I had intermittent meetings with a golden masculine figure. Later, he became an all-encompassing still, silent presence within everything. Initially, when I was still immersed in the winter of being skinless, a winter that spanned many years, in the dark, with no way of understanding, Melchizedek was a secret man-spirit who sometimes made love to me at night. I understood how much someone can get 'under your skin' because I felt him within me. Waves of ecstasy surged through my body, and my whole body pulsed with this energy so that I might experience an orgasm in different parts, in my stomach, my heart, my elbow, my fingertip, or even in my entire body. I was left with the feeling of being blanketed in pure, undiluted Love. Love in the darkness of unknowing.

I kept these trysts a secret because, firstly, it was weird and because, secondly, I knew it was unlikely to go down well with my Buddhist teachers. Paranormal experiences were sensibly dismissed in case we got so caught up in how special they made us feel that they created a kind of spiritual competitiveness. Of the few people with whom I checked in about it, my long-time teachers Thanissara and Kittisaro were dubious, although understanding, but Akong Rinpoche, an enlightened Tibetan lama, told me very clearly and sternly that I was misusing my energy.

The truth is that I could have become very stuck in my attachment to this figure of light. And of course, Melchizedek and Mother Mary were not only archetypes that I aligned myself with; at the deepest level of my being, they were me. I took his advice seriously and waited to see what would happen next.

Melchizedek eventually grew larger, more like a giant father figure in whom I nestled, curled up in his enormous lap at night-time. At this stage, he was about seven times my size. The image I had was of being curled up in the lap of a huge Buddha-like statue. But the feeling wasn't statuesque; it was warm, supportive and alive. I felt very cared for and safe there. I 'incubated' in his energy for about seven years, then was released from that cocoon into a relationship with him where he was a powerful god force. He lost any kind of figurative form and simply became a golden presence, much stronger but with no definable edge to his presence, and much more diffuse. It was confusing at first because I had to learn to intuit his presence on a deeper, less obvious level. It astonished me that the Divine would take such trouble to present itself in ways that I could comprehend at each stage of my journey. When I looked back to those days and nights with the Apollo-like figure of Melchizedek, I felt that perhaps the Divine Melchizedek simply extended his finger, gently brushed me with it, and I perceived that as lovemaking.

I had been learning to engage with Melchizedek out of my own volition, instead of waiting for him to arrive. These images that were filled with the flavour of scents and of colourful sounds began to transform what was happening outside of myself, and the way I began to tune into Melchizedek grew into a tactile sense of being cloaked in his energy.

I experienced it first in my heart, because I looked there first, although it was no less perceptible in my fingertips or my belly. I 'heard' his advice as a feeling in my body, as a colour, as an inner voice that was difficult to distinguish from my own. I transposed the senses to pick up the meaning of his information: a message had a scent, a colour, and a sensation. And all the while life continued its lessons.

The way that I encountered Melchizedek and 'heard' his messages was through feeling them; I was clairsentient but not clairvoyant, and not even particularly clairaudient. Melchizedek's words came through my fingers when I was meditating; I felt the quality of them in my body and then translated that into words; sometimes I also drew on some of my own learnings from external teachers or things I had read. His messages came through me, and they were flavoured by who I was in my everyday life. He and Mother Mary were also my own experience of my higher potential felt as archetypes. And yet they are, of course, also historical figures in their own right.

I think I had a soul connection with Melchizedek that pre-dated this lifetime, which is possibly why I was so drawn to him. I was both part of him (or he was part of me), and I recognized his vastness that was beyond this smaller experience of me from within a lifetime—and that, too, was also me in my vastness. I usually focused more on Melchizedek than Mother Mary because of this connection, although it could also have been because of the gender bias towards a male figure to somehow complete me in female form—but I'm not sure about that; perhaps it used to be so in the early days.

I connected with them a lot when I was working, particularly when facilitating the Soul Integration work. And over the years, it has become very smooth and simple to do so. However, I truly don't think it is necessary for people to have to take years to raise their level of consciousness to that of these great beings of light. I think it is very accessible, more so as time passes. Our collective consciousness is evolving rapidly. Anyone can connect with their guides, or their guardian angels, or their Higher Selves, in any moment, simply by knowing where to look, then lifting themselves to a place of joy and opening their hearts. It is becoming easier as it infiltrates our collective consciousness more fully.

PAST LIVES

Mother Mary took care of the direction of my life. As a result of the first set of Soul Integration sessions, where I had met her in my early thirties, she had inspired me to undertake a two-year training in Soul Integration. This was the first direction she pointed me towards and it felt exactly right. I wanted to understand her better. I wanted to emit an electric blue light. During the training, which took place in Amsterdam, we were expected to work about ten hours a day, including most weekends, in six-week-long modules, each spaced six months apart, with supervised home practice in between. I was living in Botswana at the time, where I had been running a craft centre and bringing up three rowdy boys. Charlie patiently cancelled his other plans during the six-week training modules, took care of our kids, held everything together and fitted in as many parties as he could in my absences.

The Soul Integration work taught me to become comfortable as a tour guide taking other people into their own Liminal Lands, and this work fascinates me to this day. I loved being a sleuth. My clients and I figured out together where they needed to dig to mine for their own gold and where they needed to look to release the sticky, tarry emotional gunk that they had hidden away from themselves. Their gold was called their Higher Self. Using active imagination, their deeply wise Higher Self guided my clients to look in their Liminal Lands for the symbolic stories that moulded their external life experiences. My Higher Self taught me to be centred and still during sessions so that my clients' soul wisdom could guide them with pure clarity to uncover their own soul truth. Despite the dramas held in the stickiness of the stories in the Liminal Lands, these lands became a place where I felt at home. I loved the language of symbol and metaphor; it is was natural to me as breathing.

I worked with people from all walks of life on creating soul connections with themselves, their loved ones, their unborn babies if they were pregnant, and with their Higher Selves. Soul Integration work requires a truthfulness that is prepared to dive deep down into the dirtier underbelly behind the conventional masks we usually show the world.

Clients sometimes access what might be termed 'past lives' through the process of active imagination. The past lives can seem authentic but can as easily be 'symbolic stories' or accounts which come into their awareness from what Jung terms the collective unconscious. From the perspective of a greater reality, linear time is a construct, and 'past lives' are in fact simultaneous ones being lived out in parallel realities.

Through my own healing and working with clients over the years, I have learned to trust and value the deeper wisdom that is found within all our imagined stories. I also learned through experience to trust the places in our bodies where these stories are stored and to trust the authentic images my clients compose.

While clients do sessions for a myriad of reasons, from working through relationship or health or work issues to investigating their purpose or direction in life, as time went by, I focused more of my work as a facilitator on helping parents create deep, spiritual bonds with their unborn babies. I recognized that I was drawn to this because birth was a place of disconnection for me. Many of us choose our work because it can help us to heal ourselves. Yet the work of healing my own disconnection at birth has also enabled me to have greater empathy for babies who are being born today.

This is the way of life: our deepest wounds are often our greatest teachers, and we often teach others our greatest lessons.

I had previously asked my mother about my own birth, and all she related to me besides the fact that her labour lasted only half an hour was a memory of standing on the toilet seat in St. Joseph's maternity home the night I was born and looking through the casement window to watch the Sputnik, the first satellite to be launched from Earth, glide past in the night sky. It coincided with the day of my birth, the fifth of October, 1957. She didn't remember much about me, though, and it was probably because, like almost all 'privileged' babies born in South Africa at the time, I was whisked away from her immediately, scrubbed down, bundled up, and trundled off to a remote and lonely cot in the nursery.

I did a Soul Integration session where I regressed back to my birth. The warm safety of my mother's womb disappeared after a rapid induced labour where I was trying very hard to slow things down. I shot out of her womb into coarse efficient hands that cleaned me, clothed me, swaddled me, and placed me in a cot among other helpless babies who were yelling or mewling nearby. For days on end I saw my mother at predetermined feeding times. Even then, I didn't see her heart; it was turned away from me towards an unknown.

The first moment I felt safe, I was a few weeks old, although time had no meaning for me then. I was lying on Dan's sturdy shoulder. She was patting me while her strong feet trod up and down, up and down the old wooden floored corridor of her home in Highwick Avenue. She was my father's mother. She smelled of starch and she was trustworthy in a way that my younger mother had yet to become. I relaxed a little and softened into the safety of her. I sucked on my fist because it was not yet 'feeding time' and I dropped into sleep, then drifted back to the liminal lands, which were still familiar to me. For a while, I was able to move between the two places, but as time went by the liminal lands slipped away, and I became solid, more stuck in my ways, more forgetful. Distractions began to weave their foggy lens over my life. The session came to an end.

BECOMING A MIDWIFE

After directing me towards studying Soul Integration work in Amsterdam, the second direction Mother Mary gave her approval to was for me to become a midwife. Having figured out through the Soul Integration work that I was not the only one whose primary trauma occurred at or around birth, midwifery seemed to be a good place for creating less traumatic experiences for the incoming babies. Birth is also one of Mother Mary's domains, and perhaps I was drawn there to be closer to her.

At the start of the millennium, while I was still living in Botswana, in the early days of learning to converse with Melchizedek and Mother Mary, I was looking for guidance to negotiate our new era, wondering how it might be different to the old one. I had recently signed up with a distance-learning, direct-entry midwifery programme in Oregon, which was a big change of direction for me. The Soul Integration work was intense, and I had decided I wanted to do something more down to earth and practical, kind of like gardening. Only I chose midwifery. In retrospect, being responsible for saving the lives of mothers and babies at birth, which is a time when life and death are inextricably intertwined, was equally, if not more, intense.

In a meditation that felt like an important milestone because it took place at the turn of the century, Mother Mary arrived. As the caretaker of babies and mothers, I was delighted to see her. I wanted to ask her if I had made the right decision. She turned towards a vast open plain extending beyond us, and with an expansive gesture murmured, 'The way ahead is open and free.' It looked delightful. I was overjoyed. But instead of 'open and free', I moved headlong into a decade of encountering obstacle after obstacle after obstacle.

I trusted Mother Mary, so I didn't question her guidance. It felt very clear. But I didn't understand how I could have misinterpreted it so badly. Over the next decade, the midwifery training institution embezzled the money we students had paid for the programme. The bureaucracy for getting registered as a midwife, first in the US, then in Botswana, then in South Africa when I moved, was ridiculously difficult to negotiate. I found the abusive treatment of patients by the nurses and midwives in maternity incredibly distressing. I got divorced. I upset all sorts of people. I had to learn to live on my own. 'Open and free' just didn't seem to fit this picture.

About ten years after she had given me this advice, I decided that she must have meant that I should have been looking for life routes where there were no obstacles and follow those. That when life unfolded easily ahead of me, it meant I was properly aligned with my path. That didn't feel right either.

I thought of Chogyam Trungpa, a reincarnated lama from Tibet and founder of the 'Shambhala' training method in the US and of Naropa University, who walked for nine months over the Himalayas to escape the Chinese invasion of his country. He left together with 300 other people, monks and refugees, but only a few of them arrived safely in India. They had to boil their belts and bags and eat the leather eventually, as they had no other food. I thought of Nelson Mandela, who spent twenty-eight years in prison. These men were not living lives that seemed 'open and free'.

Finally, I turned to Mother Mary to check with her about what she had meant by 'open and free'. She pointed to Chogyam Trungpa and Nelson Mandela. *No matter the external circumstances,* she said, *they were open and free.* And when I looked at their internal mind states, those were open and free indeed. In the face of enormous obstacles, their equanimity and serenity changed the collective consciousness of those they encountered, either face to face or through the media. I didn't feel it was altogether fair that Mother Mary expected me to have the deep understanding held by world icons of compassion and wisdom; it felt daunting, but I had chosen to work with her and Melchizedek, and as the old saying went, 'If you wanna play with the big dogs, you gotta learn to piss in the long grass.'

BIRTH EXPERIENCES

At births that I witnessed as a midwife, I saw so many newborns shocked by the over-efficiency of their caregivers; parents, despite loving their babies deeply, often allowed the hospital staff to take them away and interfere with bonding because it was the "way things are done here.' Babies were being cleaned up, wrapped up and placed nicely out of the way in nurseries, while the birth team were efficiently clearing up the messiness of the mother and of the birth to make space for the next arrival, almost as if babies came in on conveyor belts.

I knew from the experience of regressing back to my own birth and from the research findings of perinatal psychologists that when we are forced to shut down emotionally to protect our tender hearts at birth, we become more defensive. A natural human reaction to defensiveness is hostility. I questioned what kind of impact harsh birth experiences were having on our communities when almost no one was being trained in awareness of the newborn's highly receptive psyche at birth. It is still too rare in our clinical hospitals, which have done so much good in lowering infant and maternal mortality, to find doctors and midwives who are deeply conscious of the impact that birth has on the infant's hugely sensitive psyche, or the importance of the birth team dimming the lights, lowering their voices, focusing on the first 'golden' hour after birth to help the baby feel welcomed and safe.

Occasionally, though, I saw babies who were given the time to enter their bodies properly. I thought of Lyra, who made just the tiniest one-second greeting when she was born, a sweet cooing sound, and then snuggled onto her mother's tummy, into that soft bowl that minutes before had been a tautly stretched pregnant belly. She snuffled on her hand and gazed around the room in what seemed like awe. She looked at me, at the midwife, at the walls, but most of all at her parents. She listened to their soft murmurings as they smiled and welcomed her into their world. For a full hour she remained alert and silent as she happily squirmed her way up from Anna's belly to find her own way to the breast. Finally, she fell into a contented slumber with her mother's nipple resting gently in her mouth.

After some years of being a midwife, I continued working in the birthing world but stopped being the primary care provider at births. Midwifery had taught me a lot and opened many doors for me, but I moved on. And yet the title of midwife still suits me. My work these days focuses on 'midwifing' people to give birth to an expanded form of consciousness. I need to recognize my own shadows and where I am resisting life if I'm to help other people work through theirs. Mother Mary can nudge me to love those dark and murky parts of myself when I want to dive under the covers rather than confront them. She loves them despite the fact that some of them are unpleasant, smelly and un-fresh.

Mother Mary then pointed me towards the third direction she wanted me to follow, which was the one I resisted the most. This was the Compassionate Birth Project, which took place in government health care facilities, and with all its bureaucratic negotiating, sometimes felt like trawling through mud. During a meditation, about eight years after I had moved to South Africa, I asked Mother Mary to open the doors that she wanted me to walk through, as I was not sure of the direction I should be taking in life. This was often the way I conversed with Mother Mary: show, don't tell.

That day six different people contacted me by phone or email about the Compassionate Birth Project. The Department of Health in the Western Cape in South Africa was looking for solutions to the poor maternal and neonatal outcomes in their maternity clinics. There were a lot of patient complaints of staff abuse; reports were written about this behaviour, which included midwives and doctors shouting at patients, slapping them in labour, telling them if they didn't behave they would kill their babies, ignoring them and refusing to attend to them because they were screaming in pain, and yelling at them for bleeding on the floor or for speaking a foreign language.

The Compassionate Birth Project recognised that the staff were frustrated, under-appreciated, over-worked, highly stressed and very burned out. Midwives have almost no voice and less power in the hierarchical system of government maternity wards. The concept of the Compassionate Birth Project was to give the midwives a space to be seen, heard, appreciated and loved so that their frustrations had a healthier outlet, and the labouring women could be supported rather than harangued through the difficult process of bringing their babies into the world. It was a great idea but a nightmare to implement, especially since I hated admin and bureaucracy.

Before asking Mother Mary for direction, having worked on the idea for a couple of years, I had pulled out of the project in frustration, and it had collapsed. Now another year later, after not thinking about it for ages, out of the blue, without any prompting from me, the day that I asked Mother Mary for direction, suddenly everybody was contacting me because they wanted to be a part of it. Mother Mary was definitely hard at work. With a sigh, and because I truly trusted her guidance, the project got underway once again, and five years later, actually worked; brilliantly, in fact.

I worked with an amazing team of women, all of whom were volunteers, and we all believed in it fully. We had designed the programme based on extensive research on the best interventions to reduce stress, burnout, cynicism, and compassion fatigue in the health care sector, particularly among nurses and midwives. Then we added practices that we noticed had had similar benefits in other sectors like the corporate world or education. And then we included a few practices that we had personally experienced, that had reduced our own stress levels. We had looked at the literature reviews to ensure that they were also likely to be of benefit to the outcomes we were seeking to achieve.

Our solution was to take all the staff from a particular maternity clinic, including cleaners, admin clerks, security guards, midwives, nurses, and management, on a three-day retreat to dance, sing, relax, listen to one another, and to feel appreciated, loved and more resourced. During the pilot project with our first clinic, we didn't tell the staff how to treat their patients; we only spoke to them about how to treat themselves. They went back to the clinic, and for three months there were no patient complaints. They started singing to the patients waiting in the antenatal clinics. They sang to babies as they were being born in low, soft, very gentle voices about healing the world one birth at a time.

Over the years that we had been creating this programme, we watched in some amazement at the burgeoning international focus on increasing compassionate care in maternity. It felt like we were cresting a wave of innovative thinking around improving birth outcomes by caring for the caregivers. It seemed that Compassionate Birth was an idea whose time had come. Finally, when it was strong enough to stand on its own two feet, my involvement in it became more peripheral.

Those five years were hard work. They involved hundreds if not thousands of hours of unpaid bureaucratic negotiating, admin, and adapting the project to fit into a system that was hard-wired against heartfulness. Much of it did not feel like fun. Part of what Mother Mary was teaching me in her enigmatic way was to be in the world, with all its difficulties, but to slowly, day by day, release the anguish the system caused me by rising above it: in the world but not of it. She was teaching me that, ultimately, even the will of God held in integrity and truth could be playful, and that it all depended entirely on my attitude.

ANOTHER DIRECTION
The fourth direction both Mother Mary and Melchizedek drew me

towards—and this one I threw myself into with an open heart—was to become a teacher. The topic I wanted to teach more than anything in the world was the quality of being that they emanated. This created a massive conundrum for me because they represented a great Mystery. And it seemed impossible to pin this mysteriousness down without massacring its numinous quality. Yet I longed to uncover the essence of it in a way that was communicable, though I hardly knew how to describe it to myself. It was through this fourth direction that Melchizedek introduced me to the Gateways.

SOUL INTEGRATION:
THE SEVEN GATEWAYS

Like the apple blossoms unfurling out of buds, wintry me, led by Melchizedek, fumbled my way towards springtime. He funnelled his consciousness downwards through the images I created of him so that we found a meeting point where we could resonate strongly enough for me to be able to pick up his messages. The meeting place felt trustworthy, although it took a long time for my trust to develop to a point where he grew in immensity and became a deeper stillness within me.

On a cool morning in April when I had settled onto my zafu for a quiet moment of reflection, Melchizedek's presence permeated my bones as he told me that the book-to-be was calling me to journey inward to find an archetypal vision.

Seek the alchemy that turns base metal into gold. Discover Shambhala, that mystical realm deep in the mountains of the Himalayas, with its etheric counterpart hovering over the Gobi Desert. Retrieve the Holy Grail. You believe these visions are out of reach, far beyond your human grasp. Yet they are closer than your backyard. Look inside the warmth of your home, where the fire crackles with contentment. Look deeper still, Beloved; come inside your soft skin, inside the flesh and bone and contraction of your little separate self. The Alchemy, the Holy Grail and Shambhala are within you and without. Their Gateways are discovered in the midst of your pain and your joy and your connection to the Earth on which you live.

Melchizedek explained that there were seven Gateways through which I had to pass to find this mystical land of Shambhala. Obstacles blocked each of them, and it was my responsibility to identify and remove the obstacles.

Every Gateway is a facet of the whole. It provides an expanded view of your experience on Earth. Come back to your own self to find them. In the school of life, each of these windows to your soul is the curriculum: seven subjects to illustrate life's purpose, each one weaving together your

connection to your body, soul and spirit. Mother Mary as soul and I as spirit will be there as your guides if only you remember to look for us.

No one person could do this alone, he explained, but simultaneously, we each had to do it on our own. From this I understood him to mean that I was the only one who could actually do the work of expanding my consciousness. And yet, even if I didn't know they were doing so, other people doing similar consciousness expansion work, made these liminal states of being beyond my usual limited perspective of the world easier for me to access. Each time somebody else, somewhere else in the world locked a deeper insight into his or her own body, so would I be strengthened on my journey.

Before I looked at how to access the Gateways to Shambhala, I needed to acknowledge where I was right then. Shambhala seemed so unreal as to be almost untrustworthy because life on Earth for most people was nothing like Paradise. If I was to embrace the possibility of us all creating more peace and harmony on Earth, I had to begin from the starting point of a planet in crisis, and I had to look at the causative factors for the mess we had created so far—which, I was just beginning to realise, happened deep within our own psyches and not outside in the world at all.

 Collectively, all of you who undertake to heal yourselves, and through that to heal the world, are strengthening the collective consciousness. You are raising it into a heightened awareness that is as subtle as it is profound.

Through this I understood that the task of weaving Shambhala and the Holy Grail, soul and spirit, myself, Mother Mary, and Melchizedek together was simply the task of experiencing and tasting life more fully by finding, clearing and anchoring the seven Gateways into my body, mind, and soul. Doing so, Melchizedek explained, would transform me on a deeper level of consciousness. Changing myself, I would alter my interactions with others past, present, and future, and this metamorphosis would radiate outwards in a ripple effect. Mother Mary flickered an image at me to remind me that a butterfly flaps its wings on one side of the ocean and a thunderclap is heard on the other.

The Holy Grail is an archetype that feels similar to Shambhala in that they are both states of consciousness worthy of our spiritual aspirations. I see the Holy Grail as a feminine representation of a spiritual goal and Shambhala as a masculine symbol. The Holy Grail is more secretive and earthier than Shambhala, just as in Taoist philosophy, the Yin, or feminine force, is more womb-like and earthier than the Yang, or masculine force, which is lighter and more ethereal.

Shambhala felt like it belonged to Melchizedek's energy, and Mother Mary felt like the Holy Grail. The visions of alchemy, Shambhala, and the Holy Grail resonated in different parts of my body, same-same-but-different from one another. They all sounded mystical and magical, yet when Melchizedek mentioned Shambhala, I felt it light and airy above the crown of my head, and when he spoke of the Holy Grail, it was a dark, mysterious secret in my perineum. The alchemical process of gold-making had a resonance within my heart and spread from there through my body.

These were all experiences I felt as energies flowing through my body. The *kundalini* energy had awoken a wildly energetic sense of the Liminal Lands, which was stronger but similar to the tingling I feel when I know something is right, or when I meet someone for the first time, but it feels like I've known them my whole life. Because that was the language that I understood best, I realised that I would only uncover Shambhala and The Holy Grail through my body living its everyday life of walking in the mountains, seeing clients, chatting to my kids, occasional meditation retreats, supper with friends, and spending too much time on my computer.

THE STILL POINT

Five years after the turn of the millennium, two years after meeting Melchizedek, three months after his advice about the Gateways, I was still unsure where to take this direction. It all felt a bit esoteric. I needed simple, practical advice. I asked Melchizedek for an overview of the journey. I sought to understand what the journey entailed on a day-to-day basis. He gave me only a brief glimpse. Each Gateway had a particular lesson that I needed to learn. It felt that Melchizedek expected me to integrate the insights that arose through these explorations firmly back into my physical body. He required my perspective of my everyday life to become more objective. I had a hunch that if I could observe my life more playfully, my potential for transformation would increase and that if I lost my centre, I would become blind. *Your responsibility*, Melchizedek said, *is to know that from the centre you create these worlds of experience on Earth. To become the puppeteer rather than the puppet, you must first become the Still Point at the centre.*

I sat with that for a few days until Melchizedek elaborated:

 To have a clear vision for your journey, retain a connection to your centre at all times. This still point is the vantage place, the place of clarity and wisdom. When you need tools for your journey, find them here, my love. When you need to understand the obstacles, come back here. The key to each of the Gateways can only be retrieved from this centre, so you must come back here to reconnect. Return daily to the Still Point within. It will keep you safe, and from your centre, playfulness will bubble out of you like a wellspring of joy.

Stillness is.

The quieter I became and the more deeply I listened, the more I had access to the Still Point within myself. This was a place of absolute peace and calm, and when I held myself in the Still Point, I transmitted peace and calm into the space around me. Attuning to the infinite power at the Still Point, I could come into alignment with everything outside. I became one with everything within and without myself.

By harnessing the energy of the Still Point, I had the potential to transform not only myself, but also the people around me—the people in my environment, and society at large. It was only through experience that I could come to know the power the Still Point held for deep and sustained transformation.

I needed to remind myself to come back to the Still Point every time I remembered to come back to my breathing or the present moment.

But mostly I forgot all about it.

SEEKING THE SOUL-SELF

Melchizedek gave me these vague glimpses. The still point was a powerful tool. But the journey of seeking a land as ethereal as Shambhala, a Holy Grail which may or may not have included a cup from King Arthur's realm, or an alchemical process of turning lead into gold, which presumably would make me richer in feeling than in actual wealth, was perplexing. Google was still only a seven-year-old. There was not a lot of useful information available, and I didn't know how to interpret it in relation to my own life. So instead, I continued with my emailing, the gridlocked traffic, the bank queuing and supermarket shopping, the looking for distraction with friends and family and to-do lists.

Eventually, I found myself, early one morning, curled up in the comfy camp chair on the porch of my little wooden house overlooking the sea near Cape Town, drinking Earl Grey tea, which tasted insipid. It was hot already, and the cicadas were chirping. I had moved jobs and house and country, and my frown lines had come with me, my issues had come with me, and the anxiety I had inherited from my mother had followed along too.

My admin was piling up in ugly mountains. Work, which I usually loved, was tedious that day because I was addressing the long-ignored admin, and there was too much of it. Life felt distasteful and wearisome. I wondered where all the fun had gone. It was a whole lot easier to have fun by drinking wine or whiskey and smoking ciggies in the old days. I had spent years married to that lifestyle, though, and despite some excellent parties where I misbehaved badly in the most fun way possible, I had already decided that that kind of fun ran out too fast to be sustainable.

With a sigh, I turned to Melchizedek. Grumpy at first. 'Right then,' I said, 'give me some directions. How do I Grail Hunt when I don't even know what a Grail is?' I looked out at the protea bushes below my house and inhaled the scent of the sea salt permeating the early morning air. I took a final sip of by now rather lukewarm tea. Melchizedek's smile seeped into my heart. I could tell he was grateful. It melted me. 'Okay, Melchizedek, my purest love, I'm ready for the trip.'

I expected an introduction to the Gateways. Instead, he advised me:

There is a foundation required of you before you even begin the journey. This foundation is built on your recognition that your ego is a servant to your inner wisdom. Your ego's job is to maintain your discipline, moral integrity, and humility. This will keep you harnessed to a middle path where you do not harm yourself or others, where you are connected both to the earth and to the heavens, where you balance both heart and mind, and where you bring them all into service for the Divine.

Melchizedek didn't speak about this again. If you ask someone to write a book, you don't keep going back to check if they know their ABCs. However, I did know that it was important, and he did make sure that life knocked me hard when I strayed into any misuse of my energy, or when I became too fuzzy or disorganised. I remembered that at university, our lecturers had spoken about mysticism in all of the different traditions as something that demanded a certain level of responsibility as a prerequisite. This didn't mean that mystics were sturdy, upright citizens who behaved properly. Rather it required that they hold fast to the foundation of moral integrity, humility, and discipline. In fact, many mystics were outcasts. Some of them seemed mad; some wandered around naked, with eyes glazed over with love for God. Rabia of Basra lived in Mesopotamia in the eighth century. She was an influential Islamic saint and mystic who loved God in a way that was sometimes sensual and sometimes downright erotic. She wrote the following poem, translated here by Daniel Ladinsky.

The sky gave me its heart
because it knew mine was not large enough to care
for the Earth the way it did.
Why is it we think of God so much?
Why is there so much talk about love?
When an animal is wounded
no one has to tell it, 'You need to heal';
so naturally it will nurse itself the best it can.
My eye kept telling me, 'Something is missing from all I see.'
So I went in search of the cure.
The cure for it was His Beauty.
The remedy, for me, was to love.

Rabia knew that following her heart also meant that she experienced being one with everything, and so she couldn't intentionally cause harm to herself or others. Her responsibility lay in trusting that her God was reliable and that His guidance came from a source that was wiser and more loving than that of her ego. She laid down her little self in service to the Divine.

These mystics travelled into the lands of spirit and came back whole and renewed because their journeys were grounded in reverence and awe. Without this respect and a sense of belonging to God, they would have struggled to survive. Mystics, shamans, meditation masters, spiritual seekers, and psychotics know that the vast territory of other dimensions of being is also the land of the deeper levels of consciousness. R.D. Laing, an unorthodox Scottish psychiatrist, once stated that a mystic is swimming in the same water that a psychotic or schizophrenic is drowning in. Practicing reverence and respect was the way that mystics built the courageous heart they required to face the demons lurking in the deeper regions of their consciousness.

I was slightly in awe of mystics and wondered how they got to be so mystical. I preferred to imagine that I simply had special, invisible friends called Melchizedek and Mother Mary, the way small children sometimes have invisible friends. I think it felt like too much pressure to be a mystic myself. I didn't rip my clothes off and dance naked under the moon while worshipping god; I didn't go off and live in a cave for twelve years; I didn't dream of prophetic visions. I didn't feel I had what it took. But, if I wanted to go on this journey, Melchizedek required that I committed to being responsible in the same way mystics were held responsible—through being reverent, respectful, and willing to hand the direction of my life over to him.

There was still no sign of the Gateways, though. And the next directive he gave me had nothing to do with them either. *Start and end this journey with finding yourself,* he said.

I still thought I was Robyn, which was a Great Cosmic Joke.

 Your True Nature, said Melchizedek, *is pure and changeless. It is obscured by the obstacles you constructed to close your Gateways to Shambhala. Shambhala is within you already. It is within every molecule of your body, waiting*

patiently for you to find it. Discover it in yourself, and you uncover it in every sentient being. Your journey to uncover your True Nature is your journey to find Shambhala.

Melchizedek wanted me to understand that the progression of clearing the obstacles in each of the Gateways was like the settling of the mud to reveal the natural clarity within each Gateway. Since I already knew that I could only find the Soul-Self through clearing the obstacles, I tied this to an analogy which one of my meditation teachers gave a group of us in a dharma talk describing the awakening of the Soul-Self. The Tibetan Kagyu tradition described the inherent quality of the Soul-Self as the sesame oil that is already present within the sesame seed, or the gold that is already present within the gold ore. It was already there; it simply needed to be purified.

Melchizedek had previously described this to me by saying:

 Like the vastness of space revealing itself once the clouds disperse. Out of the stillness of your unobstructed mind, the luminous clarity of your Soul-Self will naturally emerge.

However, in the early days, it was still quite difficult for me to do so. Once I started unravelling the question of Who I Really Am, things got more confusing because most of the time I had absolutely no idea who I was. Unravelling began with my noticing that I was so many different people that my life looked like a multi-coloured one-man band playing reggae and blues and chopsticks to the background rhythm of the Songs of the Earth.

To find out Who I Really Am, I first identified the parts of me that were not the Soul-Self. I was in my late forties. I had already moved back to Cape Town from Botswana; I was living on my own, working as a Soul Integration facilitator and waiting for the South African Nursing Council to register me as a South African midwife. My kids felt very far away. I was often lonely and sometimes unsure of myself.

Initially, I seemed to be made up of many selves, all jumbled into one body—masks upon masks of personalities that I discarded as not being the Soul-Self, one by one.

I'm a mother, and my sense of who I am was integrally bound to this.

It was clearly only a role, however, albeit my strongest one, even after my kids had long since left home, and it was not Me.

Among other things, at this stage, I had been trained as an artist, a counsellor, a hospice worker, a Soul Integration facilitator, a doula, and a midwife. These were what I did, not who I Am.

I also loved dancing. The dancer had something a little bit real about it because it helped me release some of the stuck tension in my body. Being in my body might have felt like a distraction from finding the essential Me in the centre, but paradoxically, it filled me with a love of life that was closer to the truth than many of my other masks. Nevertheless, my body was undeniably mortal, so its limitations excluded it from being the Soul-Self, which was most definitely changeless, without beginning or end. I knew these things already, from my years of meditation practice, knew them not only as intellectual concepts but as the felt experience of being so much more than my body. Yet I forgot them in my daily life.

I am a meditator. I wondered if my Soul-Self was to be found within meditation. As much as meditation delighted me and seemed to point towards truth, it frustrated Caetano, my grandson. He thought my Soul-Self would be better employed in playing with him early in the morning. 'But Bindy,' he declared when I refused to play along by leaving my meditation cushion to build train tracks with him, 'you're already a vegetarian.' Seen through Caetano's eyes, meditation was a very definite limitation.

I loved the role of Soul Integration facilitator because, although the work was intense, sticky, and messy, it was alive with potential. The client's Higher Self (their own form of Melchizedek) guided the work, so it was trustworthy, contained, and it touched something deeper in me. At births and in Soul Integration sessions, I was given a window into the souls of the people I worked with, but I dipped in and out of this state all the time. Buddhists have a term called Stream Entry. Being in the zone, where my sense of self fell away, was like dipping into the Stream. I swam and then clambered out again, swam and clambered out. Midwife, Soul Integration facilitator and teacher were roles, but Stream Entry as an experience had something about it that felt a little more real.

My perception of this consciousness felt delicate initially. I dropped into it, and it felt like a flutter, a momentary awareness of my potential, much as a foetus is felt in the belly when we first discern its movements.

The foetus is already there—we have received the pregnancy test results, seen the scans, yet the first felt movements are like a whisper we cannot quite believe. We begin to feel the baby's movements without having to focus so intently on them, although the movements are felt more strongly when we are quietly aware. Some women who are very perceptive can feel their babies moving very early in pregnancy, even though women are only supposed to feel them at between sixteen and twenty-two weeks.

Rose described the first movements in her belly of her eight-week-old baby, and then she described how well she knew him on a soul level when she looked deeply. Her descriptions during a Soul Integration session were brief, almost terse, because she was so immersed in the experience that it was difficult for her to talk: 'He's very active . . . he's joy, ease, and certitude, it's all truth, and he's very comfortable with that, nothing to defend . . . He's a bundle of love and joy.'

Rose's experience of her baby was like the stream of consciousness that we are gestating as a collective human potential. I've no idea how far into the pregnancy we've got, or whether we will see it through without miscarrying, but on a group soul level, our new form of consciousness is imperceptibly growing in love, joy, honesty, and truth.

Finding my own inner stillness was like becoming Rose's baby. I became present. I listened with deep and alert awareness. I quieted my churning mind, my emotions, and my loud bodily demands in order to sink into the moment. It was the awareness of being a part of and One with a Universal flow of energy that was always there. A few years later, when discussing it with a group of friends, I called it 'coming home', Ruth called it 'not interfering', Annika called it 'doing less to create more', and Zo called it 'being present'.

We all agreed that the value of settling back into ourselves and holding space could become a guiding principle. If we cherished this as the core reason for being here, it could serve as a reminder that this was the only work there is. It helped us to transform our worlds, each in our own way. Stream entry was a profound Gateway to Shambhala. It was the entry point for bringing Heaven to Earth, and it was right under our noses.

Melchizedek didn't sweat the big stuff. He said, *Breathe deeply and take great care of the small silent self at the centre of your orbiting selves. This self takes up the least space and has the most impact.* (And thereafter he wanted me to take care of my admin.)

THE FIRST GATEWAY:
LIFE FORCE, PRESENCE

The obstacle: Distraction.

Questions to ask: Where am I right now? Can I embrace this too? Can I be present without resistance? Am I aware of my body all the way down to my toes? Am I aware of the subtle language of my prana or life force?

The Soul-Self was vague, ephemeral, and too quiet to keep me entertained for long. During my early stages of being on this path, I was easily distracted and quickly diverted from the task of finding it. With free will to choose my path forward, it was my choice if I wished to take thousands of lifetimes to learn what I had come to Earth to learn.

Nevertheless, Melchizedek was always right there, non-judgementally supporting all my deviations onto more scenic routes. In the meantime, he assigned me the task of grounding what was not earthbound by asking me to spin spiritual stories out of the mud, bones, and breath of this world so that these tales could merge into the mystical realm that lay beyond. He asked me, as a scribe, to forage for stories that emphasized the cracks where my soul depth could shine through my crusty, outworn defences. Writing became the pure fantasy of embedding his ethereal world into mine, because his world could only become solid if it could find its way through my blood with a haemoglobin count of 12.5, through my weary muscles, my splintered nails and my greying hair, through my beautiful, beautiful body that carried its scars like a proud warrior of light.

Eventually they became stories that were woven into this book, but initially, all I did was to find out how to gather stories. 'What kind of stories? Where do I look for them?' I asked Melchizedek.

Right here, said Melchizedek. Of course. Anyone who has flicked through half a self-help book knows that *Now* is the only moment there is. Looking around, I found myself unsure how to make writing in my journal while wearing stripy cotton pants and a red t-shirt dusted with flour from baking cassava cheese puffs into a story.

Melchizedek continued. *Now lift your vibration into the ethereal realm.*

I closed my eyes and leaned back in my chair. I could hear evening bird song, dogs barking in the distance, far-away traffic mixed with the bass beat of tinny, amplified, Saturday shebeen music. It was insistent and jarring. An aeroplane flew overhead, closer than the ethereal realms, which seemed very far away.

 Then connect to the solid, ancient wisdom of your Mother Earth. Become a bridge between the two. The more you clear your constrictions, the easier this will become.

A mosquito buzzed around my ear and landed on my cheekbone.

 On the journey to find Shambhala and the Holy Grail, there are seven Gateways, obscured by obstacles. Clearing each Gateway of obstacles will create a reliable bridge to Shambhala. You will not only become the bridge, but the bridge will lead you where you need to go.

An itch was developing at the site of the mosquito bite on my cheek-bone, and it demanded my attention. It was more insistent than the unrelenting Kwaito bass beats across the valley. Instinctively, I raised my hand to swat the mosquito on my cheek. But I had previously committed to not kill anything unnecessarily. Could I sit through my meditation with Melchizedek without killing the mosquito? The itch was becoming unendurable, a siren call for attention.

The first obstacle is the obstacle of Distraction.

'Is this itch a distraction, or is it an acceptable focus because it is happening Right Now?'

The itch is not a distraction. But your response to the itch is.

His advice was clear, but I was not sure what to do about my irritation at the mosquito without swatting it first. Melchizedek was serene as always. I felt his presence as an astute quietness, listening so purely

80

he could feel right into the very core of me. It radiated out from him with no judgement whatsoever.

His intensity was not even slightly disconcerting. I could feel him hearing the subtle nuances of my thoughts, his quiet eyes reading my every movement, his touch perceiving my feelings through the faint vibrations circulating between us. His heart-mind tasted the flavour of Who I Was and Who I Am, with no discernible antipathy to the shrieking itch of my mosquito bite, or to the mosquito that was still attached to it. As his gaze rested on my cheekbone, the itch rapidly subsided. The cause of this little miracle was abundantly clear to me. As Melchizedek's force field touched mine through his presence, I instinctively relaxed and released my resistance to the itch, whereupon it quite simply disappeared.

 Every one of the obstacles, Melchizedek resumed, *is inside and outside you on all levels of your being: physically, emotionally, mentally, energetically, soulfully, spiritually, and consciously. You will meet these obstacles one by one as you become whole. Learn about them, overcome them, and you will learn about yourself. Learn about yourself on all the many dimensions of being and you will see that you are none other than Shambhala, none other than me, none other than Oneness itself. You can release the obsta-cles through mystical visions, through feelings, through intuition, through your body and through your intellect,* continued Melchizedek, *but you cannot avoid them, and you are required to live among them without resistance and without their leading you astray.*

I couldn't even identify the obstacles initially. My life seemed frag-mented, chaotic, un-synthesized. I drank tea, was overwhelmed by emails, by social media, by to-do lists. I dashed to the supermarket, got stuck in traffic, ate a salad and some chocolate on the run, answered more emails and phone-calls and SMS messages, had a Skype meeting, saw a client for a two-and-a-half-hour session, grabbed a bag of peanuts, ate most of them even though they were stale, noticed that my plants needed watering, answered more emails and phone calls and SMS messages. It was not easy to see the big picture from within the bittiness.

I decided that I needed to create a map delineating the way I negotiated the obstacles and challenges that Melchizedek promised to show me. And I did this by creating practical guidelines to remind myself of the things I had learned but forgotten and learned and forgotten yet again.

The many dimensions of my being.

The issue: Obstacle One is the obstacle of distraction.

Melchizedek wants me to investigate it from many angles and from all the many dimensions of who I am, physical, emotional, etc. It seems that I need to look more deeply into the obstacle of distraction rather than just through my everyday eyes.

Reminder: Look into all the other obstacles as deeply in the future.

Question: What does looking deeply mean to me?

If I look deeply at someone, I can see him or her more clearly. Melchizedek wants me to look through their layers of defensiveness, and to imagine what they would look like if they hadn't been hurt by life, as all of us have been hurt in some way. The Soul Integration work also teaches me to do this. There is something tremendously inspiring about having a client tap into their own inner wisdom to be guided to recognise their negative patterns of behaviour that were created by the hurts and injustices of their lives or the lives of their ancestors. When I observe my clients doing this, I see them on a soul level, see the beauty of their intentions which have become hurt and warped by their hardships, making them into people that they don't want to be but often don't know how to control.

I woke in the night with Melchizedek humming in my centre. I could feel him inside of me, his golden glow radiating from my heart and through my body. Outside, the darkness was thick and close, and the faintest sounds were muffled by distance, but inside myself, I felt a warm and spacious well-being. He said:

Distraction will keep you from being present. Initially, Presence is fleeting and elusive, Beloved. To capture it requires stealth and patience, like a lion intent on its prey. When the sun is hot and fierce, a warm breeze ruffles its mane, flies twitch the skin on its back, but nothing disturbs its focus. The lion's intention is so pure that even the birds hold their breath. Watch how it prepares itself. Feel its stillness and absorption. Every muscle is alert; the marrow in its bones tingles in anticipation; its paw-pads hold the Earth steady. The lion's breathing is slow and sure; its eyes do not waver; its ears quiver this way and that, listening to every shifting moment.

Wait like the lion. Your prey is this very moment. Let nothing distract your watching. Not your cell phone in your bag, a mosquito on your cheek, or an ache in your shoulder blade. Gather your attention like the lion. Hold this moment in your awareness as if your life depended on it. Become still and absorbed. Allow each muscle in your body to relax into responsive alertness.

Just so.

The waiting is the capturing, Beloved. You will not find it elsewhere than in this very moment in time.

I had been thinking of distraction as something that happened in my head when I drifted off into stories about my past, and fantasies or fears about my future. Now I recognized that it happened in my body too. Presence in Melchizedek's description sounded like a felt experience. It was not only here and now, it embodied here and now. I got up to take a pee and drink a glass of water. I felt the cold floor under my feet, saw my blurry witching-hour face in the bathroom mirror, smelt the cool night-time silence. I realized that to overcome distraction I must not only put aside my vague concern that I would forget to phone Susan in the morning to tell her I had changed the dates of an upcoming class but that the trick was to slip into the absolute simplicity and stillness of a lion's awareness. If I were present like a lion, I would be present with my body, with my emotions, and with all the mental clarity I could muster. I became aware of my breathing, of the blood flowing through my body, and of subtle energetic shifts. My awareness changed to include the presence of being larger than my physical form. I discovered that when I was really quiet and listened as closely as a bat to the night outside, I was aware of the connection flowing between my body and the room and the thick, dark sky. It was very simple, like a lion's attention.

I wandered into the kitchen and made myself a cup of hot chocolate. I made it with raw Peruvian cacao sent to me from my son Rory who was living in Lima at the time. It was frothy and smelled homely, earthy even. When I gave it close attention, it was a soothing blend of malted flavours, of slow, luxurious, creamy sipping which expanded into quiet deliciousness as it filled my mouth and warmed my belly. It evoked blissful images of satisfied, sleeping babies smiling in contentment, quite drunk on mother's milk. The hot chocolate was an interval of pure indulgence, a moment of contemplation that lured me into the security of feeling fully alive. I sniffed it, licked it, savoured it, and schlurped it.

It reminded me of a poem by the painter of flowers, Georgia O'Keeffe. *Nobody sees a flower really; it is so small. We haven't time, and to see takes time—like to have a friend takes time.*

I went back to bed, and back to sleep because it was 3:45 in the middle of the night.

Presence came and went. Having moved from Botswana to Cape Town in South Africa, I then moved to the mountains behind Stellenbosch to escape the city because I need to live in nature like some people need coffee in the morning. And all the while I practiced being present, and forgot to be present, practiced and then became distracted by emotional disturbances.

I made a recording of my thoughts one morning when I became aware of my distracted state. Over a period of a minute, the transcript looked like this: My calfskin has ridges on it like the ripples of a mini Saharan desert. Am I dehydrated? Dehydration is a major cause of disease linked to inflammation, cell death, memory loss, fatigue, asthma, and histamine production. I wonder if it could lead to cancer? Do I have cancer? I wonder who would come to my funeral? Yvette dealt with her cancer by changing her diet. I need a more alkaline diet. Three cups of green veg, three cups of orange fruit and veg, three cups of sulphurous veg: mushrooms, onions, and was it cabbage? Or an *ayurvedic* diet, a *sattvic* diet—that would be nice. A *sattvic* life in a *sattvic* diet. Very nice. I haven't heard from Nix in a while; how is he? I must remember to call Lesley tomorrow; I should write it down because I'll forget. Is forgetfulness a sign of dehydration? I can't remember. Oh look, there's a pied kingfisher, I wonder what he symbolizes?

What hope was there for me against such a huge obstacle of distraction?

I liked the feeling of being present, though, and I was especially proud of myself if I could remain present when I didn't particularly like what was happening at the time. But mostly my emotions and my thoughts got in the way. I found it was difficult to stay aware of the miracle of being alive. Instead, I readily moved into crisis mode to cope with the chaos of my life. The size of the crisis was irrelevant – at different times in my life, it could have been as simple as a broken coffee machine, a child's lost shoe when they were late for school, an unstable marriage, a warring nation or a disintegrating culture. I usually chose the crises to distract me from being present and became quite easily caught up in the dramatic maelstrom of it all. At those times I climbed into the turmoil with a sense of outrage or judgement or distress. I reacted to the crises because they felt alluring. Somehow, my emotional response to a crisis validated my sense of who Robyn was at that moment. I became caught in a delusion created by emotions that were exciting, and sticky, and interesting to me. This delusion gave me a sense of Robyn that I could clothe, put make-up on, and parade out in the world.

Eventually I learned that all these crises offered me the opportunity to take a deep breath and drop into the very midst of what was happening right then—not with a sense of excitement at the drama but with a heart that could smile and embrace this as a circumstance like any other. I became aware that there was nothing I could afford to turn away from any longer. There was nothing I could afford to react to with venomous rage. I realized that we could no longer avert our global crises by fighting them; I wondered what would happen to the dramas we created if we each decided to be fully present and to respond appropriately to each and every moment.

Through engaging with the obstacle of distraction I realised that the drama and hectic pace that was blowing our world apart was not only global, it was intensely personal. I was staggered by the number of people I knew who were exhausted and dealing with some kind of emotional tsunami. We all seemed to be living in a vortex of chaos, and unless we could drop into the middle of it, into the eye of this storm, with the surrender of a soft and gentle heart, the vicious spiral would only increase. Melchizedek patiently taught me that if I could stay more centred without closing my heart, I could develop the appropriate clarity and wisdom to discover the purpose of this grand all-fall-down experiment of life on Earth. I recognized that Shambhala, as a vision of an Earth filled with light and love, was nothing like the experience most of us were having. But we were the ones creating our experience. No one was going to create Shambhala for us. It seemed to me that the Earth was going through the most tremendous spring cleaning, where so much darkness that was previously hidden was being exposed, and it wasn't much fun.

I also realised that our sacred soul essences were tugging at us to spring-clean. Our yearning for connection to one another, and ultimately, to The Beloved in whatever form it took for each of us, was dragging us to see what was hiding in the dusty corners of our souls. Concealed in the midst of the darkest places, there was a seed of purest light. We could only find the seed through our soft-hearted, present-moment opening towards our chaotic and hectic lives. Nurturing this sacred seed of potential was simple. Through noticing the miracle of each moment, and giving it our pure and undivided attention, the soul seed of light could begin to germinate.

GUIDELINES

Soul seeds.

I have to look deeply to recognize what the seed looks like in different people because each soul seed has an individual fla-vour. Someone's soul seed may really care about other people or be very sensitive or very strong or majestic. Perhaps something in the way I see them on a deep level reminds me of the way Rosa Parks or Nelson Mandela stood up for the rights of the oppressed, or the way Lily's young daughter looks after stray an-imals. I can relate to that because it is particular to an individ-ual. Everyone has these unique and beautiful soul seeds within themselves. Soul seeds thirst for appreciation. When someone else recognizes my soul seeds in me, then I am more likely to nurture those seeds in myself.

Melchizedek had an expand-ed view of what being present meant. He did not simply require that I be mindful of my physical surroundings. When I became aware of those, I observed that my windows needed cleaning, that the lemons were ripe for picking, or that the young girl next door, whom I could see out my dusty window from my fairly untidy desk, was getting better at doing cartwheels. Melchizedek wanted me to be aware of more than my surroundings and more than my

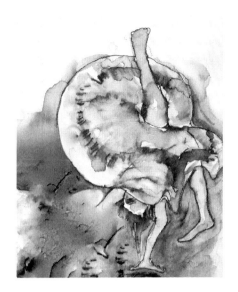

emotional state as well, with its small anxieties about an inappropriate email I sent or about unmet deadlines. To him, my being present was greater than being aware of my thoughts flitting from an upcoming meeting that needed my attention to concern about the state of our society. He wanted me to recognise that when I was truly present, I experienced a calm solidity and a deep-breathing steadiness that allowed for my life to be precarious and changeable. My presence was my equanimity. Instead of presence, it became Presence. It felt like a clear and wholesome home. It was a trustworthy state that didn't minimize the drama but didn't attach to it either. Melchizedek explained that the archetype that symbolized this state of Presence was called Shambhala.

Eventually, after years of distraction, when I focused on Presence, my mind gradually cleared until I occasionally experienced being as present as a great, immovable rock. I sat like a rock in meditation, and eventually, I became rockness. Rockness was patient and solid, but most of all it was spacious. Sometimes I was present in a way that was vast and ancient and timeless. Rockness as an experience was very, very simple. And simplicity, I began to recognize, was a powerful key to letting go of distraction.

Out of the growing simplicity of rockness, which hovered at the edge of my awareness and the periphery of my dreams, I awoke at 5.30 in the morning. It was still dark outside, yet my mind was clear and crisp, and I focused particularly well during meditation until a fly landed on my face and began crawling towards my mouth. The world had not yet woken up, but already the flies were bothersome. This farm was the only place I had lived where the flies were up and about before the roosters.

Mosquitoes and flies. It seemed like they were being called upon to be important teachers for me. The farm owners had seven dogs, twelve geese, two potbelly free-wandering pigs, and accompanying flies. If the number of flies were evaluated in cyber rather than farmyard space, they would be described in terabytes. They drove me to distracted, irritated tears at times. So when the fly started exploring my face at that early hour, I made up my mind to follow the conventional route hereabouts of purchasing some of those sticky flycatchers that you hang from the ceiling, the yellow, spiralling, sugar-coated strip ones to which the flies stick and presumably die a horrid death

Melchizedek threaded a poem through my ears.

Have you ever melted to the touch of a fly as it caressed your cheek, picked your nose, or savoured the moisture in the corner creases of your lips? Have you ever welcomed a fly buzzing in your ear and let it guide you into the delicacy of the present moment? Have you ever quietly opened to a fly's fascination for you, and let go into its tender touch? Have you ever recognized your fly as the gatekeeper and blindly followed it home to God? Try it sometime. A fly is the most intimate of lovers.

This was his poem, and I knew I had the capacity for that kind of presence somewhere, but I wasn't there that morning. I decided that before going to the shop to buy the flycatchers, I would hike up the mountain on the farm and find a peaceful fly-free place to meditate on my decision. Given that I had committed to not killing animals or insects if I could help it, I wanted to make sure that I felt okay about killing the flies. Accompanied by four of my landlady's seven dogs, I found the perfect flat rock halfway up the mountain with a gorgeous view of the sun shining on the mist nestled in the valley below. This time my meditation was deep, spacious, still, and centred. Until I asked for guidance about the flytraps. Within one minute, Sabrina, the Great

Dane, had deposited a steaming mound of dog turd five yards from my lovely rock. The stench sent out homing signals to all the flies in the area, and they arrived instantaneously. I ignored them for a while, then moved a little way away since I could feel irritation creeping in. Then Jessie, the Jack Russell puppy, jumped on my lap to escape attack from Sally, the Great Dane puppy. Their war continued unabated on top of me. Rufus, the Great Dane Labrador cross, licked my face and began gnawing through my arm with dedicated purpose. The flies got worse. It wasn't the kind of meditation I had planned, and I was starting to get seriously edgy. I recognized that if I were going to be a good meditator, I would just stick with experiencing the edginess until it abated. My options were limited: either be a good meditator or a murderer, with my preference veering strongly towards the latter. I gave up any ideas of resolving the situation at that point, because while I might kill the flies and still sleep okay at night, killing the dogs would have had significant karmic consequences, and besides, my landlady would have revoked my cottage lease. I breathed in the slow, early morning air. I leaned back against Rufus and watched the eagles soaring over the crags above me. The sky was ridiculously blue against the mist. The cliffs felt old and solid in the way that African mountains do. As I settled down, the dogs relaxed, and the flies miraculously disappeared.

When I arrived back home, my neighbour appeared bearing gifts; she had been early morning shopping and discovered some citronella candles to chase my flies away. They weren't perfect, but I worked too hard anyway, and as I typed this, the few flies that were still buzzing around my ears were whispering, 'Go outside and play. Go outside and play.'

GUIDELINES

Overcoming the first obstacle of Distraction leads me through the Gateway of *Presence*.

Presence is the Alpha and Omega of this journey. I start with being shown that I need to become more present, but Presence is also the end of the road, and there is nowhere to go but here, and nowhere to be but now. Omega presence is deeper and fuller than Alpha presence because it has moved beyond the world of everyday form represented by teacups and bathtubs and watering cans (among other things).

Presence is not simply the act of drinking tea or brushing my teeth, having let go of the past and the future. To create true Presence, I will need to work through all the other obstacles that I have yet to encounter and release them one by one. Each obstacle forms a veil of illusion that takes the magnificence of full experience and distorts it into the small, misshapen thing that I think is me. I cannot build up a sense of presence; rather, I break down what masks true presence until it eventually reveals itself in all its simplicity and purity. Clearing the other obstacles one by one will enhance my ability to be present in a way that is deeper, more embodied, and simpler.

I was beginning to recognize that Presence was something that happened at the base of my being. When I was disconnected from my legs and my pelvis, I was not fully embodied. I knew that I had never descended fully into my body right down into my toes at birth because as a midwife I had been at births where babies were not disturbed in those first tenuous minutes. Instead, they were given time and patience to simply arrive. And I knew that instead of having a calm and undisturbed birth myself, I was held upside down, roughly dried and cleaned, and then immediately removed from my mum to spend ten days in the nursery, except for the scheduled feeding times. I had learned that the best way to midwife a birth was to be like the rock: slow, sure, and imperturbable. The babies that were born into warm, serene environments that were still and sacred had a different quality about them as toddlers. It took me a while to figure out what the difference was, but then I realized that those babies had simply sunk more comfortably into their bodies, whereas I tended to flutter about mine like an anxious bird that couldn't quite settle into its nest because there were distracting, possibly dangerous humans close by.

I learnt slowly and with great perseverance to come into my body. It took years, both before and after meeting Melchizedek, and I still easily left my body to go wandering off into the stories in my head. Dance helped a lot, mostly because I loved dancing. As the dancing eased the long-repressed tension stored in my body, it also brought up long-repressed emotions. During a three-year dance training I undertook, I soon learnt that on the once-a-month intensive weekends I moved joyfully into my body, and on the Wednesdays thereafter, I was a tearful mess because all the emotions that were locked into the tension in my body wormed their way out once the tension had been released. When I wasn't dancing into Presence, I had to let go into Presence. In doing so, I finally began to sink down into my legs and my toes.

Besides dance, the other effective way I learned for sinking into my body was meditation. I also recognised the pathway to Presence was different for everybody.

There are many roads up the spiritual mountain, and it is not necessary to try and persuade someone else to come trawling all the way down just to try mine. It isn't even necessary to climb this spiritual mountain. Many people far prefer to go surfing or to listen to R&B. If someone else has practices that expand them into a more joyful, loving, exuberant appreciation of life like yoga, marathon running, gratitude, virtual reality, horse riding, laughing, bungee jumping, weight lifting, or playing bongo drums, who am I to question them? Those are most probably the ones they should follow. If those practices lead them to a place where they feel passionately alive, so long as they are not hurting themselves or others, and so long as the practices are heart opening rather than escapist, they should stalk them all the way to enlightenment.

Who am I to know what is best for someone else? They might unconsciously repeat the same spiritual lessons lifetime after lifetime after lifetime for aeons because that, too, is a choice. If I don't think it is a particularly wise one, then I also don't know what the soul choice of that person might be.

Reminder: Having followed so many different Buddhist teachers in so many different traditions over the years, I eventually recognise that it had possibly been a bit of a time waster. I decided that if I wanted to travel up the mountain, it required making a commitment to one path. No point going up and down and up and down and up and down testing this path and that, a spiritual slut for whatever caught my fancy.

I felt like I was developing a clearer sense of what the first obstacle was now, and I was nurturing more simplicity in my life, which allowed me to be present with less distraction.

Simplicity, I discovered, was the true key to overcoming the obstacle of distraction. It allowed me to be present in a very different way. Simplicity was nothing more than unpretentiously putting one step in front of the other. 'Fetch wood, carry water', was how Zen Buddhists from ancient times described being present; when you fetched wood, you didn't get distracted by thoughts about your mother-in-law or your Tinder date. When you carried water, you didn't get distracted by anxieties about your ugly hair-cut or about skipping your yoga class for the fourth time in a month because you were just too lazy to get off your butt in time.

Simplicity caused calmness to expand my heart, joy to float upwards into my stomach, and a weighty, solid quietness to sink down into my feet.

True simplicity was Presence on steroids.

As the simplicity grew, I sank into my whole being, so that eventually I experienced a shift when out walking one day, where everything I identified as mine dropped away. There was a falling into the felt experience and a simultaneous rising into the numinous. The distractions of past and future dissolved. I was moving through the landscape, but because I was not projecting forward in anticipation of what was coming, or to escape my less than perfect past, I had settled all the way down into my body. The shift was quite sudden and noticeable. Instead of me walking past the pecan trees, or the scent of the Buddleia bushes, or the grasses on the side of the path, they moved past me. I experienced the world as if I were seeing it from a moving car in a film where the landscape was rolling past me while all the time the screen and I were not moving at all.

I loved this feeling of the landscape moving past me instead of me moving past it. I started walking every day so that I could get caught up in the wonder of it again. It was as if from the very centre, where was there to move? The feeling was vast and ancient, but my understanding of it was clear. In the immersion of being present all the way down to my toes, irritations, thoughts, and planning dropped away, and a sweetly tender, sacred quality of God as everything emerged. Moment by moment, when I let go of distraction, I became the lucidity of God. Life became a dance where there was nothing other than the dance. And yet the steps of the dance were merely the form; it was the soul of the dance that condensed everything into the utter simplicity of the moment. Like Anthony Quinn teaching Alan Bates to dance at the end of *Zorba the Greek*, the dance or the walk, step by simple step, became a revelation. I became like a wild animal that did not differentiate between form, movement, or the stillness within. The soul of the dance, the soul of each grace-filled step gave birth to an unbroken woman who emerged with a powerful fluency that could be as quiet as a bush-baby, as lunatic as a wolf, as unbroken as a feral horse.

And busy, distracted Robyn dissolved in a puddle of awe in the face of her drum-beating, heart-syncing, hip-swishing love of this very moment.

THE SECOND GATEWAY:
PRANA

GUIDELINES

Prana, creativity, balanced and wholesome self-esteem, healthy sexuality, ease with money

Obstacle One: Shame.

Questions to ask: Do I hold shame? Where is it stored in my body? What incident locked it in there? How do I relate to my shame? What does my beautiful body need to feel whole and loved?

Obstacle Two: Lack of self-worth.

Question to ask: How is my relationship with money related to my self-worth?

The Gateways intersected one another, so my experience of them was not time-bound in a linear movement from Gateway One through to Gateway Seven, although it started with Presence in Gateway One and very definitely came to a completion with moving beyond the sense of a separate self in Gateway Seven. In between these two, the Gateways flowed and overlapped, each informing the next and the ones before.

I could feel Melchizedek behind me and through me again. He stirred in my heart. His energy flowed through my body, a golden colour the consistency of cream. He whispered inside my head, *This is the pathway to who you truly are*. My feet tingled in recognition, my heart thrummed

93

in synchrony, ready to continue the journey. I kept my eyes closed to anchor Melchizedek firmly into my cells. I was still hovering on the edge of sleep and not yet quite ready for the day ahead. The finches chattered, and in the distance, the Hadedahs began their mournful *aaack, aaack, aaack* as they lifted off to bring those of us still drifting in our dreamlands back down to earth.

My interior world was vibrating gently; a pulsing, fluid spaciousness beyond my time-bound daily life. A high-pitched hum wafted through my body, surging up to haunting peaks and ebbing back into quietude again. Pinpricks of light glimmered in a pale, pink-grey gas, a swirling rendition of my internal Milky Way. I sighed and stretched my limbs outside the duvet, feet touching the cool pre-dawn air. The Liminal Lands still floated in my centre as the sounds of daybreak began to percolate through my peripheral awareness: the purr of my fridge waking up, a plate clattering next door, doves warbling amidst the twittering of the house sparrows.

If Presence was the Alpha and the Omega, and distraction was the major obstacle to Presence, why did I need to engage with the other obstacles at all? Surely 'letting go of distraction' on its own would do the trick? I knew that there were many meditative traditions that decried any technique other than Presence. They believed everything else simply created more confusion. But Melchizedek wanted me to work with all seven Gateways. I asked him about this, and he responded:

 You become entangled in emotional responses when you attempt to bypass your obstacles, my Love. Your emotions create veils of illusion which distract you from being fully present. Clear your emotional reactivity, and you will see that the obstacles are simply challenges in your path. Then your Presence may become wider and deeper and richer.

Melchizedek waited as patient as the rock for me to come back to him for further instruction. His references to 'Shambhala', 'the Holy Grail' or 'an archetypal vision for turning lead into alchemical gold' all seemed to be going down the same road. It was a Hero's Journey of seeking my Soul-Self, which, as it turned out at the Second Gateway, was not a road I would willingly have chosen to negotiate.

He suggested that it was now time to explore this Gateway, which entangled most people one way or another. It was the Gateway of *Prana*,[6] the seat of which was held within the powerful and often problematic vital force of our sexuality. Melchizedek motioned for me to look back at the Gateway of Presence and to use what I had learned there to engage with the obstacles in this Gateway.

Releasing the obstacle of distraction from the First Gateway was simple because simplicity was the key through the Gateway of Presence, but when I turned to face the obstacles barring entrance through the Gateway of Prana, things became complicated.

Melchizedek said:

Presence is Wholeness, leading to Oneness. Sexuality is the spark that divides the world into two, and from there it creates the ten thousand things. The obstacles in the Gateway of Prana are numerous. God explores His world through your tentative expansions and hasty retractions. Imagine His gratitude for the gift of your courage to experience.

Unless I had a mirror to reflect it back to me, I couldn't see my own face from inside my own head, so it made sense to me that consciousness of God as Oneness might not be able to experience itself.

Sexuality was the driving force that divided Oneness consciousness into many beings, and procreation was our most primal drive. It was magnificent, beautiful, and raw.

All those chastity belts among Crusader's wives, and celibacy among monastics, and stoning of adulteresses and female genital mutilation illustrated just how fearful the church and the mosques were of sexuality's power. All the wife-beating and rape and incest and sex trafficking and child molestation indicated that they were right to recognise its power. However, suppressing it was likely to subvert it into weird deviances, like paedophilia among priests.

6   In Hindu philosophy including yoga, Indian medicine, and martial arts, *prana* comprises all cosmic energy, permeating the universe on all levels. *Prana* is often referred to as the 'life force' or 'life energy'. It also includes energies present in inanimate objects.

If we suppressed our sexuality, it snuck out as perversion, and if we expressed it forcefully or wantonly, we created havoc. Either way, it seemed we were nailed.

SEXUAL WOUNDING

It seemed to me that despite the potential that sexuality had to link us to healthy, compassionate, caring communities, the Second Gateway was highly charged and fraught with intense emotions. As a midwife, I had been a witness of sexual trauma. Women slammed up against their own sexual wounds or the sexual wounds of their ancestors, which were locked in the cells of their wombs and vaginas when they were giving birth. These ancient memories caused them to constrict in fear against the power of birth, and the constriction created frighteningly intense pain. The more they resisted labour, the more it hurt, and the more they carried wounds and traumas in their reproductive organs, the more they were likely to be frightened of their bodies.

As a Soul Integration facilitator, I worked with many pregnant women to release their history of sexual wounding before birth. In the deep, inner process work of sessions, I witnessed people accessing and then releasing sexual trauma. It was always a disturbing and difficult issue.

Even though I did not have personal experience, in this lifetime, of direct sexual trauma, and my own history of sexual wounding was more genetic than personal, I had developed great regard for the damage it created and for the emotional loops that we tied ourselves in around our sexuality.

I looked to Melchizedek for guidance again, because our human sexuality was too warped for me to know how to harness its vital energy in order to get through the Gateway unscathed. He said:

The wounds of misused sexuality have tainted humanity's bloodline in a systemic infection that has seeped into the life force of you all. Heal your sexuality and you can begin to heal the world.

AWAKENING PRANA

Sexuality has the potential to become *kundalini* energy unfurling itself, and it was *kundalini* energy that flung me into those six months of exhaustion when I first began meditating. From early childhood until my thirties, shame held my sexuality, curled like a sleeping snake in the centre of my belly, hostage. I hadn't thought of myself as sexually repressed. But I knew nothing then of *kundalini* energy, and I had no idea that something as lily-white as meditation could lead me directly into a massive confrontation with the obstacles entangled with my sexuality. I also had no inkling that shame was anything other than an appropriate way for my internal judge to ensure that I behaved as well as possible. I had yet to meet Melchizedek or Mother Mary. I simply thought it would be fun to learn to meditate. I had no idea what I was doing, and I only discovered in retrospect that because the obstacle of shame was entwined around my internal organs and my spine, my body didn't yet have the capacity or strength to handle its *kundalini* power. The *kundalini* experience was my first encounter with the power of sexuality.

I considered the other obstacles in this Gateway of Prana. I had identified the fire of sexuality as a powerful *kundalini* force that was difficult to manage. Next, I considered the shame that had previously made me and many people I knew think that our bodies were less than perfect.

I recognised that the expectations that we all placed on ourselves were so immense and the need we had to be perfect was so ingrained that it was often very hard to be present to the stories held in our bodies. My body may be the temples of my soul, but it is most definitely not perfect. It's a shabby temple at the best of times, and it only becomes a sacred house for my soul when I accorded it recognition in all its shabbiness.

When I was five, and in love with Gavin, son of Auntie Kay and Uncle George, I was given my first taste of my body's imperfections. Gavin was a massive three years older than me, but because I loved him, he was warm-hearted enough to lift me on his bicycle. I must have been very heavy because he grumbled to Aunty Kay about it. 'I suppose I'll have to marry her,' he said, 'But I do wish she wasn't so fat.'

Despite being chubby as a youngster, I became skinnier at school, although with a child's waist and the round healthy cheeks of a child. Nevertheless, I held the usual adolescent girl's criticism of my beautiful, gangly body. I didn't realize back then how beautiful youth is, simply because it is young and so often also explorative and hopeful.

The first time that the fat-feeling really slammed into me in a big way was when I was a second-year student at university. I was sitting on the loo at a pizza place, facing a full-length mirror on the back of the loo door, looking at my thighs which were distorted by the loo seat so that they looked way broader than my upper body. I felt physically sick because they weren't supermodel skinny, which meant they weren't anorexic.

Even a wafer-thin model's thighs would likely spread out on a loo seat when viewed from the front, but I hated mine in that moment and hated myself for having no control over their blobby expansiveness. I just loved food too much. In fact, I had just ordered a huge pizza in the restaurant. The mirror ruined the pizza and many other pizzas and pastas thereafter. It made them both delicious and distasteful at the same time. Food became my *tsundere*.[7] I felt both *tsuntsun* (aloof, irritable, cold) and *deredere* (love-struck) towards it.

As a 21-year-old, I used to imagine that getting older would be beautiful—how my personality would shine more clearly, how my face would express wisdom and love. But as I aged, I became the owner of a frown that ran from the bridge of my nose to my hairline. My lines of anxiety and sadness went in all the wrong directions. However, as I aged, I discovered that there was a difference between the old me and the one beginning to emerge. There was something a little more real about her. I loved the new one. I loved her as Melchizedek loved me. I might have been soft and raw on the outside, but inside I was becoming strong as a warrior.

This is your test, Beloved. Can you be God, not only on the mountaintop, or in the hermit's hut, but also in the hur-ly-burly, wonderful chaotic melange of daily life? And when you quite simply can't, and you fall back into very human reactions of despair and despondency, anger and regret, can you find the Godliness within you to love and appreciate your humanness as you experience it in your body?

---

7   Tsundere: A Japanese term derived from the terms *tsun tsun* (ツンツン), meaning to turn away in disgust, and *dere dere* (デレデレ) meaning to become 'lovey dovey'.

RELEASING THE CONSTRICTION OF SHAME

Shame is the fig leaf of society's conventions, and it ejects me from the Garden of Eden into a miserable place of mistrust in myself. When I begin to let go of shame, I start the long journey of releasing my need to cover up and hide my imperfections.

Without shame, I have more authentic feelings that I don't try to hide. Overcoming the obstacle of shame leads to a delightful sense of self-worth and a deep joy in simply being myself.

But shame is sneaky as hell. It pretends to be important, moral, and good. In a society where self-worth is healthy, shame is healthy too. But in our culture of self-flagellation and low self-esteem, where, no matter how hard I try, I'm never quite good enough, shame is a mangy cur, with a dreary, unpleasant odour and a sulky countenance. Perfection is an impossible ideal, and shame is its conjoined twin.

Shame grinds me down into hopelessness and despair, but it has a positive flipside called remorse. Shame itself seldom serves me; however, regret or remorse for the things I have done and that I wish I hadn't can be a powerful ally. Remorse lifts me out of the murkiness and helps me to reorient into a more wholesome approach to life.

Melchizedek wanted me to revisit the obstacle of shame, the one that had created the problems with my *kundalini* energy. I had secretly been hoping to avoid this obstacle. Now it seemed I was going to have to start digging in the muck to see what else was lying hidden there. He started by reminding me what shame felt like. I felt his words in my body as if they were real:

Shame emerges from the entrails of your little self. It sneaks out and exposes its undigested dregs for all the world to see. It is the dirty laundry of your unclean life. It is your menstrual blood spilled on the white linen sheet. It is the

*ejaculate of your wounded soul-self. It is the sordid fruit of
the knowledge of good and evil. It is the original sin made
manifest.*

Bleurgh!

Despite this, Melchizedek insisted that *Shame is the mud that nourishes
the lotus.* Shame felt like a very muddy part of my spiritual path. Therefore,
maybe it was rich in nutrients to feed the lotus of my awakening.

To get to Shambhala, Melchizedek wanted me to open every skulking
Pandora's box in my soul, hiding nothing away, so that the light might
infiltrate every dark crevice. Soul work was grounding because our souls
are ardent and, like the Black Madonna, they are full of love. If I was
to integrate soul and spirit into my body, I couldn't do it by rejecting
the earthier wisdom. Spiritual evolution could only become real when
I integrated it into the muddy shambles of my everyday life.

At this stage I was living on a farm on the slopes of the Helshoogte
Mountains. Utopia was present in the sheer beauty of the scented roses,
olive trees, king proteas, and craggy mountain backdrops. As I engaged
with Melchizedek's instructions to look at the obstacle of shame, it
was mid-winter and there was snow on the peaks, which I couldn't see
but could feel through the tile floor. Although the fire was blazing in
the hearth, I was wrapped in a fluffy, tartan blanket. At the base of the
mountain was a shanty-town built of tin shacks, plastic tarpaulins, and
a lot of crystal methamphetamine. There the blankets were not fluffy.
Sometimes they were wet, and there weren't enough to go around. In
the vineyards between us, pesticides waged war on the insects, the birds,
and the bees.

I considered the villagers at the bottom of the hill who lived in
windblown, muddy hovels, and with my vague longing to be free of the
first-world drive for perfection, I wondered if they, too, had time for the
romance of a flawless existence.

At the top of the hill, I watched entitled youngsters bitch and gnaw
away at one another's self-esteem in their hopeless striving for a life of
unattainable purity and polish. And all the while they missed the scent of
bread baking in the oven, and all the while they forgot to water their sense
of humour, thankfulness, and forgiveness. Instead of their lives blooming into rich, wild gardens of thorns and roses, in the underappreciated

sweetness of their human frailty, they desiccated into dried-out, hollow shells of bitterness and regret. For a moment I wondered if it was more difficult for them to move beyond their quest for perfection. Didn't Jesus say something about the rich having as much likelihood of reaching the kingdom of Heaven as does a camel walking through the eye of a needle?

I looked back over my sixty years lived on the tops of hills built out of colonial privilege, where the birds did sing more sweetly, the beds were softer, and the laundry was starched with stiff upper lips. I wondered who got to be closer to God—those in the castles on the hill, those in the hovels in the valley? And it seemed to me that no matter if we were trying to be perfect or not, there was one thing that levelled the playing field. Here, on top of the hill or there, in the hollows, it made no difference: we all experienced shame. Shame at having too much or too little. Shame at being innocent or guilty. Shame on the virgins. Shame on the whores. Shame at our imperfections. Shame because no matter how hard or how little we tried, somebody somewhere would judge us for it, and if they didn't, we might judge ourselves. Shame on us all.

I looked for the places where shame still resided in my body and found mounds of it stored in my hips and my womb. It was also in my gut and my bladder. Judgement at my shame lived in my shoulders and my jaw. Shame was a feeling I wanted to avoid at all costs in the years before I met Melchizedek. But it was there, all right.

Shame, with its potential to tie me up in knots and constrict my passion and my love for life had mangled my ability to be real or healthy. Shame was the biggest obstruction to the clear flow of *prana* when my *kundalini* energy first awakened. I was brought up to Behave Myself. Shame was a thick, gnarled rope running through my life, an ugly grey-blue umbilical cord that first attached itself to me in the womb as I imbibed all the shame of my ancestors lurking in the DNA of my amniotic fluid. And then to make doubly sure, it transferred itself to me once again as I entered my body at birth. I picked it up passing through my mother's vagina. Her shameful vaginal residue stuck onto me as if I had been dunked into a vat of tarry meconium, cold and congealed. It hunched my shoulders and twisted my jaw into a tense knot that extended all the way up to my frown.

All this tension restricted my joy for life. It monkey-wrenched me notch by notch into a tense and anxious-to-please person. My best escape

101

was to party with my friends or play with my children who didn't judge me, but inside I was governed by a purse-mouthed harridan, proper, stiff and severe, who told me that only when I was perfect would she relax her grip on my shoulders. And her standards were impossibly high. If I reached for perfection, she increased her demands. Her requirements were always beyond my grasp.

Perfection, I discovered, was not the antithesis of imperfection; it was the antithesis of joy. It was the outward mask of tyrannical self-condemnation which I inherited from Mum and it dwelt beneath my shoulder blades—that place that anchored my wings to my bones. Wings were surely a symbol of perfection, yet it was perfectionism which clipped my wings by shrivelling them. In a Soul Integration session where I was journeying through the Liminal Lands with my beautiful mother, she gave me a symbol of her legacy to me: a pair of perfect, soft, grey kid gloves. They had little pearl-like buttons on the back of them and were small, the size of my grandmother's tiny hands, so perhaps Mum had inherited them herself. The kid gloves symbolized treading delicately through my life instead of embracing it with wide, open peasant's hands and a hearty guffaw of inelegant laughter. My kid gloves could waggle their pretty fingers at me when I didn't behave in a way that deserved love or admiration.

Twenty years down the line, I had wanted to rip off my kid gloves and dig my roughened hands with cracked fingernails deep into the musty earth of this imperfect present moment, but I hadn't known how to do it. I had turned to Melchizedek and Mother Mary. They too were perfect, but at the other end of the continuum, where it was an expression of self-love, not self-judgement. I was sitting on my meditation cushion, placed in front of open bedroom doors in my cottage under the Helshoogte Mountains. I felt them expand outwards from me, touching the mountain and moving beyond it. They expanded backwards in time, holding my mother in a gentle embrace that loved her sweetness and her longing to be whole, and they expanded forwards into the future that may be what it may be. They contained it all. With a sigh of relief, I recognised that this was joy, this was imperfection in all its wholeness. I recognised that this was where I wanted to be. It took me a long time to get there, though, and I couldn't bypass that shame.

SHAME

 Savour the richness of your cracked and brittle vulnera-bility, its contracted throat and bitter belly, Ah, that path leads directly home to God and to the pure, raw beauty of imperfection.

It was my choice if I wanted to live as a constricted perfectionist. I thought of Ruby. She was one of the most badass people I knew. She had the most wonderful laugh, which bubbled out in youthful vitality. She was irreverent, trusting, naughty, and drank too much. She also spread happiness and irrepressible smiles about her, whether she was at work teaching autistic children, down at the pub, or playing pranks on my sons. Her joy was infectious, and it opened doors for her wherever she went. Ruby's joy seemed to be the very opposite of the shaming harridan.

Finally, with a sigh, I turned towards my own shame, and to all the little memories that had tied me up in knots of awkwardness, each of them rolling past me, one by one, like the carriages on the outworn Kenyan train track. Clickety- clack.

My first memory of shame was of Mother's Day on the Sunday after my friend Jean and I had decided, in a flourish of childlike generosity, that we would buy our mothers presents with our weekly Saturday pocket money. We each received a *tickey* a week—two and a half pennies in 1964, enough to buy a pale marshmallow fish from Charles's shop on the farm. They were stacked in a cardboard box smaller than a shoebox next to the bright pink star sweets which gummed our teeth together, the bubble-gum I was not allowed to buy, but Jean was, and the niggerballs, which we didn't know was a bad word yet. I didn't like their liquorice flavour anyway. The marshmallow fish were packed in wax-wrap inside the box. On this day they looked soft and fresh. Sometimes they were dry and dusty. Resolute, I turned my altruistic self away from them.

We had come into the shop through the whites-only entrance, and because my dad was the manager of the farm, we had ducked beneath the counter to explore the merchandise. On the other side of the shelves was the non-white section of the shop, which was much noisier and dustier. Charles always left off serving his customers there when we came in, because even though we were only 7, we got preferential treatment.

Charles was in his thirties, bald, and smelling of pipe tobacco. He was friendly enough, although gruff with us. He was brusquer with the chattering crowd on the other side, where the large wooden bins stored flour, mealie meal and rice, and where the racks displayed matches, Omo soap powder, candles, and greasy twines of pungent chewing tobacco.

Jean and I looked at our options carefully. The small packs of safety pins could make a thoughtful present, or there was a pencil, or a thimble. But then I saw it, nestled between the motley reels of cotton and the knitting needles: a lace handkerchief, pure white beneath its slightly dusty edges, delicate, with two little women in dirndl skirts embroidered in one colourful corner. It was beautiful, and I longed to buy it for my mother, but when I asked Charles how much it cost, he told me five pence—double my weekly allowance.

I was crestfallen and thought about it for ages, played with Jean in the back of the shop among the tyres and paraffin, overalls and gumboots, and finally came up with a solution. My father was the *Boer maak 'n plan* variety of farmer. This South African expression describes men who create resources for their farms where there are seemingly none available, out of barbed wire and ploughshares if necessary. It's genetic. I asked Charles if I could pay for half now and half with next week's pocket money? In the meantime, I could put the remaining *tickey* that I owed him onto my parents' shop account. He was unsure if that was allowed but, after some pleading, he agreed.

Pipe clenched between his teeth, he packed the lace handkerchief into a little brown paper bag, and I bicycled home with my treasure and spent the afternoon creating a Mother's Day card with pencil crayons. It read, 'Roses are red, violets are blue, sugar is sweet, and so are you.' In my family, we didn't get lovey-dovey with one another. Love was either something slightly embarrassing that adults spoke about to each other when they kissed, or that I felt for puppies and horses, so it seemed very courageous for me to tell her how I felt about her in a card.

That night I was in the bath with my younger brother when my mum marched in. 'Robby, have you been stealing?' She knelt down at the side of the bath, grim-faced. 'No!' I was bewildered and scared. She asked me again, and once more I denied it, confused and tearful now. She pulled me up to standing. My tummy glistened roundly, water droplets trickling off it. Head down, I watched the little rivulets of water,

104

watched my tummy. Why was it so round? I wished it were skinnier, like Gail's. Gail was proud of her skinny tummy. My mum asked me if I was lying? 'No!' I wasn't!

'Charles phoned me and said you bought something on my account, but he said he wouldn't tell me what it is. Why you are lying to me?' She spanked me on my bum. Not hard, but the shame, remorse and hurt at how my beautiful idea had gone so badly wrong burnt through me. My belly, an obvious expression of just how unlovable I was, glared up at me, too white and too round. I tried to explain but although Mum begrudgingly conceded that it had been a thoughtful gesture, she still wanted me to know that 'stealing' was 'wrong'. We gave up on celebrating Mother's Day. I had hoped she would love me more, not less.

I look down at my belly now, still carrying the scars from its seven-year-old sadness, and I hold it gently, aware that it took such a small and insignificant rebuff from my mum to create this lurking monster that had been waiting to leap out and disembowel me, waiting to reject any life-loving passion.

A long line of shameful incidents trundled past my memory, accompanied by the set teeth and grimace of the Disapproval of Others and my internal harridan.

I was eight years old, sitting in the front row behind my desk, looking with trepidation at acerbic, astringent Mrs Wilson, ancient, dry and brittle as bone in her grey twinset jersey, brown plaid skirt and brogues, hair primped and mouth prim. She was teaching history, and I could not hold it in my head that it was in 1652 that Jan Van Riebeeck discovered the land of South Africa, which wasn't there before his arrival. She sent me to stand in the corner. Outside the window the eucalyptus trees were ugly, and I hated them. Behind me, Willem, who was clever and whom I never talked to because he was a boy, was giggling at my misfortune. He was whispering to my friend Sarah. Sometimes Sarah and I played 'doctor-doctor' in the shed behind her parents' hotel, but on this day she was revelling in my misery and bobbing her dark, shiny hair at Willem as they sniggered together. I was stung by her treachery, hurt by Mrs Wilson's dismissal of me. I detested Jan Van Riebeeck and suppressed hot tears of anger at him for putting me in this position.

The images were coming fast and furiously. I was 14, and Bernice and Farrah were mocking me because they didn't want to be my friends.

105

Farrah was pretty and popular; Bernice was not. They had teamed up in tightknit rejection of me as they sat on the bench near the high school hockey field and taunted me.

Then the sunlight faded into cool shadows, and I was kneeling in the quiet stone school church in front of the priest the week before my confirmation. It was my one and only attempt at confession, and I was unable to confess to masturbation. It was too enormous a sin and much too dirty. My failure to get the words out of my mouth felt immoral and wicked.

As a 17-year-old art student in my first year at university, my lecturer humiliated me in front of my peers by referring to my immaturity as a burden to him. The intimation was that my youthfulness was inappropriate to the weighty intellect required to produce meaningful art. The remark stung all the more because he was correct. I was young, tremendously immature, and had yet to produce even one piece of authentic art. I was still timid and had no real opinions about the world or myself. But his comment contracted me further. I judged myself for not being an erudite, intellectual 17-year-old. I felt small and insignificant for a very long time.

I tumbled forward into theory of art class at university, sitting in the row behind the young man, name long since forgotten, on whom I had a crush. I stared at him through the lectures, all through every lesson, and he avoided me as much as possible because, in the presence of his mighty intellect, I became mute and stupid. Whenever he was nearby, I tripped over my takkies and bumped into walls.

My next memory was from Botswana, and it was of being continuously and insatiably hungry when I breastfed my kids. I was having a third helping at a barbecue. Kingsley, colonial appraiser of women, age 70 or so, with bottle glasses so thick that I'm amazed he could see me at all, made a very disparaging comment about how I seemed to be 'letting myself go', and 'what a shame' that was. Rory was less than two months old. I slunk off to my chair. And even then, even when the food tasted as if it were poisoning my beauty, my body was so demanding that I polished off this third plateful and practically licked it clean. In fact, the food—and letting myself have it—was the only antidote to the fat-feeling.

As a young woman, I did not have the courage to resist society's disapproval for not being Beautiful Enough. I simply felt inadequate because I was not a careless, carefree, dark-red, flamboyant woman of the night, sinuous as a prowling panther, eyes glaring wildfire.

Much of my shame was and is collective, not only for being a woman but also for being white and privileged in South Africa. When I looked into the hidden recesses of my body, my country's history was a shameful wound that I still carried. It was ugly and dirty like old, grey dishwater that stank from being dammed up for too long, and which had consolidated into lumps of hard matter in my shoulders. When I had left South Africa in my early twenties to live in Botswana for twenty-five years, those foul slabs of shame dropped off in a noticeable thwump of relief. But I was back here now, many years post-Apartheid, and this wound had reconsolidated its keloid-like lumps. It was still dammed up in all of us who were white, unrecognized or not, matched only by the wounds of anger that simmered furtively in the hearts of the shantytowns.

And there was the shame of my sexual misdemeanours, evidenced by the telephone call years after my children had grown, when I had divorced and returned from Botswana to South Africa.

'What?'

I tried to keep my voice as low as possible. The door between my bedroom and the dining room where Gilly was working on my admin was open. My voice got stuck in my throat anyway.

'I have what?'

The doctor's voice was filled with malice and *schadenfreude*. She didn't like me because I was having an affair with a married man. He was supposedly in an open relationship, but my presence triggered something for her. I saw it in her eyes when she spoke to me, and I could hear it in her voice on the phone. 'Gone Or Rhee Yah.' The syllables echoed through my head, dropped like lead into my stomach and then burped up into a ball of bile in my throat.

I had thought I was having a pap smear, although she had asked me if I was sexually active, and I had admitted to the affair. She hadn't told me she was testing for gonorrhoea. Was it even legal for her to have done so behind my back?

'You need to come in for scripts for treatment, for you, your partner and his wife.'

She sounded satisfied, like a great lizard blinking in the sun. Watching me through the phone line. This was her moment of revenge, perhaps for her own unfaithful husband, and she was suitably censorious.

I protested. 'But what will this do to his wife?' Actually, I felt very protective of his wife. In an attempt to make sure I felt okay about the affair, the deal I had with the married man was that we could only be involved so long as it didn't hurt his wife.

'You should have thought of that beforehand.'

Who would have known that Gone Or Rhee Yah could turn me instantly into her husband's whore, into the slut that breaks up marriages, into a traitor towards women, into a shameful woman with a dirty secret in her genitals?

The antibiotics took care of the gonorrhoea within a week, but the aftershock lasted for years. It was the end of the relationship, the end of my sex life for at least five years, and the end of his marriage, which, it transpired, hadn't been so open after all. An innocence died in me that day. All my churchgoing Scottish ancestors rose up out of their graves and judged me with their stony ghost-eyes whistling cold through my bones. For misdemeanours like this, villagers shun women; they cast them out of their communities or stone them to death.

'Be grateful, wretch', they said to me, 'that you can get off so lightly. You do not deserve it.'

There was one last image that arose when I looked at shame. It was a memory of a dream rather than an actual event, and it took me full circle, back into the birth world, but from the other end of the spectrum, creating wheels of repetition and ancestral cycles of indignity.

In the dream, I was an ancient crone giving birth, observed by a group of medical students who were violating my sacred birth space. I groaned through a quavering voice box, shat through haemorrhoids, leaked colostrum through sagging breasts, vomited through yellow teeth, wept through cloudy eyes, dribbled urine out of an incontinent bladder, and pushed my baby out through a prolapsed uterus and grey pubic hair. The students chattered to one another like little birds in their gaudy prime-of-life colours and took notes on their clipboards. Their lack of respect for my experience and the isolation of being treated like something sordid froze my bones.

Finally, I turned to face this shame. Hidden far behind the malodourous monster, vague and formless to begin with, I sensed a wanton and audacious female who was bewitching in her glorious self-confidence.

She was the Black Madonna buried deep inside of me.

Love your beautiful body, she whispered, moth-close. She threaded pink and silver tendrils through it, ever so gently, lovingly, as if it was the most beautiful creature in the world. *It has been poorly treated and dishonoured. Wash the stains of misuse off it, pamper and nourish your skinless skin, breathe love into its tender heart, let warmth and acceptance melt down into the Grail of its womb, dissolve the hardened calcifications of bitterness and disappointment and clothe it in the reassuring frequencies of your patient Earth Mother.*

Grateful for the gift of the pink and silver filaments of love woven through my body, warming my heart, softening my Not Good Enough fears, I turned back to the younger particles of myself. I picked the naked young Robby up out of the bath-tub and rocked her gently, humming lullabies to her white, round tummy, giggling with her about the fairies circling it in the steamy bathroom, inhaling the smell of her fresh, wet seven-year-old hair, telling her how lovely her Mother's Day card was. She nestled into my shoulder and relaxed, then fell asleep. That little Robyn belonged in my heart. I placed her there very gently so as not to wake her, and then moved to Mrs Wilson's classroom to find Robyn-in-the-corner. The two of us made paper aeroplanes and threw them at Willem. We pulled faces behind Mrs Wilson's back as I encouraged her to do cartwheels. Little Robyn squealed with delight, much to Mrs Wilson's displeasure. But before the Ice Queen could express her condemnation, I tucked Robyn-in-the-corner safely beneath my collarbone.

One by one, I revisited each of my shame-filled selves. Teenage Robby facing the Bernice-Farrah combo laughed as she linked arms with the 60-year-old Robyn with the sagging breasts, and they wandered off to try on some illicit lipstick that she would be disciplined for wearing on the school grounds. Instead of being afraid, she felt daring, as teachers, headmistress, and Bernice-Farrah forgot to reproach us.

The priest stood at his pulpit giving a sermon about the wonders of sexuality and how masturbation was not only natural but was healthy for adolescents. The headmistress promptly fired him. He went on to become a Bishop in the Anglican Cathedral.

Seventeen-year-old Robyn shrugged off being young and immature at art school, along with the expectation that she should be intellectual and preferably driven by angst and meaningful despair. She decided to

109

have fun, and to create a series of images about Zhoma and the flow of life between them.

Robyn flirted with the young man in the theory of art lectures, who might have been intellectual but had no idea how to dance on a table-top. She ignored bottle-glasses-Kingsley's remarks. Whistling a Harry Belafonte song to herself, she returned to the serving table to pile up a fourth plate of food while doing a little jig of happiness to the ditty: 'If you wanna be happy for the rest of your life,' she warbled, 'never make a pretty woman your wife. So from my personal point of view, Get an ugly girl to marry you.'

And she embraced the GONORRHOEA by writing about it. Even though contracting gonorrhoea was such a tiny transgression, just a blip in a microcosm, it united her in some small way with the shame experienced by millions of men and women with HIV, with queers and trans-gender folk made into society's misfits, with children who had been raped and sold into sexual slavery and made to feel like outcasts and with all of humanity and its shameful sexual secrets.

There, there, beautiful body, made to dance on this Earth like a Maori Queen with strong and sturdy thighs: except this body was papery me, skinless light-walker, tiptoeing around Other People's Feelings to keep myself safe, 60-year-old with slender ankles, humming the Earth Mother's song as I danced, paper-light, to her beat. This body of mine, uniquely me, it too had its own peculiar song, if only I could learn it well enough to sing as a glorious soprano, meeting the Maori Queen's deep bass voice, aligning with the patient thrum of the Earth, and composing a powerful symphony of light for all the world to hear.

THE THIRD GATEWAY:
PERSONAL POWER

GUIDELINES

The obstacles: Constriction of the self, misuse of power, disempowerment, anger, and insecurity

Question to ask: Who holds the power? What does true equality look like? Can there be equality between a parent and a child, or a boss and an employee, or a banker and a homeless person?

I noticed early on in my meditation career that spiritual guidance came in many forms:

- Kwan Yin for Pure Land Buddhists.
- Avalokiteshvara for Tibetan Buddhists.
- Melchizedek and Mother Mary for me.
- The ancestors for sangomas or traditional African healers.
- Pranayama, meditating and doing yoga for a Hindu.
- Focusing on the Absolute for an Advaita practitioner.
- Returning to Jesus for absolution and forgiveness for a Christian.
- Mindfulness for a secular person who was appalled by the harm caused in the name of religion.

We go to the places where our soul draws us most strongly. Kittisaro's love for Kwan Yin guides him in making decisions. His humility flowed through aligning himself as closely as possible to her wisdom and humble presence. He was the friend to whom I could talk in detail about Melchizedek because he had a similar deep connection to Kwan Yin. It felt wonderful to have someone understand my inner world. His wife Thanissara, on the other hand, is spunky, with intelligent eyes and a dry, subversive sense of humour. I love her impish lack of respect for authority that blends curiously well with her ability to listen deeply to my problems. Thanissara doesn't put up with inauthenticity or bullshit, and yet she is very humble in the face of truth and vulnerability.

Over the years these two wise and precious teachers also became my friends because they were insightful and supportive and because, like their mentor Kwan Yin, they listened to the sounds of the world with a humble sense of ease. Humility is an underrated quality. The word derives from the Latin word *humilis* 'low, lowly'. It reminded me of how

Taoists use water as an analogy for humility. Lao Tzu, Taoist Master from the fifth century BC, author of the *Tao Te Ching*, described the 'Way of water', which Ursula Le Guin has translated and explained in this quote:

> The weakest, most yielding thing in the world, as he calls it, water chooses the lowest path, not the high road. It gives way to anything harder than itself, offers no resistance, flows around obstacles, accepts whatever comes to it, lets itself be used and divided and defiled, yet continues to be itself and to go always in the direction it must go. The tides of the oceans obey the Moon while the great currents of the open sea keep on their ways beneath. Water deeply at rest is yet always in motion; the stillest lake is constantly, invisibly transformed into vapour, rising in the air. A river can be dammed and diverted, yet its water is incompressible: it will not go where there is not room for it. A river can be so drained for human uses that it never reaches the sea, yet in all those bypaths and usages its water remains itself and pursues its course, flowing down and on, above ground or underground, breathing itself out into the air in evaporation, rising in mist, fog, cloud, returning to earth as rain, refilling the sea.
>
> Water doesn't have only one way. It has infinite ways, it takes whatever way it can, it is utterly opportunistic, and all life on earth depends on this passive, yielding, uncertain, adaptable, changeable element.

It was surprising to me that the way to discover freedom of movement through the Third Gateway, the Gateway of Power, was through learning about humility. I had associated the word 'humility' with fawning, obsequious lackeys trying to curry favour with their masters. Yet when I came across teachers displaying true power, they were humble as apple pie, lowly as water. And they always made me feel as if my ideas were worthy, so I left them with a deeper commitment to follow through on those ideas.

Nelson Mandela was a good example. He was considered a fool to engage in dialogue with the Afrikaners and British colonialists who were responsible, either through their actions or their ignorant disdain, for imprisoning him for twenty-seven years for challenging the Apartheid regime. After his release, he didn't trust that what they had done to him was acceptable or good; he simply trusted in the underlying goodness of their souls beneath the fear that caused them to incarcerate him for all those years. He said, 'The best weapon is to sit down and talk.' Our response to his humility was a global, unanimous love for the man. He imagined the best in his oppressors and brought out the best in them.

When I considered his approach as a powerful world leader, what stood out was what a good listener he was. Being a good listener seems to be synonymous with being humble. Being a good leader seems to include being genuinely more interested in others than oneself.

Listening deeply was something that belonged to this Gateway of True power. My father-in-law was a man who listened well. It was a remarkable gift. I always felt that whatever I had to say was truly interesting to him, even when I was pontificating as a 20-year-old know-it-all about how the world worked. He would nod and ponder and ask more questions with a small smile of pleasure on his face, and I would dig myself into ever-deeper holes of pretension that he didn't seem to judge at all. Listening deeply seemed to me to be the key to allowing true power to flow strongly and easily though the world. If only we could all recognise its gift.

Nineteenth-century British politician Lord Acton famously said, 'Power tends to corrupt, and absolute power corrupts absolutely.' Engaging with my power, that source of sunshine and nourishment, benevolence and warmth, without becoming corrupted by it, required that I let go of everything within me that yearned for fame, success, glory, competitiveness, or more money than others. It required that when others clambered over my head and put me down in their scramble to the top of the spiritual or material mountain, I had enough inner self-confidence and wholesome humility to not get caught up in the race.

This wasn't easy for me. When I was a child, I was rewarded for my achievements and disapproved of when I didn't meet other people's high expectations of me. This was not unusual, growing up in the sixties and seventies; however, Mum was very concerned that we should never grow up vain, or 'too big for our boots', so praise was fairly hard to come by in our family. A grunt of approval from Dad, or a 'well done, Robby,' with a small smile from Mum, would keep me satisfied for weeks.

Disapproval from my parents, teachers, colleagues, anyone in authority—to be honest, even from my children—filled me with dread. My stomach would turn into a knot of anxiety, and I would scramble to make them like me again. Apparently, there is a personality type identifiable by their preference for anything, even death, above humiliation. The word 'humiliation' comes from the same root as 'humility'—to be 'brought low—but we can be humble by choice, whereas we are forcibly cut down by humiliation. It only cuts down what is not needed, the false sense of power that comes from trying to scramble away from low self-worth. I was not particularly afraid of death, but my fear of humiliation was colossal.

Try as I might, this fear never actually stopped me from being humiliated, it just slowed me down from being brave enough to smoothly follow my dreams because I was so busy fulfilling other people's dreams of me. In primary school, my teachers disapproved of me being loud; my friends disapproved of me being quiet. In high school, my parents disapproved of make-up and bikinis, and my friends disapproved of bobby socks and the 1950s clothing that my mother thought was appropriate for a teenager. My parents disapproved of bad boys; I wasn't attracted to good ones. Disapproval didn't stop me from doing what I wanted to do, but oh, the tiptoeing around in an effort to make it all right again wore out the points of my shoes and cut deep furrows into my forehead.

Taoists also speak of another principle that has to do with true power. This is *wu wei*, which translates as 'effortless effort', or non-striving. It is about appropriate action, and like water, which simply flows along its path, *wu wei* encouraged me to choose my direction in each moment with a grace and ease that was seemingly effortless. This kind of effortless effort was not concerned about What Other People Thought. *Wu wei* is expressed through the big-wave surfer or the ballerina whose focus is strong and one-pointed, but whose fluidity and grace in responding moment to moment to the direction of the wave or the music are effortless. This is true power, where actions are taken for the sake of the actions themselves, rather than for some distant goal, like money or fame or Pleasing Other People.

Melchizedek buzzed with pure power; there was a high-voltage, constant force radiating from his core.

As always, he mirrored our highest potential, and in absorbing his energy, my centre awakened to its steel strength and the blistering coolness of a pure electrical charge. Melchizedek's heart was sweet; I could lie curled in the centre of it like a purring cat, but his power was fierce, glittering, calm and cool.

Melchizedek's clear centre had a message to humanity:

Plug into this Power. It is your birthright. How else do you think you will change the world? The electrical charge of pure power can fry lower, denser energy, transfiguring the detritus into crisp, clear vision. Power that is untainted by greed is truth in its purest form. Power does not belong to you, yet its clarity can cleanse the world. This is the free energy your world has been looking for.

The centre of your body is a powerful generator that transforms higher vibrational frequencies into electrical storms of mighty strength that shift physical matter by realigning its energy into light—light on which you can travel, light which holds all the knowledge and wisdom you need to birth peace onto your planet, light of the pure, white heart.

And powerful as Melchizedek's message was, there was nothing about it that made me feel I was unequal to him.

He continued, this time with more down to earth and practical advice. He wanted me to come back to my centre. *The Still Point at the core of your being.* I could find this Still Point in my heart or my *hara* or my fingertips, but at that moment he wanted me to find it in my emotional centre. He indicated my solar plexus area, the little soft, hollow space beneath my sternum where my ribs met the front of my chest. *Find the effortless effort of non-striving in this Still Point,* he said, *and connect it to the natural rhythm of the Earth.*

If I was to find the Still Point at the core of my being, I needed to find ways to recalibrate and to come back into harmony with the slow patient song of the Earth. When I was a baby, my body remembered the frequencies it needed to disarm disease. As an incoming soul, I wafted in on the chords of my unique song, consonant with the Earth. But it didn't take long for discordance to arise. Now, computer and cellphone smog interfered with my natural frequencies, which were set to resonate with the frequency of the Earth and its geomagnetic fields. My hurried, harried world interrupted the melody of my song. This was the way of things; there was nothing unusual about it. To learn what we had come here to learn, we all had to experience whatever it was that disconnected us individually from the wisdom of the Truth in the centre of our beings.

In writing your new song, compose a symphony that reverberates out into the heavens, find the tune that lights your heart and then harmonize it with the Earth to create a symphony that is sonorous, vibrant, rich, and evocative.

Walking barefoot on the earth, looking at the stars, and realigning with the natural world helped me to tune in more easily. When the Earth held me steady, I breathed more deeply, and I settled into my body. When my body was in harmonic resonance with the natural world, I could pick up insights from Melchizedek more easily. It was from walking barefoot on the Earth that I settled down enough to tune into the still point at the centre.

When I considered how this related to the Gateway of Power, I noticed that when I was attuned to the *wu wei* rhythm of Melchizedek, Mother Mary, or Mother Nature flowing through the cells of my body, the issue of who held the power in interpersonal dynamics became irrelevant. Instead of the irritation, rage, fear, or anxiety other people might have ellicited within me, I was more likely to experience a strongly felt sense of ease and confidence where I was no longer playing Myself Against Them, so that our communication slowed down into a clearer rhythm that enabled me to listen with less judgement.

ANGER AND INSECURITY

The biggest obstacle blocking the Third Gateway, said Melchizedek, was false power.

Humanity is scrabbling for the false power of kings and riches. You cling to the fairy-tale belief that they are the secret to happy-ever-after endings. Ride the pendulum swing of tyrant and victim until you tame it. Guide it gently home and come to a halt in the centre of your being. There you will discover the purest gold of true power hidden in the quiet certainty and humility of your Soul-Self.

I received this message from Melchizedek after I had returned to Cape Town and had lost the protection of husband and kids. I knew it was time for me to continue the journey of self-discovery, yet all this work felt too self-centred and isolating. Everybody else seemed to be having fun on his or her Friday evening, so why was I alone at home, having to focus on recognising the difference between true and false power? I remembered the Friday parties of my now long-ago life, all the people, the vivacity, and the alcohol. Then I remembered the hangovers and still feeling lonely. I turned back towards Melchizedek. *You are never alone,* he reminded me, *unless you believe that you are.* I stretched into that and remembered the times when I had felt so alone that even the air I breathed didn't belong to me. These were not times I was on my own; they were times like the day I made a stupid comment in a group of students I was working with, which showed that I wasn't listening. I contracted into a tight ball of self-condemnation that felt utterly disconnected and very lonely.

Feeling separate as Robyn against the world not only caused my feelings of loneliness, it caused me to feel rage, discrimination, manipulation, jealousy. and all the other emotions that lined up to defend the Me Against Them section of myself. Usually I felt absolutely justified in hanging onto those judgemental feelings. They seeped from the intuitive intelligence in my solar plexus, which I identified as an extension of my gut brain. From there they seeped into my analytical, censorious head brain, and then they circulated in my blood, creating jaw-clamping, finger-clawing tension.

My anger arose from a sense of me against the world. My loneliness arose from a vague disquiet about the world against me. My anger and loneliness were linked in an unconscious dance of power that I couldn't quite rationalise, but I had a vague feeling that they were both associated with judgement, either my own or other people's. The places where I felt most alone were not hermit dwellings in natural surroundings where I was solitary out of choice. Such places felt expansive and welcoming to me. Because I was fairly introverted, I would find myself a little lonelier at social gatherings than on my own, although if I was having fun, my sense of loneliness dissipated. I had in the past preferred bolstering my unease at parties with padding in the form of beer, wine, flirting, or whatever took my fancy. The worst forms of loneliness for me, though, and the places where I personally had felt the most disconnected, were in institutions where the rational, cognitive left-brain functions that drove them made me stupid with unease. There was something about the power dynamics of such places that made me feel rejected and outcast. Hospitals, schools, prisons, corporate power structures, army barracks (I had never been in an army barrack, but they looked hostile from the outside), all carried the potential to leave me trembling with dismay. Even though I realised that this wasn't normal, it didn't stop my dislike of such places. Why did I have such a reaction to institutions, apart from the mistrust of them engendered by boarding school? I rationalised that perhaps it came from my experiences in maternity wards where the stress levels were ridiculously high.

This feeling of being pitted against the world outside meant that I even ran cowering from the left-brain tasks that defined me as an individual. Organisation belonged to the part of my brain that was linear and time-bound. It was the part that knew that I needed to boil the water before adding the teabag, or that writing an email required a hello before the body of the mail and a goodbye at the end. I got that those were useful skills. It was the part that liked to line up all the little Robyns in rows and make sure they were all presentable and polished. But that part of me didn't know that the silent pinpoint of Robyn at the centre even existed. That part of me could crush my heart's longings with its judgement.

As a result, I was cowed by tasks such as admin and organisation in case I got caught in their cogs and ground down to nothing. Deep down, I was a little organised, and pleased on the odd occasion when my ducks were neatly lined up in tidy, feather-dusted rows. I had great admiration for intelligent people and for other people's organisational skills. I recognised that human life as we know it could not function without organization. But I was smacked sideways by how it ran the global show. As a heartless tyrant of megalomaniacal proportions, it

118

isolated and distanced me from the quiet, humble power at the centre of my being.

Of course, it is not only possible, but imperative for balance, that we learn to do left-brain work and simultaneously stay connected to the creative flow of the Universe through right-brain intuition. Many people love the organized, structured experience of using their left-brains efficiently. Genius is nothing more than the trick of connecting and balancing right brain and left brain, intuition and intellect, Oneness consciousness and everyday life, Heaven and Earth.

When the power between my own left and right brains was not balanced, it made me edgy. Doing left-brain work often disconnected me from my true power at the silent centre of my being. It shouldn't have, but it did. Robyn felt judged and discriminated against. And I realised that the real cause was that Robyn was judging and discriminating against herself, comparing herself to others. She shouldn't have, but she did. And so she preferred escaping from day-to-day organization into creativity and communing with the gods.

And beyond my unhealthy relationships with institutions and organisation was an aspect of the sense of separation that seemed to create power dynamics and loneliness. This aspect comprised the feelings I associated with hatred, including resentment, irritation, and anger.

I had assumed that hatred would have been the major obstacle to the Gateway of Love, and I had already figured out that love would be the Gateway centred in the heart. Weren't love and hatred on opposite ends of the continuum? It became apparent once I felt into it that hatred closed this Gateway of True Power. Hatred belonged to the obstacles of conflict and misuse of power. It arose in response to my feeling thwarted in some way or another. It was so easy for me to get caught in the false and judgemental power of comparison, where I was weighing up who might be trying to control or disempower me, especially in institutionalised power structures.

I thought back to when I was standing next to the bed of one of my clients in obstructed labour as she waited for a caesarean section. Passive aggression was seething out of my shoulders while my jaw tightened with frustration. 'Theatre is busy,' we were told. 'There are emergencies more urgent than yours.' 'Another half an hour' was the refrain we heard, but we had been waiting for six hours, and there was no relief in sight. My client was hanging onto her husband, moaning, and I was rubbing her back. It was like this sometimes.

The midwives were underpaid, overburdened and exposed to terrified, helpless women in pain, day in and day out. They were also under-appreciated and frustratingly limited in their power to change the bureaucratic decisions constantly made on their behalf without consulting them. I knew, as a midwife myself, how it was to feel that level of frustration, and I knew how easy it was to take my frustrations out on those lower than me in the unyielding hierarchy of the medical system. I observed it happening over and over among my colleagues. It was soul-crushing. The entire hierarchy of the medical institutions caused uneasy power dynamics between all the staff.

I was working as a doula, or labour support person, that day, and we were in a large government hospital where I didn't know the staff. As a result, I was lower in the hospital hierarchy than the cleaners. I was as disempowered within that hierarchy as an ant, and I was trying to ignore my shoulder-clenching frustration. It was directed at a paediatric registrar who, ten minutes previously, had marched through the curtain screening our small labour room off from the corridor outside. Young, with an important jaw, she didn't acknowledge our presence, let alone greet us when she entered. We heard sounds of grief coming from the curtained-off room next door. A registrar is a qualified doctor who is training to specialise. This one was specialising in paediatrics, and I would have assumed she had chosen this specialisation because she liked babies and children. However, she had come in bearing a tiny bundle of a newborn baby in front of her, and she didn't look as if she liked her at all. I glanced at the mite, who was translucent, shiny-red, maybe ten centimetres long. I guessed she must have spent only twenty-one or twenty-two weeks in the womb before her birth, and therefore she was only just over halfway to full term, way too premature to be considered viable. The doctor was grim; she continued to ignore us, which we should have been used to by then. She wrapped the baby in a clear plastic bag, a special hospital plastic bag designed to keep her warm, so no doubt an expensive plastic bag, but it looked like a large sandwich bag. And she hooked the baby up to a heart monitor at the resuscitation table in our room. There were other resuscitation tables in other empty labour rooms ten metres away, and there was the mother's breast, which would have kept the baby warm and loved, but the doctor chose us as her audience instead. For some reason, she preferred to be busy and impatient in our labour room.

The almost-but-not-quite-feasible-baby's heart was pumping at thirty beats per minute instead of 120 to 140. The sound of it through the monitor was slow and tenuous. She was alive but hanging on by a thread. Once she was strapped to the monitor, the doctor obviously felt she must wait a while to observe the baby, but it looked like she found it boring. She continued to ignore my client who was sobbing softly into her husband's chest. She looked up at the corner of the ceiling, one arm across her chest, the other hand on the baby, disdain on her face.

After ten minutes or so, without glancing at us or the baby, she removed herself. She left the baby to die alone while its heartbeat still pumped through the room with a slow, unsure beat. I felt anger welling up inside of me at this ugly doctor who represented everything cold and mean about the institution. I fantasized about grabbing her by her white collar, squashing her stethoscope between my fist and her white, thin-skinned neck, where I imagined I would see a blue vein pulsing. The fantasy fascinated me, because the vein had a dusky, blue-grey pulse that I had the urge to snuff. I observed my immense self-righteous strength and imagined a strange hiss coming from my throat. It felt as if thick smoke was pouring out of my eyes. I visualized myself lifting her off the floor and striding to the window where I planned to throw her three floors down to the road below. She didn't belong in my life.

Melchizedek's hand touched my shoulder. *Put her down, my Love.* He breathed the words into my head where they cleared the smoke and the anger away. Confused, I dropped the fantasy, and a weird calm settled over me. The doctor, who still hadn't even noticed us, brushed her coat down and walked out. I had been shaken by the intensity of my rage, trembling at her unconscious, busy importance. Melchizedek continued, *Write a report and submit it to her superiors, so that this bitterness doesn't harm you.* I felt my anger drain away as I softly rubbed the back of my labouring client. Without discussing it, the three of us prayed silently for the baby in her plastic bag whose heartbeat picked up to forty beats per minute, then forty-five. We joined into a rhythm of baby's heartbeat, labour contractions, sighing and moaning; our trio, together with the tiny mite of a baby, settling into a kind of timeless peacefulness at life coming in and going out. I knew she would die shortly. I knew she should be with her mother at this time. I knew if I said anything, I would be escorted out of the hospital immediately and my client would have to manage without me. The mood in the room with its hospital disinfectant and its torn plastic curtain had transformed into a tranquil silence that resonated beneath the sounds of labour and hospital and heartbeat.

PLAYING WITH POWER

As a baby, I couldn't differentiate between my mama, myself, and the bed. As a baby I only experienced the place of meeting, my hand fondling my mother's cheek, my skin touching the bed linen, without a sense of hers or mine, and therefore without a sense of needing to fight anyone else to get my share.

As a toddler, I demolished this idyllic picture in moments. As a toddler, I was heartbroken that some of the love and attention I had received before my baby brother arrived had been diverted to him. I had less power over my mother, who was still my world, and I panicked. I became angry, sullen, manipulative and strategic. I pretended to love my brother sweetly in order to curry favour and win back my mother's love. I was no longer Monarch of All I Surveyed. I had lost power in our family dynamic, and please God, Beelzebub, Mum, or whoever was in charge here, I wanted to find a way, any way at all, to regain it.

As soon as I developed a sense of self-identity, I became embroiled in the comparison of myself in relation to everything that was not myself, and out of that came a primal, instinctual urge to control and manipulate whatever wasn't me. As a two-year-old, I began to play with power. And power-plays became an everyday part of my life. Most of this expression or suppression of power happened unconsciously, often through anger in one form or another. Then my parents taught me that anger was unacceptable, and after quite a number of years of pushing back with whinging, I learned to hide it, where no one, not even myself, could find it.

My emotions, though, are outside of time, just as the astral lands are outside of time. I remember how, a couple of years ago, I reverted to a five-year-old stuck inside my 57-year-old body. The five-year-old me watched my father taking sides with my mother who was not coping with my whinging. This little me was overwhelmed with five-year-old rage because I was impotent to make life behave the way I wanted it to. We had just returned from a learning-to-swim outing at Uncle Fred's swimming baths in Worcester. It was the middle of our summer holidays, and we were each permitted to choose a treat from the café before the nine of us kids plus the three mothers piled back into the Kombi van to drive home to the farm. I wanted crisps or a cool drink, but I got Star sweets because it took me too long to decide. I didn't want Star sweets and had a meltdown.

Mum reported to Dad in the evening, who told me off for being insolent since I was still sulking. They were just a few stern words, but with the force of massive disapproval behind them. I was a BAD daughter.

The 57-year-old me was attending a workshop. I had wanted decisions to go one way; others had disagreed. Immediately, I reverted to age five. I could feel the disappointment and disempowerment welling up inside me, and I badly want to cry or sulk. My tummy contracted in five-year-old fear, and the feelings of the disapproval of others were still as strong and hurtful as they were all those years ago. My emotional body was the body of a five-year-old without crisps, who had disappointed her mummy and daddy once again.

When I realised how I had been triggered, I started investigating my anger more carefully. As my guide through the Liminal lands, Melchizedek advised me to,

explore the sticky astral stuff that impacts so significantly on who you are, my love, and then let it go. Breathe a deep sigh of relief and feel the spaciousness that remains when you release the individual and collective wounds from the cells of your body where they have been imprisoned.

I noticed that some people flung their rage about indiscriminately; others suppressed it in passive-aggressive resistance, and a lucky few simply dealt with it by addressing the issue squarely. Those were the people who neither expressed nor suppressed their rage, but who took responsibility for the difficult feelings it brought up in their bodies. They could then respond appropriately to the situation by being centred in their own power without playing power games of either dominating others or playing the victim themselves.

I wasn't allowed to express my anger as a youngster, so my unconscious tendency was to fall into the passive-aggressive box. As a young adult, this tendency was so unconscious that I didn't even know it was there. I thought I was the good guy, and everyone else was attacking me for no reason. Then I recognized that I needed to deal with my set jaw and stiff shoulders, but I hated the feelings buried underneath them and didn't know what to do with them. I tried to bring things back into alignment by expressing my anger. However, anger and I were uneasy bedfellows. The few times I expressed it, it backfired on me hopelessly.

Once I yelled at Tim from the craft outlet in Gaborone. I was fed up with waiting for payment on old invoices and was so mad-angry that I told him to 'fuckoff and don't tell-me to calm down.' I had slammed the phone down after he said in a self-righteous voice that he hadn't paid me because he hadn't received part of the consignment. I had never yelled at anyone before. But he was such a liar! The power of having expressed myself so forcefully felt quite exhilarating. I decided this was the new me: strong, independent and, watch out World, I was a force to contend with. Then I opened the drawer beneath my desktop to retrieve a pen. There were the thirty teddy-bear passports that were supposed to complete the order to the craft outlet, neatly bound in an elastic band. Shame-faced, I had to phone him back to apologise.

Another time, a colleague told me that the tension between the two of us was entirely my fault because of my 'mother issues.' She looked at me smugly, having checkmated me. A surge of anger at the disempowerment and unfairness of her behaviour blasted through me in a tsunami so strong that I felt as if I had the strength to lift the huge wooden table constructed of railway sleepers and to throw it at her. My eyes launched fireballs of black rage at her. One, two, three, four black fireballs of rage. Although I didn't throw the table, my rage was palpable, and I was terrified by its power. It left me shaking and battered.

Mostly, though, the person that I judged harshly was myself. Much of the time I relented and backed off from any confrontation. But if I looked deeply, I was only outwardly calm. Inwardly, I could either be seething, irritated, or in such denial that the anger had become entirely invisible to me. It emanated through my cold jaw, my haughty arrogance and my bitter mutterings, but I didn't see it, except occasionally in my dreams.

When my anger built up inside and I had no outlet for my exasperation, my frustration got bigger and bigger, and I shrank into a hand-grenade-size bomb. If the bomb had exploded, I would have become huge, and everybody else would have either contracted in response or have fought back until it ended in bloodshed and tears. Because I hated confrontation, I seldom lobbed my hand grenade at people; I was more likely to contract. so that even though my resentment was everywhere, like dark matter, I still felt tiny and unhappy.

BALANCE OF POWER

Two years after Melchizedek had asked me to investigate the Gateways, I was at a market in Australia with my three adult sons. We had all met up for a few weeks after spending a year apart. I was distressed and feeling judgemental. All three of them had appalling hangovers, having stayed up all night catching up with one another. They looked unwell, unshaven, and unkempt. Much as I adored my kids, they were not conventional and proper. I wandered off in an irritated frame of mind, and on my return noticed my middle son sitting on the grass with three mentally  challenged kids, two of whom were severely autistic, and one who had Down Syndrome. Maf is a musician. He was barefoot, having lost his shoes the evening before, and he was smoking a roll-up cigarette to ward off his exhaustion. He was playing the guitar for them and showing them how to play it themselves. They were entranced. The Down's kid was drooling into the guitar and making soft, cooing sounds. She was thrilled with herself, and all four of them were captivated by their delight in one another. Something about the true power in this Down's child, and the equality between all of them in this huddle, made me reconfigure my understanding of where I wanted my power to be.

I came across an article by Dennis McGuire from the Adult Down Syndrome Centre in Illinois about what the world would be like if people with Down Syndrome ran it.[8] It sounded a whole lot more in alignment with Shambhala than our present world order did. Some of the things that would become commonplace would be affection, hugging, and caring for others. All people would be encouraged to develop and use their gifts for helping others. People would be refreshingly honest and genuine. The words 'hurry' and 'fast' would be not be uttered in polite society; 'plenty of time' would take their place. Art, music and dancing would be big. John Travolta in *Saturday Night Fever* would be even bigger. People would not hurt the feelings of others or lie or keep secrets. I bet they would all have stuffed animals tucked under their pillows at night too.

It seemed to me that these Down syndrome kids were not caught up in power games. Power describes the dynamic between us and others. Almost every relationship we have is a dance between who is more powerful and who is less so. A baby can be powerful and demanding. A president or a terrorist can play the victim. I could get caught up in feeling uneasy because I hadn't tried hard enough, or had expressed myself too forcefully, or was feeling side-lined.

That type of uneasiness is created by unequal power dynamics. And in negotiating my way through this gateway I was beginning to recognise that competing for power in even the simplest relationship never served me. I thought of people I knew who were comfortable in their power. They were often easy-going and funny, sassy and sexy, quiet and calm, effective and efficient. They breathed deeply and easily, and they carried a quality of serenity that arose from being unaffected or distracted by money, fame, power, or society's expectations.

Balance of Power:

GUIDELINES

If I look deeply into the continuum of power, an interesting pattern around masculine and feminine archetypes emerges. These are not gender classifications because I know plenty of aggressive women and wimpy men. In Chinese medicine, the archetypes are termed yang and yin. In the West, the same

8   http://www.nads.org/pages_new/news/ruletheworld.html

archetypes are described as masculine and feminine. I have learned from various teachers, especially within the world of Soul Integration, and from my own experiences through using Soul Integration sessions, to address the issue of power. There is a continuum of power from the extreme exploitation of the tyrant through balanced equity of power down to the total disempowerment of the victim. Negative masculine energy holds the most power, and negative feminine energy the least. Positive masculine and feminine qualities sit balanced in the centre. A chart defining the way we play with power might look like this:

Power Traits

Negative Masculine	Positive Masculine	Balance of power	Positive Feminine	Negative Feminine
Abusive	Wise	Standing in truth	Loving	Victimized
Dictatorial	Providing	Integrity	Maternal	Manipulative
Tyrannical	Protecting	Authenticity	Nurturing	
Raping	Intellectual	Equanimous	Tender	Secretive yet gossiping
Killing	Rational	Respected	Abundant	
Autocratic	Grounded	Respectful	Fertile	Scheming
Closed-hearted	Warrior energy	Deep listening	Peaceful	Martyr complex
Judgemental	Benevolent	Clear speech	Listening	Helpless
	Transcends emotions	Humility	Serene	Pained
		Patience	Intuitive	Vulnerable

Victims and abusers feed one another within this dynamic. Fighting aggressively for the oppressed or trying to torch the system to bring justice to the disempowered doesn't heal the problem because the dynamic remains the same. Everyone has simply switched sides. And they are all still caught in a negative feedback loop where nobody is happy.

A centred place of power is a place of wisdom, truth, authenticity and clarity, but it is also a place of love where one can listen deeply to everybody.

The place of balanced power was in the centre of my body, in the still point at the solar plexus or stomach area. It was the seat of my emotions and one of the major centres of my intuition. It was also my place of my power in relation to the world around me. This was the place where I could bring the sun down to earth. Having a healthy solar plexus would allow me to be sure of myself, joyful, confident and filled with self-worth. However, my solar plexus was also the centre of my emotional turmoil and often where I first experienced and then suppressed my anger. It was the place that my rage exploded from; it was my place of being a tyrant or a victim, where I could swing from outraged emotion to downtrodden martyr, back and forth, each swinging more wildly in response to the other.

Many of the struggles in our world seem to reduce to the pendulum swing of who holds the power. This could be as obvious as the pendulum swing of political power between warring nations or as nuanced as wondering whether my slice of apple pie was bigger than the slice that was given my brother who was sitting on my right at the dinner table when we were children. Freeing the flow of *prana* and clearing the obstacles of constriction in the Second Gateway gave me a more expansive capacity to move beyond the conflict of being caught in a fight for a place in the pecking order. Yet the correct balance of power often remained unclear to me. Power struggles were murky business.

I considered scenarios where initially the power dynamic seemed obviously imbalanced, such as in an abuser and victim cycle. After closer inspection, one may find that the abusers had been previously abused themselves. I thought of the fathers who beat their children in undiluted frustration, and of their own fathers beating them as children—an ancestral cycle of rage.

I imagined the schoolboy who threw rocks at lizards and bullied the smaller boy with braces and pink eye who smelled of urine; and the teacher who threatened the bully with expulsion and hatred because he terrified and irritated her in equal measure. I looked at the power dynamic between the thoughtless mass of humanity who spilled carbon and plastic, boredom and despair into the air and the rivers and the land, and our beautiful Earth retaliating through the droughts and floods and earthquakes of climate change. Her retaliation is not abusive, but like a firm teacher, she can create hardships that I don't always like.

When there is abuse of power, it is our responsibility to address it. Yet as soon as I became emotionally embroiled in the sticky power dynamics in my solar plexus area, I perpetuated the cycles of imbalance. But when I could dig deep within myself to discover compassion enough to embrace even the perpetrators of abuse, a small glimmer of hope revealed itself. In that place, it was more likely for conversations to begin that could unravel some of the drama, and we could start to investigate solutions.

In Soul Integrations sessions, if someone experienced a past life where they were an abuser, I could be sure that their Higher Self would also lead them to another lifetime where they were the abused. On a grand scale, everything always comes into balance. But sometimes it is hard to be that grand.

I had asked Melchizedek what he thought of being peaceful in the face of our global crises.

 Breathe deeply and come back to your centre, my Love, he said. *In this place of peacefulness, does screaming and fighting seem like the resolution to your problems on earth?*

Often, he used external events to illustrate his point. As he was explaining this to me, I could hear yet another mouse in my kitchen. It was eating through my kitchen cupboards; not just the food, but also the plastic containers, the wooden shelves, the electrical wiring. Mice like this, of the *rhabdomys pumilio* genus, can apparently infect humans with the hantavirus. My heart sank. Part of me wanted to kill it because I had tried so many other solutions, and none of them had worked. The mice disregarded the expensive mouse cage that was supposed to catch them alive without harming them. They were unbothered by the sonic mouse repeller that sent high-pitched sounds into the room that humans couldn't hear but that mice were supposed to hate. A few months earlier, I had killed one mouse by guillotining it. It had felt awful, and I really didn't want to do it again.

 You perfectly reflect the level of consciousness you are resonating in your world. Your environment is not separate from you; it is a manifestation of what you reflect.

129

It seemed to me that the issue was more important than one little, rather pretty mouse with stripes down its back. The resolution to the way we all treated the planet and one another had to start with each of us taking responsibility. And that included me. If I killed mice because they irritated me, how far removed was that, philosophically speaking, from killing Kurds, Syrian rebels, Assad's armies? If I couldn't manage to control my emotions around a mouse, how were we as humanity going to do so around the mass genocide of humans in North Africa or colossal corruption in our governments so that we could respond appropriately from a place of calm?

I turned back to Melchizedek again, feeling hopeless.

 Move beyond your little self. The mouse is a reflection of you, just as your car when it breaks down is a reflection of you. Or your arguments are a reflection of you. So too are the beautiful mountain and the orange blossom scent in the air. If your environment irritates you, move out of the judgement in your head and into your soft, but sometimes painful heart. What does the mouse represent of you, Beloved? Where is your resistance to it held? What does that feel like?

This sense of symbolic awareness, that my environment was also a reflection of me, was a minefield. I was utterly disinterested in having other people tell me that my sore tummy or flu or headache represented some unresolved emotional state. Or getting advice from someone else that I should be grateful for the teaching the Universe was giving me when my car broke down or my mother died. People did that sometimes. It drove me crazy.

I had heard a professor of oncology being interviewed on the car radio at around the same time as I was slogging through one of my grittier periods. He was speaking about the tremendously transformative, life-changing obstacle of cancer. An enormous percentage of his patients were renewed by developing a much richer and deeper appreciation of life as a result of their diagnoses. His words expanded the concept of cancer for me because as I knew that the disease induced a gut-clenching fear in people rather than being seen as an opportunity for spiritual alignment.

130

But I also recognised that if I were the person with the cancer, I would feel unseen, unappreciated, and probably angry if someone else had the gall to ask me to see my awful experience in a positive light. I mention this man's theory because it does work on an intellectual level for me. I believed him. But one must come to it on one's own. To point out to someone who is struggling with a painful situation that they were responsible, through their unhealed emotional debris, for creating the shit-storm is a gross insult and an unkindness.

I had respect for the underlying elements behind my experiences so long as I was the one choosing to do the investigation or sincerely asking for someone else's interpretation. My son Nix told me of an Australian man that he met at an Ayahuascan medicine journey in Peru.[9] The man had terminal cancer with, according to his doctors, only a few months left to live. He was looking for alternative remedies for his condition. He had signed up for a three-month healing journey in the Peruvian rainforests, where he was doing repeated Ayahuasca ceremonies under the guidance of a powerful shaman. During one of the first ceremonies, while in a trance state, he met the 'Spirit' of the Ayahuasca vine who took him to meet his cancer, and a conversation ensued. The cancer was full of love and concern for his spiritual well-being. It told him that it was there to heal him from feelings of disconnection and from rejection or blame towards other people in his life. The relief he felt was tremendous. He resonated with the advice and resolved to fix his problem now that he understood it. He thanked the cancer profusely and bade it farewell. 'Oh no,' replied the cancer, still full of concern for him. 'I can't and won't leave you now! You are not ready yet. You will simply return to your old ways within months if I were to do so. Your psyche isn't healed yet. I am here to help you!' The cancer was warm, tender, and firmly attached to

9   **Ayahuasca** is a hallucinogenic mixture concocted from an Amazonian vine brewed together with a DMT-producing leaf from a different plant to create a foul-tasting purgative drink. DMT or dimethyltryptamine is a mind-altering substance that is also produced by our brains at birth and at death. Participants in a ceremony will imbibe ayahuasca under the guidance of a shaman or traditional healer, with the intention of going on a spiritual journey. People who have consumed ayahuasca report having revelations regarding their purpose on Earth and the true nature of the universe. Individuals often report they gained access to higher spiritual dimension and made contact with various spiritual or extra-dimensional beings. (Wikipedia.)

him. So he stayed with it, drinking the bitter, purgative brew every day for ten days, taking off a week, and then diving into the next intensive ten-day journey of communicating with the cancer. It took three months of courageously facing his deepest, darkest shadows for the cancer to finally acknowledge that he had done the necessary work and was free to go home to Australia. The cancer had left his body and, apparently, a small part of him was slightly sad to see this beautiful teacher go.

Ditto the mouse. I didn't want anyone else interpreting the symbolism of the mouse or telling me that it was probably hanging around so obstinately because my guilt was gnawing at me.

But I didn't mind doing it for myself. Symbolism is deeply personal. Only I knew what something represented to me. The mouse felt stubborn. It was nimble, destructive, messy, and very astute. I'm messy and quick, but neither of those qualities resonated deeply with me. I thought about it some more. It felt like the mouse represented that heady part of me that kept on and on and on, gnawing away at things that didn't serve me (like the mouse was unlikely to be served by eating empty plastic tubs). Aah, that resonated more deeply! Symbolically, the mouse reflected not only the part of me that gnawed at things, but also that part of me that felt gnawed at by others. Caring what other people thought of me was a trait I continued gnawing at long after I knew better. I held onto it stubbornly, as stubbornly as the mouse. Guilt gnawed at me in ways that sometimes felt out of my control; sometimes the guilt made me feel like the chewed-over plastic tub.

Recognising this, I immediately felt friendlier towards the mouse. The next morning it was running around my lounge, and I shooed it out the front door into the garden. Maybe it would come back, but it didn't bother me as much any longer. It came back the following day and then that night conveniently hopped into the mouse cage that it had been assiduously ignoring for two months. At six in the morning, I carted it off to an uninhabited shack near the graveyard five kilometres away, where it could find shelter from predators without disturbing other people.

Of course, that wasn't the end of the problem. A week later, one cute little high-maintenance mouse made a cosy nest for her babies out of chewed-up scraps she had harvested from my alpaca cape, shawl, and jersey, all of which were special, very beautiful mementoes of my trips to Peru, where my son Rory and his family used to live. The mouse saga continued, just like our global problems continue. How could they too be a reflection of me? If I couldn't listen deeply enough to a mouse to be able to see things from its perspective, how were people supposed to listen deeply to others who had killed their families and destroyed their homes or to governments that were seemingly unaware and uncaring?

I didn't have answers, just questions, and a faint glimmer of hope that perhaps the questions were where the conversations needed to start.

TRUE POWER

True power had nothing forced about it. Even the *prana* flowing through my body flowed freely when I wasn't fighting for a place in the pecking order. I learned a lot about empowerment from Niall, who had promised us all a surprise for his fortieth birthday party, which turned out to be a fire-walk over a bed of hot coals. I didn't believe it was possible for me to walk on coals without getting burned. However, all I needed to do was to move into my place of true power. The theory behind fire-walking, we were told, was that so long as we projected as much *prana*-power out through the base of our feet as the burning coals were radiating towards us, we would deflect the heat of the fire. I gave it a try because other people just like me were walking over the coals and they looked so empowered afterwards. Facing the one-metre wide, three-metre long, ten-centimetre thick bed of burning coals, bordered on either side by deeper mounds of the stuff, was daunting. I took a great gulp and launched forward, breathing as hard as I could through the base of my feet, powering all my energy down onto the coals. It felt like I hardly touched them, and within a few seconds I was standing on the other side, looking back at the bed of fire that I had just crossed. I felt invigorated, like I could take on the world.

I walked over the coals a second time because the first had been so exciting, then a third time because I wanted to be less tentative as I walked, then a fourth because I wanted to dance over the coals, and finally a fifth time just for the hell of it. I was so blasé by the fifth attempt that I forgot to focus my *prana*-power out the base of my feet, and I ended up with a cigarette-sized burn under my left foot. In bed that night it felt sore, and I was having difficulty falling asleep because of the pain. I recognised that the burn was on a reflexology point that corresponded with my solar plexus, the place of power dynamics in my body. The moment I made the link between the two areas of pain in my body, the burn completely disappeared. Not only did the pain disappear, the burn mark itself vanished as well. Some magic I just can't explain, not even to myself.

THE FOURTH GATEWAY:
DEVELOPING THE HEART

 I am wholeness and fractions, bliss and fiery truth, tranquillity and grief. I am the Great Mother, hips as broad and solid as Africa. I am your Home—Mother Mary

The obstacles: Fear and clinging

Question to ask: Am I making this choice out of love or out of fear?

Hints: A fear-based choice is constricting. That made from love might require great courage, but it is expansive and inclusive.

A choice made from love is compassionate (*com* = with; *passion* = suffering). It includes my willingness to be present to the suffering, with a gracious, tender, open heart. And it includes my willingness to love and take care of myself. If I can't love myself fully, with all my imperfections, my capacity to love others is diminished.

When I finally arrived at the Fourth Gateway, just before I turned fifty, Mother Mary spoke to me quietly. *Remember*, she said, *the bicycle that brought you here.*

The bicycle. I had forgotten all about the bicycle.

When I had arrived in Amsterdam to start the Soul Integration training, I sat down on the double bed in the attic of a three-storey heritage Dutch building converted into a bed and breakfast and meditated until I found Mother Mary again. I asked her what I needed to do to ensure that I became the very best facilitator. I was hard on myself in those days; the best facilitator meant best in comparison with every other facilitator who had ever lived. I hoped to be transformed—if possible, into Mother Mary, living in peace and harmony while dispensing bountiful blessings in radiant arcs to all and sundry. Well, that was a vague fantasy I had anyway, but mostly, I simply hoped to catch more glimpses of her, feel her peaceful acceptance of me, and have her teach me how to become more like her.

The bed-and-breakfast was next door to the Vondelpark, which was full of tulips, ancient Dutch elm and poplar trees and stalls selling *appelpoffertjes* in spring time. Mother Mary didn't answer me in words. Instead she showed me an image of me cycling through the Vondelpark, meandering along the twisting pathways, wind blowing through my hair. Somewhere in the park a busker was playing a flute. The sound of it wafted through the trees in a sine wave of light and sound, where it tangled into my heart-strings and played with the bicycle bending and looping this way and that, with a tender, natural quality of reassurance that matched Mother Mary's presence.

You must be joking, I responded. I was serious; I planned to work hard. How was I to become a great facilitator on a bicycle? This was not about playing around in the Vondelpark. Once again, she showed me the bicycle weaving between the trees. I sighed in frustration, then went out and rented a creaky, black Dutch bicycle with high handlebars. Every day I cycled between my hostel, the house where we were training, the cheese shops, and the bakeries. The Vondelpark was centred between them. The work was  hard. It was emotional. To become facilitators, we needed to be both vulnerable and sure. Our wounds were exposed, our scabs were scrubbed off, and we were expected to breathe deeply and come back to a place of power. We had been receiving or facilitating sessions of three hours each,

135

usually twice every day, weekends included, plus spending time unpacking sessions and learning how to hold the highest level of consciousness for our clients. Working with our own unconscious material was intense; our deeply hidden traumas came barrelling out when we received sessions. We had to process these while simultaneously setting our own stuff aside, to hold space when we were giving sessions. Exhausted at the end of each day, I climbed on my bicycle. In the late evening twilight, the Vondelpark breezed through my hair, blowing away the cobwebs and replenishing me with its charm. It was the very best and most healing part of my entire training. If I became a good facilitator, it was in spite of myself and because of the bicycle.

PRESENCE

 The mountain belongs to the Earth, as you belong to Love. As rock shatters into separate shards under the pounding forces of life, your stone self-erodes into fine, white sand, weathered by the patient unfolding of the seasons. The sand receives the imprints of your experience. It moulds itself back into the land, and the Glass Maker blows your sand body into a crystal Holy Grail. An elixir of love so pure pours out of it that it dissolves all the edges while your core remains anchored in the bedrock of the Heart.

I was learning that as I turned to face each new Gateway, I should hold onto the insights gleaned from the previous one. True power and the ability to listen well allowed me to stay present to more of the fear and anxiety that had closed down my heart.

Melchizedek pointed out that if I were to open the Gateway of Love, I would draw closer to the understanding that I created my own Universe. If I was responsible for creating my world, then my responsibility to live with integrity increased. I would become beholden to God. Shambhala, he said, was not a place of perfection from which to judge the chaos of earthly interactions or our human ability for mass destruction. It was a resource available for integrating ourselves into this tumultuous reality, to hold onto it with care and tenderness.

You do not change humanity's consciousness by forcing humans to see their shortcomings. You can only change yourself by taking responsibility for yourself. As within, so without. Change who you are, and you change your responses to your environment. Be the still point at the centre of your world. Your environment will come into harmony with that centre as surely as night follows day.

Being human is never perfect. Your greatest strengths develop from your greatest weaknesses. Moving through the Gateway of Love does not require that you be kind or sweet or generous all the time. This gateway asks you to be as you are, without judgement or blame. See things as they are with all their imperfections and beauty. Respond appropriately to every situation. Do not deny or resist the truth of your humanness even for a moment, my Beloved. Be open to it all.

Melchizedek had taught me at the beginning of this journey that Presence was both the alpha and the omega of the trip. Therefore mindfulness—the art of coming back to the simplicity of beginning again and again—would have been classified as a cornerstone that held Presence in place. Being present was the very foundation on which all other practices rested. But to get from the alpha to the omega, from the beginning to the end, I had to go through the middle. Which meant that I couldn't arrive at the end without passing through the heart, because the heart was slap-bang in the very centre of it all. The heart was where I learnt about earthly things. It was rich with the compost of my daily life, and it did not always smell as fragrant as a cathedral, mosque, or temple. This Great Heart taught me through the slow, pumping heartbeat of the Earth. I learnt its wisdom through the quickening in my own heart when it made a connection with the old lady in the grocery store who dropped her shopping, or with the horse blowing soft tendrils of warm steam into my hand as it nuzzled me, or when the tender shoots of young carrots that emerged from the seed trays I had been patiently watering for days stirred something very soft inside my chest. My blood-red heart taught me through the same compassion that Mother Mary so generously shared with all who prayed to her, 'Hail Mary, full of grace, the Lord is

137

with you. Blessed are you among women, and blessed is the fruit of your womb, Jesus. Holy Mary, Mother of God, pray for us sinners now and at the hour of our death. Amen.' And I learnt heart wisdom through the dark, mysterious knowing at the heart of the Black Madonna, who could see and know and love all of that which is hidden in the shadows. She was the fierce and protective mother of the wounded, including even those who were so wounded that they lashed out at others. The heart of the Black Madonna understood the deep truth of all experiences, both seen and unseen.

OBSTACLE OF FEAR

 The biggest obstacle barring entrance to the Gateway of the Heart, said Melchizedek, *is fear. Fear cast a dark trawl net around your heart and yanked it tight. Your love suffocated in this constriction, for it couldn't breathe without the wide ocean of awareness flowing through its gills.*

Be brave enough, Beloved, to begin to clip the fear that holds your heart hostage. Cut a small hole in the trawl net and invite the great beasts of humanity's burdens back into your heart. Welcome them all. In the squashed discomfort of inclusiveness, they will sever the bonds of fear. And once again, you will breathe freely in the ocean that belongs to you all.

It was easier to address my fears after I had faced my issues of low self-worth that I encountered in the Third Gateway, and after I had learned something about moving into my quiet, inner power. But, of course, fear was always there, waiting to be acknowledged. I slowly became aware of the ramifications of fear in my life. It was fear that caused me to cling to what I wanted most. I wanted my children to stay safe; I wanted people to love me; I even wanted my breakfast cereal to have nuts and diced apple in it and was vaguely dissatisfied if it didn't have just a pinch of salt added to bring out the flavour. I might not have thought that my need to have my cereal be a particular way was caused by fear, but it was caused by clinging, and clinging was caused by fear; usually a fear of change.

It was also fear that created anxiety, and mine was often a low-grade underlying current controlling the choices I made. My own anxiety, as I've mentioned, was often governed by what other people thought, but I noticed that the same kind of anxiety in those around me could be sparked by expectations about how well or badly they did in exams, whether they'd get the promotion they deserved, how much money they had in the bank, whether their partner was cheating on them, how to come out of the closet, whether a child would recover from illness, or how they should deal with their burgeoning wrinkles or painful ingrown toenails, or the disturbing cough that was keeping them awake at night.

Fearing what other people thought seemed very minor in comparison to some of the options available for falling into fear. But fear doesn't work on an objectively calibrated system where it is rationed out according to what other people think its value is on a scale of one to ten. I've known a person who faced death without fear, and I've known another to have a nervous breakdown over picking up a few extra kilos over Christmas. Who was I to judge one response as somehow worthier than the other? I knew nothing of the context. I didn't live in the other person's head

What I realised was that when I loved myself more, I carried less fear about external appreciation., Fear is like that; when we bring enough non-judgemental love into the equation, fear, no matter its cause, disperses like fog in the sunlight.

Letting go of the obstacle of fear was my task at this time. Mother Mary smiled at me and with her sunshiny fingers carefully lifted off some of the constriction of fear that held the edges of my heart closed. Mother Mary was the Delighter. Both my mountain cottage on the slopes above the Helshoogte Pass and in the valley nearby, the frosty bare-feet children playing with abandoned car tyres and  rusty tins, were gladly received with her gentle, reverent smile.

Feel me, said Mother Mary, *heal me in your heart*. Naturally, Mother Mary didn't need to be healed; she was referring to the part inside of me that yearned to have a heart like hers but didn't have her capacity, and she meant I should heal my own heart, which was nothing but a mirror, albeit a dusty, foggy one, of her own. But my heart was straining under the pressure of my wounded country. It was hurting from my little fears that were intensely personal and my big fears that were global and left me feeling powerless. My fears hurt my heart, so I turned away from them and decided I wanted to become enlightened.

 Enlightenment will distract you, said Melchizedek. *Instead of the distraction of the allure of enlightenment, follow your heart. It knows the way as surely as a blind man's sense of sound can lead him to the Music.*

My heart had painful edges to it, where it had been stretched too far. Sometimes 'too far' felt close to home and tight with tension, and sometimes my heart had a broader capacity for stretching. Paradoxically, my heart was also the place that filled with delight at the taste of chocolate, the fragrance of home, and the sounds of my children laughing.

I remembered years back when they were playing in the garden under the jacaranda trees. It was autumn, and the sky was redolent with the scent of recent rains and warm, wet earth. It hovered softly between the harsh furnace of Botswana summer and the impending icy winter. My two older boys were rigging up a zip-line from the tree, and I was sitting with Nix, the youngest, on the trampoline beneath them. Bounce, giggle, bounce. We bobbed up and down while the dogs panted in the shade nearby. I lay back and looked up through the leaves. Nix bounced on my tummy and then, bored, raced off to find his plastic tricycle. His exuberance still to this day reminds me of Calvin from *Calvin and Hobbes*. One eye closed, I watched Rory and Maf figuring out the zip-line above me, which didn't look very secure and was quite definitely dangerous to swing off.

I closed both eyes and began to drift off, aware of a vague tug of sadness in my heart at the fear that, no matter what, I couldn't really keep any of them safe. The ache tugged at me, and when I opened my imagination eyes again, I was still lying on the trampoline, still aching, but it was years later. The kids were getting ready to leave after the Christmas holidays. It was ridiculously hot, and although the trampoline was in the shade, the only real relief from the heat came from diving into the pool every twenty minutes or so and staying dripping wet. We slept with wet *kikois* wrapped around our bodies that summer to keep us cool. I was wondering if my kids had finished packing yet, aware of how I would need to move through the house shortly, picking up trails of forgotten undies, toothbrushes and love letters from already discarded girlfriends. Rory was heading back to South America. He had always travelled light: jeans, baggy shorts, t-shirts, slip-slops. He was seemingly cold-resistant and so didn't seem to own any jerseys, although I had spotted one tatty, mustard-coloured corduroy jacket for when he needed to look semi-smart for interviewing someone for an article. Maf's rucksack was full of untidy fisherman's pants, beanies, guitar strings, harmonicas and a ukulele that was unlikely to survive his upcoming trip to Australia unscathed. I wasn't even sure that the customs officials would let it in, because it was made of wood. Nix had an equally untidy, although much more expensive suitcase, which was jammed with designer-branded clothes and boarding school uniforms. He had rejected the local school in favour of one five hours drive away in South Africa, where they played rugby, and he had yet to discover his inner socialist, where his rejection turned towards all things capitalist, and the designer brands were replaced with hemp shirts.

I felt the age-old yearning creeping back into my heart of always, always wanting to protect them, to cling to them, to have them be my babies safe next to my breast once more.

Following my heart highlighted both the pains that belonged to me alone and some of the collective pain that I shared with my country. The wounds of my country were hidden deep in the back of my heart, producing entirely unconscious behaviour that I only started to become aware of through leaving South Africa in my early twenties. In those days I believed that the river of segregation running hidden in my veins belonged only to prejudiced racists, but as a result of growing up white in Apartheid South Africa, it tainted my blood too. This river carried black people past me like spectres with woes and difficulties of their own that my head as a child did not comprehend or dwell on. I never considered the pain carried by Jabulani, the groom, who lived in one of ten dormitory blocks on the farm, sharing with eighty-two other migrant labourers, one thousand one hundred kilometres from his wife, children and grandparents in Mthata. One of his grandparents was dying, and all of them were waiting for his meagre wages in the hope of a radio or some extra tobacco or perhaps, with luck, a pair of school shoes from Pep Stores. At the end of the apple-picking season, most of the men went home, carrying their wages for their families. Jabulani stayed on with the cowherds and the men who were skilled at pruning because he had a permanent job. He only went home for three weeks at Christmas.

I couldn't speak isiXhosa, and his English was very broken, yet Jabulani and I shared a love for the horses and an ability to communicate with them that bound us together in mutual understanding. I never said goodbye to him when I left home to go to university because I expected that he would always be there. I moved on carelessly into my 17-year-old life of excitement and freedom from the constraints of boarding school, and I returned to the farm as seldom as the expectations of my parents allowed. In retrospect, I recognized that the connections that we shared and that I threw away so heedlessly, partly because I was a thoughtless teenager and partly because I was still wearing racial blinkers, had in fact been heart rather than head based.

As a child, I was not taught to trust my heart fully. However, for all the neglect it had taken, when I felt into my heart, tarnished as it was, it was also very real, like a critical place in the search for the Soul-Self. The language of my heart felt like something I might have spoken fluently as a soul before birth. And although I worked with my mind when I used this pre-verbal language, it felt as if it came from a brain that was centred in my heart. Later I would discover that there was, in fact, a physiological brain in my heart called the intrinsic cardiac nervous system. This was a network of complex ganglia, neurotransmitters, and proteins exactly like that found in the normal brain that allowed it to make decisions and even feel and sense. One article I found stated that we can intentionally direct our heart to communicate to our brain and body in beneficial ways: 'When we experience sincere positive emotions, such as caring, compassion or appreciation, the heart processes these emotions, and the heart's rhythm becomes more coherent and harmonious. This information is sent to the brain and the entire body neurologically, biochemically, biophysically and energetically. You can shift into this coherent state to bring your mind and heart into harmonious alignment and have more access to intuition often in less than a minute. It can take a little practice to do this on demand, but it gets easier and quicker the more you do it'.[10]

Melchizedek simply shrugged. Although I was excited to discover that my heart had an intelligence all of its own, he expected that I should have known that already.

My heart-brain might have been wise; it might wake me up to being Real, but it was a definite stretch for my heart to contain all the beauty and the suffering in my world. I did not yet have the capacity that a Zen monk from the eighteenth century, Ryokan, had when he wrote, 'Oh that my monk's robe were wide enough to gather up all the suffering people in this floating world.'

And when I looked back at the things that had made my heart stretch wider, I recognized that they had never been easy.

Six weeks after Rory was born, I was sitting on the thick, pale desert sand in the shade of the mulberry tree in my garden on the cattle farm near Ghanzi in Botswana. The late afternoon shadows brought welcome relief from the merciless December midday heat. Smoke from the donkey boiler, which was heating water for Rory's evening bath, curled out towards us, and I could hear the crackling of the fire among the noisy thrushes, the starlings, and the tiny brightly coloured waxbills and finches. Rory was inconsolable. He had colic, had had colic for five of his six weeks since birth and I was bracing myself for the three-hour evening stint of misery as his poor little tummy clenched against the pain of the immensely difficult task of constricting his soul-self into such a tiny body.

When the doctor in the labour ward had plopped this squirming baby, slippery with birth fluids, onto my soft belly, the bottom fell out of my heart in a gush of love, incomprehensible in its intensity. It erased all the lack that made up my sense of self; it crumbled the carefully constructed walls of my persona, and it obliterated the pain of the labour. And six weeks later, under the shady tree, raucous birds fighting over the plump dark juicy mulberries above me, I had a startling insight.

The love I had felt for him at birth was nothing compared to this now. His pain over the past weeks had pulled a love out of me so deep that its potency matched and overtook his desperate cries for help. The more he cried, the more I loved him. The more he needed me, the stronger I became.

10   'Let Your Heart Talk to Your Brain' by Deborah Rozman, Huffington Post.

Thus it is in our world today; we are expanding who we are because the Earth requires that of us. We are responding to her desperate situation not because we choose to but because we have no choice. The bottom is dropping out of our hearts, like it or not, and we find our worlds tipping upside down into unknown territory.

UBUNTU

As a member of the urban, over-stimulated, stressed out and highly pressured society we all lived in, I had lost some of the sensitivity of indigenous people, who relied upon their intuition for survival. The Aborigines in the Australian Outback could not afford to be stuck in mind games or in emotional chaos because these distractions would have destroyed the close attention needed to interpret the 'songs' of their surroundings. They used 'Songlines' to navigate across vast areas of arid territory to find scarce food and even scarcer water points.[11]

The way I understood it was that the Oneness or 'Spirit' or 'Life Force' that underlies every particle of matter on earth created a web of connection that generated the Songlines. Few of us are aware any longer of this web that connects us to everything that is not us. The meeting point for this interconnection is an open heart in this exact moment in time. The present is the only moment in which we can begin to experience Oneness.

It seemed to me that I could touch into Shambhala on Earth by gathering in the essence of each of the Gateways; I needed first to be very present. I also needed a bit of imagination, an awareness of the truth that came from my body. I needed to be grateful for what I had and to trust and surrender my vision for a new way of being into the vaster cosmos, where it could unfurl and find its way back to me in its own form. But essentially, I couldn't enter Shambhala until I recognized that the life force that flowed from me and through me connected me to

---

11   Bruce Chatwin. *The Songlines*. Penguin Books. 1987 According to Bruce Chatwin, these 'Songlines' are '...the labyrinth of invisible pathways which meander all over Australia and are known to Europeans as 'Dreaming-tracks' or 'Songlines'; to the Aboriginals as the 'Footprints of the Ancestors' or the 'Way of the Law'. Aboriginal Creation myths tell of the legendary totemic beings who wandered over the continent in the Dreamtime, singing out the name of everything that crossed their path - birds, animals, plants, rocks, waterholes - and so singing the world into existence.

every other living being, including the rocks and the water and the air. This unity was something I recognized through my heart, and it could overcome the illusion of myself as a separate entity.

Interconnection sounded beautiful, but I was not so sure I could straddle the changes in our world, was not sure that I wanted to be so interconnected with the suffering as to be one with it. Sometimes the size of the problems overwhelmed me. '*Ubuntu*,' whispered Mother Mary softly, and in an image she placed inside my head, she pointed outwards over a vast crowd of people who were toyi-toyi-ing[12] in front of her, towards where Desmond Tutu, icon of Ubuntu, was delivering a sermon.

Archbishop Emeritus Desmond Tutu was a beloved figure in South Africa. He had described Ubuntu as the quality we express when we realize, 'My humanity is caught up, is inextricably bound up, in yours.'

I focused on the group of *toyi-toyi-ing* funeral attendees that Mother Mary had brought forward in my mind. She was pointing me back to 1981, to the funeral of Griffiths Mxenge, who had been hacked to death by state assassins for rebelling against apartheid. During the apartheid struggle, before the first free elections in South African history, bloodshed was a frequent occurrence in the townships. Archbishop Tutu was presiding over the funeral, and the seething mob violence was fast swelling out of control. An *impimpi*—or informer—was suddenly identified among the funeral attendees. The group's rage turned on this man, with the intent of 'necklacing' him. 'Necklacing' is a horrifying method of mob retribution, where a tyre filled with petrol is thrown over someone's head as a 'necklace' and set alight.

When Desmond Tutu, who was saying the final prayers for the deceased at the graveside, realised what was happening he burst through the crowd and pushed his way to the front of the mob forming around the *impimpi*, and flung himself down on top of the man's prostrate and bleeding body so that the crowd would have to kill him too. 'Burn him,'

12   The toyi-toyi is a South African dance that has long been used in political protests in South Africa. Toyi-toyi could begin as the stomping of feet and spontaneous chanting during protests that could include political slogans or songs, either improvised or previously created. It is a military march dance and song style that became commonplace in massive street demonstrations in the Apartheid era. As one activist puts it, "The toyi-toyi was our weapon. We did not have the technology of warfare, the tear gas and tanks, but we had this weapon.'

he demonstrated to the crowd, 'and you burn me. I am me because he is him.'

I didn't have that kind of courage, and my level of Ubuntu might never grow that deep, but I knew that the etymological derivative of the word 'courage' came from 'cœur', which was French for heart. As Buddhist nun Pema Chodron says, 'Usually we think that brave people have no fear. The truth is that they are intimate with fear.'

Mother Mary, of the red and pumping heart, knows the courage it takes to be us. She listens to the spiralling song of our journeys with a silent, compassionate awareness that is always, always there. We need only turn from our worm-grubbing, compost-churning daily absorptions to feel her presence and her support.

Chris Abani, a Nigerian poet, said, 'What I've come to learn is that the world is never saved in grand messianic gestures, but in the simple accumulation of gentle, soft, almost invisible acts of compassion, everyday acts of compassion. In South Africa they have a phrase called Ubuntu. Ubuntu comes out of a philosophy that says, the only way for me to be human is for you to reflect my humanity back at me.'

And then he said, 'You know, you can steel your heart against any kind of trouble, any kind of horror. But the simple act of kindness from a stranger will unstitch you.'[13]

AN OPEN HEART

I began noticing Ubuntu. Many of my friends and acquaintances devoted their lives to finding resolutions to the terrible mess we had created globally. I wondered if Ubuntu was the answer. Somehow it seemed to transcend the boundaries of the separate self and touch a deeper recognition of how, at our core, we were all one. Ubuntu seemed to display in outward form something of the inner journey for finding the Holy Grail or Shambhala. Ubuntu seemed to transcend fear and move into a place of deep and trustworthy love. Maybe Ubuntu was the place where I could find the Soul-Self?

As a deeply wounded society, South Africa reflected her pain through the level of crime we experienced every day. I met a woman at a Tonglen[14]

13   Chris Abani in a TED talk given in 2008.

14   Tonglen: (Tibetan: *gtong len*, or tonglen) is Tibetan for 'giving and taking' (or

meditation retreat near Cape Town who became a personification of Ubuntu in a situation that sounded terrifying. Even though it was a silent retreat, we would break into groups of ten people every afternoon to discuss our practice, and she and I were in the same group. She told us how she had used Tonglen when she, her husband, and daughter were hijacked in their car in the early evening, driven to a remote place and held at gunpoint overnight. She was threatened with rape three times by one of her attackers. I remember vivid descriptions of him trying to penetrate her and at the crucial moment being thwarted by his own flaccid penis refusing to comply. She mentioned wild-eyed anger and shaky knives held against her throat and her husband's throat while their seven year old daughter looked on. The whole family was repeatedly told that they would be killed before morning. The woman spontaneously began to practice Tonglen on her attackers, compassionately drawing their suffering into her heart and returning it with loving-kindness. She didn't focus on their meanness or anger. She didn't focus on the fear that made them freakily tense and as unreliable as unexploded mines in a minefield. She focused on the suffering they must have encountered in their lives to get them to this place of terrorizing her and her husband and her daughter. She never voiced this to the men, she simply imagined drawing in their suffering and sending love back to them in return. As she recounted the story, her eyes glowed, and her face softened.

The method of Tonglen practice that she used was to visualise a deity in one's heart and imagine the deity transforming the suffering that one has breathed in on behalf of the sufferer. For her deity, an image of Jesus had formed in her chest (not in her heart, she explained, as she could only find her heart in her throat) when the leader of the group threatened to rape her. She pointed out that, being a Buddhist, she hadn't consciously thought of Jesus for years, so was surprised that she didn't turn to Avalokiteshvara, Buddha of Compassion, at this time. However, what she got was Jesus, looking exactly as he had looked in the photo frame above her bed as a child, dressed in a brown robe with a crimson heart beating in the middle of it. Jesus breathed in all the pain and suffering

sending and receiving) and refers to a meditation practice found in Tibetan Buddhism. In the practice, one visualizes taking in the suffering of oneself and of others on the in-breath, and on the out-breath giving recognition, compassion, and succour to all sentient beings. As such it is training in altruism (Wikipedia).

of her attackers and exhaled kindness, care, and compassion towards them. After long hours of doing so, despite her assailants continuing to threaten her and her family, she loved them like she loved her own daughter. The men were unable to kill them, and the rapist finally gave up after three unsuccessful attempts at raping her, no doubt because she had protected herself and her family with the love that was pouring out of her. Eventually, she, her husband, and her daughter were left tied up beside their car as dawn was breaking.

She recounted that although her husband was deeply shocked by the event, not only were she and her daughter left un-traumatised but both felt stronger and more energised as a result of it. In fact, her daughter was sent to four different psychologists because everyone was certain that after such a horrific experience, she must be suppressing post-traumatic stress. But none of the psychologists found that she displayed any symptoms whatsoever. I have since learned that apparently young children are likely to reflect the emotional state of a parent when they are exposed to trauma together. In the years that followed, the woman helped to raise money for their attackers, who had been caught and were imprisoned for life for previous rapes and murders. Eventually, the attempted rapist died of AIDS, and she lost touch with the other two men when they were moved to a different prison.

The attack informed her life; it became a peak experience that deeply changed who she was inside, and who she was in the world, at every level of her being.

When I turned to face my suffering with as open a heart as I could muster, our shared history was so intense it took my breath away. And I knew that our collective history ran way back before Jan Van Riebeeck 'discovered South Africa', or before Jesus, The Buddha, Melchizedek or Mother Mary were born on Earth with hearts that must have felt it all.

Ubuntu wasn't only a connection that happened horizontally, creating a web of connection and shared humanity that I recognised had the potential to exist between my fellow humans and me. It also happened vertically, connecting me to Mother Mary's heart and Melchizedek's wisdom, and connecting though my heart down into the dark, heavy depths of our collective suffering.

Learning to be human was a major challenge—so difficult and yet so simple. I wrote a poem about it years ago.

Aow,
My heart cracks open.
Its painful tenderness reveals
Lichen on the bamboo fence
And rain-splattered sand.

I felt into the still space in my heart and felt the glow of Melchizedek's presence flow through my body. I focused into Mother Mary's sweet, quiet and very subtle essence, and I slowed down so that I could listen with care.

 Be at peace, Beloved, said Melchizedek quietly, *and know that when you transmit this peace through your free-flowing Prana, through your quiet still Presence of True power, through your Heart that is the Heart of the Earth and the heart of the world, through the ordinariness of your everyday life, and through your moment-by moment-experience without interruption, then will you begin to tap into the Truth of who you really are.*

GRATITUDE

Gratitude is a pathway that is closely aligned with joy. For many years I taught compassionate care of patients to fourth- and fifth-year medical students, but it sometimes felt like compassion by itself was not enough. The students were often the only ones in the hospitals who were still laughing, albeit too infrequently. Mostly, the doctors and nurses were a pretty gloomy lot. They did not seem to appreciate one another much, and their patients, colleagues, and superiors seldom seemed grateful enough for the incredible life-saving roles they were playing. The work was simply too burdensome, and the demands of a desperately needy population too high. The student's lives were tightly compressed into studying, undertaking clinical work with patients, and staying alert to not making mistakes. The consequences of mistakes were dire not just for the patient but for the student in terms of possible humiliation by the consultants.

When we spent time together, it was useful for the students to reflect on compassion and what it meant to be more compassionate towards themselves. There was time, too, for them to contemplate qualities undervalued by the medical establishment: gratitude, joy, sacredness, tenderness, taking time, listening well, trust and the recognition that life includes death as an essential and valuable part of existence. I felt that unless the students found sustenance in gratitude and joy, they would bomb out into overly serious know-it-alls whose hearts had shrivelled up because it was the only possible way to cope. Many of the students were disparaging about the idea of compassion before they came to the tutorials; they felt it was irrelevant to the important work they were doing and an irritating diversion from the immense workload they had to deal with. Some of the consultants teaching them encouraged this attitude. It was just too far removed from their worldviews. However, most of the students changed their minds because the tutorials provided a space where the stress of obstetrics could be unloaded. For a few, it changed the direction of their lives. And the one technique that seemed to open their hearts up the widest was appreciation and gratitude.

EXERCISE

The exercise consists of partnering with another person. This person can be someone well known or a stranger. The pair take two-minute turns for each person to speak without interruption while their partner listens deeply to them. The speaker tells the listener what it is that they most appreciate about them. The listener simply receives the commentary with an open heart.

I placed such value on gratitude because in my own life it nourished me deeply. When it flowed from me, it gathered momentum out in the world and cycled back to me in magnificent abundance. It alerted me to the beauty of a threadbare carpet with dusty edges that had been worn smooth by cushioning so many hurried, tired, or uncertain feet. It magnified the mystery beneath the ordinary sound of rain pattering on the corrugated iron roof or snow on the distant mountaintops. Gratitude was one of the few things that could keep me open to the harsh, relentless realities of human unkindness or the difficulties of working alongside an overburdened medical system. Gratitude provided a glimpse into the deeper awareness of the pain that closed our hearts down. Love helped me to hold onto this, but it was gratitude that showed me the perfection of all existence.

INTERDEPENDENCE

It was a Sunday, and it had become a meditative, restful day of allowing space for stillness to arise. In the morning I wore my pyjamas and dressing gown till long after morning was a distant memory. In the afternoon I went for a walk. The recent rains had caused moss to grow on all the pathways. During the evening I made pumpkin fritters with large yellow squashes because I didn't have any pumpkin. Mostly though, I spent the day meditating, settling, and letting go. Extra-ordinary beauty began to emerge in everything as the day progressed. It arose from opening my heart to the stillness within, and the stillness overflowed into everything around. It was the ordinariness that surprised me most.

It was so simple, and yet I recognised that grace arises in the most unpretentious places and in the most mundane experiences.

 You need only allow your own inner perfection, breathed Melchizedek into my being. *Open your heart to it.*

'I am me because you are you', began to thrum at my heart. Thich Nhat Hanh, a Vietnamese Buddhist monk, told a story about his hands. 'My right hand has written all the poems that I have composed. My left hand has not written a single poem. But my right hand does not think, You, left hand, you are good for nothing.' My right hand does not have a superiority complex. That is why it is very happy. My left hand does not have any complex at all. In my two hands there is the kind of wisdom called the wisdom of non-discrimination. One day I was hammering a nail and my right hand was not very accurate and instead of pounding on the nail it pounded on my finger. It put the hammer down and took care of the left hand in a very tender way, as if it were taking care of itself. It did not say, 'You, left hand, you have to remember that I have taken good care of you and you have to pay me back in the future.' There was no such thinking. And my left hand did not say, 'You, right hand, you have done me a lot of harm—give me that hammer, I want justice.' My two hands know that they are members of one body; they are in each other.'[15]

15   Thich Nhat Hanh. Address to US Congress, September 10, 2003

You are not separate from the rest of humanity, my love. What they do to one another, and to the earth, is your responsibility too. All of humanity's actions, emotions, thoughts, and perceptions help create an interconnected web of consciousness around the earth. Each one of your actions, emotions, thoughts, or perceptions ripples out into the world like a pebble's wake in a pond.

And then he gave me directions for working with an Ubuntu heart:

Take your attention and turn it inwards now. Support yourself through present-moment awareness, hold yourself close, bring your focus into the Heart of your heart, into the pure essence of your being. This Heart resides in the centre of your chest, in the marrow of your bones, in the dark womb of your pelvis, in your brainstem, in the root of your fingernails, at the tip of your coccyx where your primal tail remembers its connection to its ancestry and deep, dark history.

This Heart contains within it all the love, fear, anger, and all the experiences that ever were or are. You know in the centre of your Heart exactly how it is to be a beggar or a king. Each painful moment not fully experienced closes the Gateway of Love, Beloved. So many obstacles obscuring your pure, raw Heart, each slammed down, boulder by boulder, in layers of defensiveness.

Acknowledge all those painful experiences with tender-ness. Gather the suffering, the aches, and the pains close. Embrace them as a mother embraces her child. Do not hold them at arm's length, so that they barricade you from your heart any longer. Welcome them all, my love. Welcome your shortcomings, your fears, and your anguish. Welcome the judgement of yourself and of others. Hold your resentment and anger with stillness and with gentle understanding. Make space for the imperfections of your nearest and dearest. Clear away each obstacle and let your long-resisted experiences into your heart space. Can you do that? Even

152

though these unwelcome experiences thrash about inside you, upsetting your life, where you had everything in its proper place, so 'neat and tidy'? In Shambhala, the angels blow gold dust through the chaos so that everything settles in its place.

Plant yourself in the centre of all your experiences with an open heart that embraces it all.

Then, when the gold dust subsides, the underlying love that resides in the centre of your heart of hearts, in the centre of the world, reveals itself to you.

Then you see that Heaven was here all along. When the Gateway of Love is fully open, you will discover that you do have the ability to heal the world.

HEART WISDOM

To know the Earth's wisdom, said Melchizedek, *you must either become her, or feel your way in a barefoot exploration through the darkness of not knowing her. Let your tentative fingertips search for the way. Feel her rock-like support beneath your feet. Breathe in her sureness and steadfastness. Despite the way mankind treats her with such ignorant carelessness, she longs to hold you close. She is your mother, and no matter how selfish, rude, or uncooperative you are, she cannot help but love you.*

Melchizedek always brought me back down to earth, and he insisted that his wisdom was only valid when it was grounded.

Nothing is too small and insignificant for your attention, my love. Do not turn away from mosquitoes, worms, or imaginary beings. They are each a projection of your larger self. Each being you encounter deserves respect. Your world needs all of them to be complete. You hold one another in harmony and balance so that you reflect every scenario back to every other scenario in perfection.

In your darkness and your fumbling, begin a patient

153

merging with your Earth. Let her inner warmth begin to shine through you, and allow its gentle glow to radiate out, enlightening your search. It tingles through the soles of your feet and binds you to her. It flows back from your heart and your belly into her womb and holds you close to her. Feel her solidity and presence. Feel the wounds you and the rest of humanity have inflicted on her. She is in pain. But even though she is gasping and choking from your treatment, she does not turn her back on you. She still retains a reassuring presence, and the safety of her strength allows you to drop the weight of your search for individuation and meaning. She can lift off the burdens of responsibility that you have shouldered for so long. Her consciousness understands the wisdom of the cycles. She comprehends your need to explore your free will to the point where you could kill yourself or her. She understands your essential human role of separating out to experience yourself so as to return enriched to Oneness. Despite the damage that is caused, the Earth honours your creative human exploration away from Oneness. She is but one of the 'ten thousand things' in material form, and she helps you to value your density, weight, and structure.

Love yourself first, in all your frail humanness. Expand this love outward towards all of humanity for its weaknesses and its strengths, and beyond that, love the Oneness that underlies it all.

Heart wisdom, for all its richness, was very day-to-day, and very down-to-earth. There was nothing that extraordinarily mysterious about it. Compassion, according to John Ballatt and Penelope Campling in their book *Intelligent Kindness*,[16] could only be 'caught, not taught'. I couldn't truly develop my heart through studying great texts, I had to live compassion, I had to be fed compassion. I had to express compassion in

16   *Intelligent Kindness: Reforming the Culture of Healthcare* by John Ballatt and Penelope Campling. RCPsych Publications, 2011.

tiny familiar ways for it to slowly develop and grow into a mighty thing that could link with other immense and thumping hearts.

My 84-year-old friend Martha has a that expressed itself in gentle daily interactions with people and with her plants. She had watched Cape Town expand beyond her seams. In the old days, people she knew, white people that is, Martha's people, my people, would holiday in colonial splendour at St. James, where householders also owned little brightly coloured wooden beach huts to store their towels and tubes, their swimming costumes and bathing caps, so that all the beach sand didn't end up back on the veranda at gin and tonic time at six in the evening. Slowly, without her even noticing initially, the suburbs grew in neatly cordoned-off racial areas all the way past Retreat where the coloured people lived, to St James and far beyond. When there was no longer enough space near the inner city, Martha watched as the city officials bulldozed the bustling vendors, spice markets, and mosques of district Six all the way out to the ganglands of Hanover Park and Mitchells Plain, where people now traded in guns and *tik*[17] instead of in spices and brightly coloured scarves. Martha observed apartheid disappear from the legislation if not from the streets. Yet even though the benches in the parks no longer had 'whites only' stencilled on their brown slatted backs, and the seawater pool in St James was populated with holiday makers of all skin tones, Martha knew that the wounds of the Mother City's history still ran deep in her veins. Martha was not an activist; I had never seen her at a protest march. All Martha knew was how to chat to people on the street about the weather, or how to listen to the stories people told her about their lives, even though her hearing aid was not always switched on.

Martha's aging inner arteries and her blood-thinning medications had recently conspired to bruise her calves into masterpieces of abstract art; glorious hues of deep purple blotches on her shins rubbed up against dusky pink-tinged brown whorls over her calf muscles, with daubs of cabernet and smudges of sepia splashed here and there near her ankles, crimson at their centres, raw umber around the edges. Her leg designs harmonized beautifully with the bottle greens and maroons of her favourite skirts and dresses. It seemed as if her legs were bleeding downwards towards the dry wasteland of her once beautiful garden, that was now parched

17   Crystal methamphetamine

from the drought that had also driven millions of desperate people to the Mother City in search of sustenance, sucking her dry. Martha ached for her garden. The Mother, desecrated with the disposable diapers of the wealthy, the two-litre Coke bottles of the middle classes and the plastic bags of the poor, ached for us all and for her beautiful Earth as she was stretched beyond her capacity to provide. And although the rich people hired those who lived in garbage bags to keep their green and leafy suburbs cleaner, the South-Easter blew the litter about indiscriminately.

Martha straddled the changes bravely. She learnt to switch her computer on and off by herself and to send emails. But because Internet banking was terrifying, she still queued in the banks along with the black people who didn't have computers. Her main concern was how much her back stretched and creaked as she carted buckets of bathwater out to her withering plants, and it drew her close to the *gogos*[18] in Khayelitsha who carried buckets of bathwater into their houses from the stand pipes down the street.

Martha didn't know it, but she was Mother Mary in disguise, tending to the little things like soft-boiled broccoli mush and crocheted quilts, and petunias and poppies, and too many funerals these days, and to her friend down the road who had Alzheimer's.

Zinzi, who worked for Martha every Tuesday morning, was also Mother Mary in a different guise. She expressed it through her careful ironing and her gentle smile. She conveyed it through protecting her children in a township filled with looters, gangsters and rapists, and through cheerfully arising at 4.30 every morning to brave the mud puddles in the dark, the taxi violence, and the stench of shared long-drop toilets with no flushing water.

So too was Nadiah, angelic hospice worker who cared so deeply for her patients, and Lubaba who worked the night shift looking after mothers-to-be and delivering babies in Hanover Park while the gang-wars continued unabated beyond the small hospital window. Even Ben, the pizza delivery boy, aged nineteen, with his shy smile displaying crooked front teeth, was touched by Mother Mary's gracious presence when he worked late nights to bring home a salary that nowhere near covered his

---

#18   *Gogo*: grandmother in isiZulu

family's hungry requirements for corn meal, rent, and electricity.

The vision of creating a new reality was expressed in tiny pockets worldwide, among people who were making choices that were inclusive. I noticed spirals of hope popping up like mushrooms around me in the smallest acts of kindness and the biggest acts of sacrifice: kindnesses like someone smiling at me in the supermarket, or someone singing opera on their bicycle on their way to work, or a beggar blessing me in exchange for a five-rand coin—a whole day of blessings in exchange for such a tiny sum. This hope also lived in the tremendous sacrifices made by the grannies who took in AIDS orphans in South Africa. There were many of these grannies in Southern Africa who had raised their grandchildren because their own children had died of AIDS. Some of them took in other orphans as well. They stepped out of retirement and raised fifteen to twenty kids who did not belong to them while living in one-room shacks. They received a small government stipend for doing so, but this was often siphoned off into the community at large where the needs were so overwhelming. Perhaps this was not Shambhala of the material world, but it was a kind of Shambhala of the heart.

Sometimes it had felt like nothing was changing, and usually that was when I was looking at masses of unconscious people caught up in busy lives, filled with cell phones, video games, junk food, and thoughtless consumerism. But it was like a parallel reality when I looked at my Soul Integration clients, or at how women were sometimes creating sacred spaces in which to bring their babies into the world, or at colleagues, who cared so deeply about issues of power imbalances. When I saw how their love and wisdom kept growing and growing exponentially, I knew we were in the midst of a consciousness revolution, and that it was gaining momentum.

Sometimes humans have acted with such incredible kindnesses towards me and other people that it has made my heart swell in hope for us all. When my two oldest kids were three years and six months old respectively, I drove them from Botswana down to Benoni in South Africa, where Rory, the oldest, had an eye appointment with an ophthalmologist. This was in the mid-1980s during the hard-core years of apartheid in South Africa. At the time, Charlie and three business partners were opening a pub called 'The Bull and Bush' in Gaborone. They had asked me to choose suitable paintings for it while I was in South Africa and had given me an enormous wad of ten-rand notes for the purchases. Ten rand was the largest denomination in those days, even though thirty-three years later they had become the smallest. It was a lot of money. At that time, we had strict exchange control regulations between the two countries, so I had removed all the paper clips dividing the notes into bundles of ten, and then spread them all out carefully beneath Matthew's sheepskin cover on his baby car seat as a clever way to smuggle them through the border unseen.

Feeling very pleased with myself at having accomplished the border crossing with ease, I gathered the money back together on arrival in Benoni and stuffed it all into my handbag. Then with Matthew under one arm, and holding Rory by the other hand, we crossed a double-lane highway to get to the eye doctor. The wind was blowing hard, the highway was busy, and Rory accidentally tipped my handbag upside down because the big city was making him anxious and he was holding my hand very tightly.

Everything in my bag fell out into the middle of the highway. The coins and passports, mascara, and a tampon fell down onto the road. The notes swooped into the wind and fluttered upwards like waves of quelea birds or like a scene from a movie. I picked up my bits and pieces off the road, found one ten-rand note and, still clutching my kids, I weaved through the traffic that was busily dodging bank notes, to the pavement on the far side. As the money flew away from us, people swarmed out onto the road chasing it, grabbing at it in the air, off the chain-link fence on the far side of the highway, and off windscreens of the cars that had slowed down to watch the spectacle. All the money-grabbers were men, all of them were black and oppressed by apartheid, and if they earned anything, their wages would have been below the poverty line. They had no reason to want to help out a white woman with so much money on her. Rory, Matthew, and I stood quietly watching them scurrying after our money. I wondered vaguely how I would explain this to the partners of The Bull and Bush. Then slowly, one by one they trickled back towards us, bringing me the money that had blown up to 300 metres away. One by one, they handed me the notes, until eventually one guy asked me to count them. Those men returned all but two of the ten-rand notes. Nobody expected thanks. They quietly returned the money and disappeared from wherever they had come.

The kindness of those men and the money blowing in the wind reminded me of an annual migration of millions of small white butterflies that came through Thanissara and Kittisaro's meditation retreat centre near Underberg one January, heading for Mozambique and Madagascar. So small and so light, and yet doing such a big job of lifting our human hearts, all of them together making possible what one or two could not do on their own.

Hope lives on in only one Sumatran tiger surviving extinction, or one 10-year-old pulled alive from the rubble of a collapsed village after an earthquake, or one president of a country driving a Volkswagen Beetle, who spent his government's money on education rather than fighter jets.

Rare political parties were popping up in unlikely places that seemed to be genuinely concerned about the real problems we were facing. We no longer all blindly trusted our governments, our media, the pharmaceutical companies, big agri-businesses, or the oil corporations. People were demanding organic food, a reduction in GMOs, and more transparency from our governments. It might never be enough, yet these tiny signals of hope, like the butterflies, lifted our human souls into a union with something more than the mundane drudgery of everyday life. Hopeful feet could carry us where angels might fear to tread.

THE FIFTH GATEWAY:
TRUTH

The Gateway of the Heart opened the way between the pre-verbal communication of instinct, which is the language that links you to your cosmic consciousness, and the communication of speech, which is the language of individual identification. This Fifth Gateway teaches you the value of will, authenticity and truth. When you made the distinction between self and other, them and us, imposed order and natural order, and between chaos and the cyclical unfolding of creation, you began your descent into imposing your will on others. When Adam and Eve were expelled from the Garden because they bit into the apple of good and evil, they moved out of Oneness into duality and separation. It was the beginning of deceit. The magnificence

159

of your humanity is that it expresses itself through Oneness and individuation, yin and yang, innocence and maturity, good and evil, creation and destruction, language and imagination, understanding and free-will. Don't let your humanity hold you back from your magnificence. Don't let your magnificence keep you from embracing the incredible gift of being human.

The obstacles: Control, lack of boundaries, and deceit

Questions to ask: Am I courageous enough to stand in the light? Can I speak from a place of truth? Is my will fully aligned with the Will of God? What can I learn from this? How can I be bold and sure enough to find anchor in the middle of this storm, without resistance, or closing down, and without being swept away by my emotions? How can I stand up for what is true, or how can I move away lightly?

Having figured out that I seemed to be moving up through my body to encounter the Gateways, and these were the challenges of the Fifth Gateway, it seemed logical to look for the next set of obstacles in my shoulders, my throat and my neck.

My shoulders were the place where I carried the weight of the world, including many of my own burdens of personal responsibility.

My throat held all the frustration of the times I hadn't spoken out for fear of retribution or humiliation. It also held the residue of words I had spoken in anger and lies I had told to protect myself and promote my agendas.

My neck was a narrow channel connecting my head to my heart, so it felt constricted sometimes, particularly because the topics Melchizedek mentioned—will, authenticity and truth—required a certain sense of individuation: me as separate from the world. I was already suspicious of the damage we humans could do when we became caught up in setting ourselves up in competition with others. I valued interconnection. I longed for the opposite of independence. I dreamt of falling in love in deep, meaningful relationships, or being loved unconditionally by my children, or merging with Melchizedek. But at this gateway the concept of individuation meant that I needed to find my own particular truth and unique power. I needed to separate myself from the whole with purpose and with intention. It was a radical shift for me.

TRUTH

My throat was my place of communication. Insincere communication often presented a great challenge to me because I still sometimes defaulted back to trying to make my life look perfect.

Having removed the net of fear and having made the decision to welcome that which I resisted into my heart, I realised that I also needed to create boundaries, chosen by me from a place of power and love rather than from the untruth of either being overly forceful or too timid.

I needed to learn how to be True to myself. Finding my Soul-Self wasn't just a spiritual exercise, I discovered. It meant I had to be True here on earth as well. I had to find out what it meant to be authentic. I had to speak out and say what I felt, both for myself and for the injustices in the world. I had to be truthful and not care what other people thought of me, even if it meant that they all got to know that I was sometimes ashamed, or bummed out by the idea that I should be standing up for oppressed minorities, or afraid to say what I thought, or was a mean bitch when I was hungry or when I felt attacked. Being real meant that much as I wanted to be Mother Mary, being me also included being terrified of being seen. Being me included being everyone else's painful hearts as well. Individuating did not seem to disconnect me from others.

Maybe being me meant that all my judgemental ancestors would not only turn in their graves but might just come bounding out of them to wag censorious fingers at me for letting the awful, mangy cat of who we really were as a family out of the bag.

Nix taught me the value of authenticity. He has his father's warmth and charisma and my father's good looks. Growing up he was a tornado of energy and emotions. He decided early on that since our family bottled things up and kept things 'nice', he would take responsibility for our emotional well-being. He once howled and sobbed for an hour and a half as we were sitting on the roof-rack of the Land-Rover searching for game on a camping trip because Charlie had driven over a guinea fowl that had flushed up directly in front of us. Nix felt that the bird required more grieving time than we were allotting it. He was about eight then, and I have no doubt that he was crying for a whole lot more than just the guinea fowl, but he also felt that it was up to him to send it off in a proper fashion.

Nix expressed our unexpressed anger when times were tough, both before and during our divorce, especially when we were pretending that everything was fine. He felt and still feels life deeply, and he has tremendous integrity that will not put up with my pretences. In his wisdom, he has always called me out anytime I tried to cover up for anyone, myself included. When I wanted peace and harmony, Nix wanted unadorned honesty. It took me years to learn the value of truthfulness, and I was initially very afraid of it. Nix was my first and most important truthfulness teacher.

If I was going to be truthful, I couldn't pretend to be other than I was. This included having to look again at everything I had written to see where I was kidding myself, or where I was portraying myself as wiser or more awakened than I actually was. Melchizedek wanted me to write a book about 'Seven Gateways to Shambhala', but I wasn't an enlightened master. The urge to pretend that I knew what I was talking about was strong. By the time I was dealing with the Gateway of Truthfulness, I was already seven years into writing this book. It had taken various forms: novel, treatise, instruction manual, and finally, the story of my life, while I searched for the best way to illustrate what Melchizedek and Mother Mary were teaching me. And then two years before it came to completion, I slammed into the problem of being authentic. How could I possibly write a book about stuff that I didn't completely understand? Being truthful meant that I could only write about what I knew. It meant that I had to draw on my own experiences. How was I supposed to write a book about moving beyond my little self and the dream-like illusion that I was Robyn through writing about the experiences of Robyn? How could I share experiences that were close to my heart, and had the potential to be seen as special, when the purpose of the book was to move way beyond being special into being nobody at all? It was confusing; it was paradoxical, and it was littered with half-truths and subtleties that I didn't altogether get. I considered abandoning the writing project altogether. I went on more meditation retreats. I tried to learn from enlightened teachers in physical form, who were a whole lot more perfect than me. And then I decided to give up trying to be like them, to just be me.

This being me in all my murky, brilliant, shadowy, sunlighty colours, in all my authentic integrity, was held in my throat because it was there that I needed to learn to speak my truth. I couldn't go anywhere near my throat area until I had strengthened my solar plexus enough that I was not afraid of my power and had strengthened my heart enough that I could temper that power with love. Even though I was weaving my way back and forth between the Gateways, I found it very hard to be authentic before I felt stronger in my heart and self-worth. And it was still discomfiting to be seen for who I was.

So even though this might have been a strange starting point to learn more about Truth, I began addressing the obstacles in this Gateway by taking up singing lessons with Rebecca to help me find my voice. I had grown up among family tales of how we were all tone-deaf, an embarrassment to any choir. As soon as somebody harmonised next to me in the school chapel at boarding school, my voice would slide off pitch to mirror theirs. Despite Rebecca being entirely non-judgemental, the singing lessons were initially unnerving. During our very first lesson, I couldn't get a sound out of my throat, so we spent the entire lesson on hands and knees simply beating out a rhythm with our hands on the floor. I eventually thought of my weekly Wednesday classes as singing therapy rather than singing lessons because I would arrive each Wednesday at 11.30 in the morning and would sing and weep for half an hour. I loved those lessons, however, and Rebecca patiently guided me through the tightly held constriction in my throat.

Through learning to sing, I learned to speak out—slowly, like a tortoise's head emerging from its shell. And at the same time, in my work and in the world, I also learned the value of silence. Silence allowed me to listen. Listening allowed me to intuit what was happening around me more deeply. Speaking and silence were intertwined, and the one only became valuable when it was held in relationship with the other.

GUIDELINES

Silence really is golden. Sharing a communal silent space for a meal, or sitting in silence around a fire, or during group meditation is an intimate gift from the gods.

The reason it can feel awkward initially is because it exposes where I'm inauthentic. Silence is more truthful than chitchat.

Note to Self: When I speak, I often use flattery and manipulative words to cover what I really think to get others to align with my agendas. I say things like this: 'So good to see you; you're looking great, glowing, in fact. I've been missing your lovely presence. Friday we're having a meeting. We couldn't do it without you; I know you'd make ALL the difference. Promise me you'll come?'

If I simply said, 'We're having a meeting. Can you make it?' it would be more truthful because often the additional fluff was only there to ease underlying anxiety in myself.

Or I mould my words into a shape that I think the other person would like to hear. They ask me, 'Do you want to go to the meeting?' Definitely not! Except my answer goes like this, 'Aah, I would *love* to, what a pity that umm, my car is being serviced, and umm, I don't think I'll have it back by then. But I can get hold of you if it is. Umm, okay?' Who was I kidding?

When we sit among others in silence, we communicate via subtle signals that are more truthful than language. *Our bodies don't lie,* and the almost subconscious messages I reflect and receive through body language are more obviously perceptible when I quieten down and begin to listen into the silence.

Reminder: Silence is like slowing down. It also takes me back to the first lesson of being present and letting go of the obstacle of distraction.

I knew from my work of doing Soul Integration with parents-to-be who came for sessions to connect to the souls of their unborn children that these little beings-in-formation spoke a more truthful language. Their pre-verbal language used imagery and feeling to communicate, and it was identical to the language of animal communication. It was the language of horse whisperers and the Australian Aboriginals who made their way across vast semi-deserts by following the Songlines. It was the language of the subconscious. It was the language of images and telepathy, and as adults we had mostly forgotten it.

Animal communicators use imagery to receive and send information or messages to animals. During the days that I was taking singing lessons, when I was working with this Gateway of Truth, Melchizedek asked me to attend a course in animal communication, and without knowing why it might be relevant to me since I didn't really work with animals, I went to one that was being held at a lion park. The facilitator of the course gave us various questions to ask the lions, which she already knew the correct answers to, and we had to visualize their responses. Astonishingly, almost all of us received the right answers every time, even though I didn't expect to, and even though none of us felt particularly telepathic or experienced in communicating with animals.

What I realised as a result of this short course was that there was a possibility that babies' and animals' intuitive communication and perception was more conscious than it was for adults, since they seemed to be very attuned to it. It helped me to realise that the Soul Integration work for communicating with unborn babies and our Higher Selves was identical to the process of animal communication.

INTEGRITY

I asked Melchizedek about integrity because it seemed to belong to authenticity and truth, and I wanted to understand it better.

He answered: *Integrity is your internal compass bringing you into alignment with God.*

REFLECTIONS

Integrity is a beautiful word. It derives from the Latin word 'integer', which means wholeness, or perfect condition; that which is sound and complete.

In 1994 I trained in Soul Integration facilitation. The sessions with clients were simply called sessions in those days. I asked Mother Mary what name I should give to the sessions, and she suggested they should be called 'Integration' sessions. Integration has become a popular buzzword over the years, but in those days, it was relatively unused. I love the word.

'Integration' has the same root as 'entirety' and 'integrity'.

The etymological root 'integer' also has figurative meanings of purity, correctness, honesty, honourability, uprightness, untainted—literally untouched, from 'in' (not) and 'tangere' (to touch).

'Integro', the Latin verb of 'integer', also means to 'begin again, to renew, to restore'. Integrity and integration infer that the person is whole, complete and always themselves and that when they aren't, they simply come back to the beginning to find their re-alignment once again. This sounds like a description of the Soul-Self that Melchizedek was directing me towards. It is integrity that most completely describes the teachings of the Fifth Gateway.

How it seems to play out in my day-to-day world is that when I step out of my integrity, Melchizedek places what I perceive as obstacles in my path, which eventually guide me back to wholeness again if I listen clearly enough. Usually, though, I just get caught up in the daily grind of managing the obstacles and refuse to see the big picture or the 'wholeness'. It becomes a battle of wills; my will against my willingness to follow Melchizedek's pointing. The outcome is a toss-up, and the more I fight, the rockier the road. This does not mean that when someone is having a rough ride and life is flinging challenges at them from every direction, they are out of their integrity. It simply means that their challenges are life's way of gently assisting them to expand their vision to the point of being able to see the big picture or the 'wholeness'.

Ram Dass was a legendary champion of the value of leading an authentic life of integrity. He wrote a book called *Still Here* because he wanted to develop a curriculum for conscious aging.[19] He had almost completed the book and was struggling with the conclusion. He asked in meditation for guidance to help him to understand what Conscious Aging really meant, and at that moment he suffered a tremendous brain

19   Ram Dass. *Still Here*. Riverhead Books. 2001

haemorrhage, a stroke that nearly killed him and left him severely in-
capacitated for four years. Slowly he learned to speak again, to receive
help from others, to know what it really meant to age well. Then he
rewrote the book from the beginning. While it might seem that he had
little choice in what happened to him and would have been unlikely
to consciously call on that experience with open arms, he was nevertheless humble and insightful enough to recognise the wisdom of the
synchronicity and learn as much as he possibly could from the event.
He transformed what would normally be viewed as a catastrophe into
pure grace. And his book is a masterpiece.

Developing integrity was more difficult than I expected. Melchizedek
showed me the way and then left me to make my own decisions. When I
turned to him, he was there, behind me or inside me. I followed the Aum-
like hum of inter-being, which is traditionally called the *nada* sound,[20]
into a subtle place of resonating with his vast and immensely reassuring
presence. It was always calm, and his wisdom felt solid. He felt reliable
and caring. Once I tapped into that, I could feel his guidance become
gradually clearer. I could also feel his presence in my daily activities; it
showed itself as a quietude in my belly, a connection and flow between
my belly and my heart, a vibration radiating outwards. However, my
external world still pulled me this way and that, and it was a conscious
choice that I had to make out of my own free will to align myself with
Melchizedek's will so that he could guide my way forward. Instead, I
often chose to detach from his power supply by distracting myself and
vegging-out in front of a movie with chocolate or popcorn.

---

20   A small part of the music of the spheres we tune into through liminal living is
that of the *nada* sound, sometimes called 'the sound of silence'. It is a high-pitched
ringing tone, sometimes misdiagnosed as tinnitus, which resonates with the hum of
Universal energy. From Sanskrit, *nad* means to flow or a stream of consciousness.
Generally, the word *nada* means sound. There are yoga schools that base their med-
itation on this technique. Kabir, a fifteenth-century mystic poet described it thus,
 '*Nada* is found within.
 It is a music without strings, which plays in the body.
 It penetrates the inner and the outer
 And leads you away from illusion.'
 The *nada* sound is a manifestation of the experience of bridging worlds. This
sound brings us into an awareness of higher planes of consciousness.'

FREE WILL

Melchizedek had guided me through this time with messages whispered inside my head. But although the insights came from him, I created the agenda and time frame. First, before he showed me anything at all, I had to show up. It was called 'free will', and he would not interfere with it. He made my way easy, and he paved the road ahead of me with golden footprints. Sometimes I followed them, sometimes I forgot. He watched with love when, I fell distracted into the holes on the side of the road again and again. And he lent a hand to help me out, but only when I extended my hand to him first.

However, free will held me captive. I would have been been so much freer with Melchizedek's will, attuned to the natural rhythm of life, not fighting for things that were Bad For Me like Chocolate or Unsuitable Men. Free will belonged to this Gateway of Truth.

I had always admired the concept of free will. Surely it was the right we humans gave one another in a democratic society to question freely and to choose freely, so long as we didn't intentionally harm others? However, now I could see that what I called free will operated from my deluded state of thinking I was a separate being. I wasn't free at all; my will imprisoned me in deluded actions. I was entangled in knots with the pretence of trying to match my will to how I thought things should be. Free will was really nothing other than a desperate urge to control my life. Melchizedek said,

Your task in opening the Gateway of Truth is to allow the experience of life to unfold without needing to make it better or different. This does not mean you cease taking appropriate action when necessary. Your world requires your thoughts and your feelings, your perceptions and your actions. But let go of the emotional drive that insists you should control it. Allow the impartial observer within you to watch this play of your life with equanimity and ease.

This was a letting go of the deepest kind. I still had choices. When I aligned those choices towards the greater good, I could easily see that it was my intention behind each and every one of my choices that not only created my reality but affected everyone else as well. *Wu wei*, the flowing in a harmonic resonance with life, was a choice. Standing in my truth was a choice. Finding the place of stillness within was a choice.

Aligning myself with Melchizedek and Mother Mary amounted to reconfiguring my intention towards *wu wei*; that effortless effort that allows the Universe to choose the direction of my life, without me forcing it towards my own particular ends.

I often experienced *wu wei* through attuning so closely to Mother Nature that I first began to resonate with her, then become her. I found it easiest to align with the flow of life force when I was out in nature. I live in rural areas because that helps me to remain attuned. Mother Nature is a tangible presence of love that I feel in my body and following the feeling leads me directly into the Liminal Lands of dreams and meditation, while simultaneously connecting me firmly to waking consciousness and the earth.

Melchizedek refers to it as *living as a walking prayer*. Sometimes it was hard for me to surrender my free will to the will of God, or Melchizedek, or Mother Nature. Sometimes I struggled with trusting enough to live as a walking prayer.

TRUST

Most of us have fears that we know are irrational. Fears of heights, constricted spaces, spiders, or babies. We are taught that it is prudent to judge life according to its ability to harm us. This attitude is like a huge monster interfering with our ability to trust life. Trust helped me recognize that life brought me exactly what I could use to make me grow, and each experience was tailor-made just for me. Trusting life didn't stop life from being difficult or painful sometimes. It did increase synchronicities, though, and it did create an ease in dealing with the difficulties. As this easiness and effortless flow increased, my worldview and my world changed. As a very practical, down-to-earth example of this, delighted people are more likely to create a delightful ambience around them.

When I trust deeply enough in the natural order of things and open my heart with gratitude to my topsy-turvy life, there is a definite consciousness shift that occurs, both in my own life, but also, no matter how miniscule, on a collective level as well. I know it occurs, but I don't know the size of it.

Trust was hard for me to surrender into completely. Even when I was giving birth to my babies, I fought desperately to maintain control. Childbirth is a time when controlling our surroundings and attempting to force the intensity of the experience into something manageable illustrates how important trust is to the business of living well. The more we resist and fight and fear the labour, the more it hurts. The more we soften and open to the experience, the more magnificent it becomes.

Ella was such a perfect example of the value of letting go of the resistance caused by fear.

As her doula, I received her phone call at 8.30 in the morning while I was having breakfast. Her primary midwife had checked her and gone home again. She had been told that her cervix was one centimetre dilated and rigid. She already wanted to ditch her plan for a home water-birth because labour was too painful, and an epidural felt like her best option. Ella believed that a natural birth would help her body to produce the most beneficial hormones for bonding with her baby, and she wanted his birth to be as peaceful as possible for him. She had researched the best options for creating a safe and peaceful birth and had decided that since she was afraid of hospitals, she was best suited to home-birth with a professional midwife in attendance.

It sounded like labour would be long and hard for her. We decided that I would drive to her house, see how she was doing, and then she could make her decisions from there. When I arrived, her contractions were coming regularly, every three minutes or so, but they were short and did not seem very strong. She timed them while gasping with raggedy breaths as the tears spilled down her cheeks. She had wanted a calm home birth so much and had practiced her breathing techniques for such a long time, that despite the intense pain, she then chose to stay at home for a further half an hour while we breathed together to see if that helped. Then if it was still too painful, we could transfer to the hospital for an epidural. She and I moved to a quiet side bedroom. Her husband preferred to wait outside and water the garden. He was shaken by birth's intensity and needed a breather. Besides, she needed mothering right then.

Initially, Ella could only breathe deeply and relax a little in between the contractions, and even that was hard for her to do. But her shoulders did soften slightly in between, and after two or three more of these still rather mild contractions that she had been feeling so intensely, she realized that as she relaxed and let go of fear, so her contractions became easier to manage. It was a watershed moment for her.

She found her rhythm within the next few contractions, and half an hour later, now in full, strong labour with mighty contractions lasting over a minute each, she was swaying on the birth ball in the lounge, her arms around her husband's neck, her head buried in his shoulder, rolling back and forth in a deep labour trance, back and forth, back and forth. Her watch for timing the contractions lay ignored on the kitchen counter, her plans to go to the hospital forgotten. Her breathing was steady, slow, and measured. The contractions grew strong and powerful while she grew soft and wild and open. She rested her head on her husband's shoulder and slept between contractions, and at one point she lifted and turned her head sideways to speak to me as I rubbed her back. I saw her eyes were glazed and dreamy, almost rolling backward. 'This is easy, Robyn,' she said, 'I could do this forever.'

Her baby arrived less than twenty uncomplicated minutes later before she had time to get into the birth pool. She had done a lot of Soul Integration work during her pregnancy where she let her inner wisdom guide her gently to a place of inner serenity, so her baby was calm and sure and peaceful, as surrendered into life as she had been in labour.

Ella's birthing was such a vivid example of how as she let go of resistance to birth, so the magnificent power of her labour could simply flow through her. Birth was identical to everyday life but cranked up to ear-splitting intensity. If I could let go of my resistance to my experiences and simply trust whatever showed up, then life could flow through me with more ease and grace.

I recognized that this tendency to remain in control at all costs was impacting severely on our societies and the earth. We killed ugly bugs; we imposed order on the land with monoculture and fertilizers and pesticides. We plundered our mineral resources to maintain the machinery of civilized society. We lived in boxes with no access to the vibrant life force of nature. Managing of our planet was becoming too much to bear, and I imagined that she was in deep distress.

The resolution had to lie deep within our own psyches. We couldn't respond to the pain of the Earth until we could tune in to the inter-being between us. Unless we could hold our own wounded little inner child or baby selves with tenderness and deep listening, we would be unable to overcome our defences that created separation and hostility. The only real way to take care of the Earth was to trust that on a cellular or soul level she was not separate from us.

It was time for me to start listening.

In this squashed-together time, between learning and reading and studying and the World Wide Web; between travelling and child-raising and marrying and divorcing; between sculpting and meditating and teaching; between piles of dusty admin, the midwife, the hospice worker, and the Soul Integration facilitator in me sought out the Liminal Lands that were so apparent in those transitional moments of people coming into and going out from their bodies. The metamorphosis of leaving that world, or leaving this one, is when we are all required to trust deeply and to let go of control. I knew that letting go gracefully was the portal to the Holy Grail. It was the alchemical secret that transformed lead into gold; it was the key to Shambhala. In the dance of life, the entrances and the exits were entrancing and exciting to me, and they only worked their magic when those who were birthing, being born, or dying could surrender like wild animals. Transformation happened when they trusted enough and became so attuned to their instincts that birth was natural, and death was not rejected. The midwife and the hospice worker in me knew that little deaths and little births were the stuff of life. Letting go into the three-year-old dreamlands when snakes lived under my bed was a Little Death at the end of every day. Leaving boarding school to go home was a Little Birth at the end of every week. I gave birth to a husband and died through a divorce. I gave birth to children, and when they left home to move further out into the world, bit by bit, a small part of me died. Embracing each moment and then gracefully letting go was like being in the boat on the river at De Mond, where our family has an old fishing cottage. My hand lazily trailed through the water as Rory rowed from the cottage to Kob Gat. This water at the cottage was not the same water at Kob Gat, but it all glided through my fingers, and if I caught onto one silver glimmer by capturing it in my fist, I lost the next.

Melchizedek used the analogy of a baby to deepen my understanding of letting go.

Look into the eyes of an infant. They have not yet closed or locked their Gateways that divide Heaven from Earth. They have not yet learned to mistrust their knowing, or to shutter the windows to their souls through their judgement of the world outside.

As you look into a newborn's eyes, notice his willingness to love you. Be aware of his vulnerable softness, his undefended heart, and his un-constricted body. Watch his flexible movements and feel him surrender into stillness on your shoulder. Breathe in his innocence and smell his unsullied newness. Let him lower your defences and permit him to show you his way.

Become a child as you enter through this Gateway because a child is not yet comparing himself to others. Let go of comparison and remember that integration is only present in this moment in time, right now, and it is only available to you in this place, right here. Look around you with the wonder of an infant seeing his environment for the very first time.

No matter whether you are dealing with daily life or are submersed in the depths of the Liminal Lands, can you allow a childlike sense of delight to be present in every moment of your life? Even when the weight of meetings, phone calls, emails, schedules, plane flights, coffee, business deals, romances, and unresolved family issues hang over your head, each one of them prodding and needling you to worry and gnaw and clench?

The weight and pressure of unmet tasks is just weight and pressure. Feel it without resistance. Explore your world with the inquiring mind of a child who is still fascinated by his surroundings.

Be like a child, Beloved, in the midst of your grown-up and important world. Be like your own child in front of this Gateway. Your infant is not capable of closing herself to the pain in her immediate environment or to the suffering she encounters around her. Your infant thinks she is you, my love. Her pain and her love are your pain and your

173

love. If you are stressed and apprehensive, she is unable to protect herself from an acute and sensitive awareness of it. Your infant becomes who she is partly through absorbing your impression of the world. If you are anxious about her well-being, she will be anxious too.

As time goes by, your toddler constructs a shell of constriction and tension in her small body to protect herself. Initially, she protects herself from being so sensitive in an insensitive world, then from separation anxiety as she grows a little older. Thereafter, she protects herself when she realises that she can't manipulate her external world to meet all her needs. The layers of defensiveness build through her life as she ages, and unless she is prepared to meet her experiences openly, she becomes progressively narrower and more constricted in her judgements, her beliefs, and her opinions.

But you, with the infant as your teacher, and with the wisdom of experience behind you, can choose to contain both the soft, open heart of your infant and the rational, separate, intelligence of your intellect. Then you can be in this world, but not of this world. A tiny individual speck and an entire cosmos simultaneously. Drop your adult baggage, let go of unnecessary accoutrements, so that you can become it all. In letting go of everything, you can have anything.

Melchizedek and Mother Mary required that I trust them. Not blindly; they required that I felt into the frequency they were beaming into my body. I did this through feeling grateful and loving them. If my love for them resonated on a high enough frequency, then I had come into closer alignment with the thought-forms that they broadcast through me. These were more likely to contain a wiser form of guidance than the muddled everyday content of my monkey mind.

Following the directions Mother Mary pointed me towards when I didn't want to, because her choices made my life more challenging, was a choice. It took me years to realize that perhaps the most profound teaching I was given by Melchizedek and Mother Mary was this one about free will. Turning to Melchizedek was a choice. Even letting him go, despite the fact that I wouldn't have consciously chosen it, was a deeper choice that I made when my soul was ready to take responsibility for all of who I was. It happened after a mediation retreat with Thanissara and Kittisaro in the Drakensberg mountains in South Africa.

A PHYSICAL PROBLEM

Sometimes I was pulled into being present through the intensity of the energy that Melchizedek brought with him. And sometimes it caused big physical problems for me.

Migraines were like an annual tooth-cleaning at the dentist; they always blasted my brain clear of plaque build-up, of stilted thought patterns. The backwash of this flooded through my body as toxic detritus, leaving me washed-up and wobbly but stripped bare and clean. Then Melchizedek's energy spanned the distance between Sun and Earth, through the mere finger-breadth of my fragile, hollow, rock-solid body as easily as if I were a lightning rod conductor. The sheer power raging through my body rooted me deep into the massive rock I was standing on. Immobile and lead-heavy, flashing fire and sun flares, I became a bridge anchoring Heaven to Earth.

Migraines weren't the only way I was washed clean. *Kundalini* energy did it to me in my thirties and left me bedridden for those six long months.

I could simply log these events up as migraines or myalgic encephalitis, as the medical fraternity would have assured me was the case and taken myself to bed with a packet of whatever the latest medication was for these things. I didn't know if I loved or hated the intensity of the energy that surged through me at these times. When I surrendered to the sheer power of it, I felt like I was plugged into the massive-voltage-high-amp-live-wire cosmos. When I resisted it, it turned into a cosmic shit storm.

Through practices such as *tonglen*, we humans were creating a cosmic sewerage system to weather these storms. It was important work, and many of us were involved in it to a lesser or greater degree of consciousness.

And then as a result of these intense energy surges in my body, a pressure build-up in my brain during a meditation retreat in my fifties popped a hole in my dural membrane, so that my cerebrospinal fluid leaked out. It was particularly difficult to deal with because it occurred when Melchizedek left me.

LETTING GO

Towards the end of the three-week silent meditation retreat, I was tumbled into a Melchizedek-empty wasteland. Melchizedek, the light to whom I belonged, became entirely absent.

Three months previously, he had nudged me in what seemed like the dead of night. I had glanced at my clock. It was 3:33. I stretched into a dozy wakefulness. Numerologically, 333 signifies the presence of the Ascended Masters in one's life. I had looked up the numerological significance of 333 previously when Melchizedek wanted to catch my attention by using it on clock times, book pages, and aeroplane flight numbers. Melchizedek was apparently an Ascended Master. No matter whether this information is valid or not, the number 3:33 must have meant that whatever he wanted to say to me was important.

 You belong to me, Beloved. You are me. But you don't know it yet. Strip away the armour that protects you from your wounded self, peel it off, layer by delicate layer. What is left behind is me.

Even though I was still lying in bed, my knees buckled, and my heart swelled in gratitude.

Really? There was nothing I wanted more. I had been asking in a roundabout way for something like this for years, both in meditation and as an evening ritual: Whenever I saw Venus hanging in the sky, which was most nights, even if I had seen other stars before her, and even though Venus was a planet not a star, I repeated the childish verse,

> Star light, star bright.
> First star I see tonight.
> I wish I may, I wish I might,
> Wish the wish I wish tonight.

Almost invariably I wished to integrate with Melchizedek, although occasionally I might have wished for collective awakening, or for Bernie Sanders to win the US primaries, or for longer eyelashes.

When he said I belonged to him, he anchored more solidly in my body, like a dependable shoreline, a country that you visited for the first time but knew was home, a friend that was always a friend even though he lived on the other side of the Atlantic Ocean. My daily practice of merging with Melchizedek's energy became second nature, and I could feel that he was always there. I just needed to turn my attention, and there he was, inside of me. Mother Mary was there too, as the sweetest breeze through my body.

I am here, Melchizedek reassured me over and over and over. *I am here*: a murmur in my heart, my belly and my toes. *I am here*. He gave me a few months to learn to trust this feeling. *I can no longer be separated from you in this body,* he told me repeatedly. Then towards the end of the retreat he added,

No more than you could live without your bone marrow or your blood. I am your survival. I am your home. I am your breath. Through this particle of me, you have a Gateway to the whole.

The entrance to Oneness is through your body. Expand into your body and find the spaciousness there. I am you. You can no more detach yourself from me than you can halt the flow of existence. I am omniscient, omnipresent. I am the vastness of your being when you release your clinging to restricted perspectives.

Let go of clinging to your children, let go of your trepidation about What Other People Think, let go of your anxiety about Messing Up, let go of your aversion to the physical pain in your shoulders, your hips and your ankles, let go of your anxiety about not having enough and not being enough and not doing enough, let go of your fear of letting go. All your tightness and constrictions and wants and desires of your little self, all these must go. Be easy on yourself. You cannot cast them away; they can only dissolve in the softness of your great being.

And then. Get this. Having assured me that he was me, Melchizedek disappeared. Completely. Gone, gone, gone beyond.

Having insisted that the only way to experience Shambhala and the emptiness out of which everything emerged was to let go of clinging to anything at all, he merged with Shambhala and vanished. He was there, but without form, without voice, without guidance or advice, a silent presence. I was left disoriented, forlorn, adrift. Melchizedek had been there as a guiding light for so long. I prayed to him; I checked in with him at many intervals throughout the day; I turned to him for a hug or for reassurance whenever I needed support.

He had told me that he was always, always there, but now he was no longer available to me. Bereft, angry, scared, I imagined the worst. I thought I had made him up, and he was never more than a figment of my imagination. There was a deep truth in that, but I couldn't see it yet. Years ago, he had told me, *I am who I am. What you see of me or others is a reflection of you.* But he wasn't even there to remind me of that.

I had come to rely on Melchizedek's presence so thoroughly that I turned to it as I woke in the morning. I felt it often during the day. I lay cloaked in it at night-time. When it disappeared, it wasn't as terrifying as the grey sense of helplessness during the *kundalini* illness because over the intervening years I had built a surer sense of becoming that energy within myself. But I hadn't fully recognized that yet, so I simply felt let down and lost. Over the years, Melchizedek had become my anchor, my place of refuge. He had felt much more reliable than my other relationships. Zhoma had died; Charlie was re-married to a lovely woman called Fran, who felt like my sister. My kids had created their own lives around the world. But I had relied on the fact that Melchizedek would always be there for me.

If he had disappeared while I was figuring my way through the Gateway of the Heart, or perhaps by the time I was working through the crown of my head, maybe that would have been something I could have figured out better, maybe I wouldn't have felt so bewildered. But instead, like the *pwhoo!* of a genie magically vanishing, he was gone just at the time when I was grappling with the task of individuating into a place of creating boundaries and speaking my truth. Creating boundaries all by itself was a paradox that befuddled me. Since it was clear that I was interdependent and knew that I was not Robyn any more than I was Martha, my 84-year-old friend, or the CEO of Monsanto, or perhaps that I was all of them, I had been grappling with the paradox of also finding ways of expressing my uniqueness. And suddenly I had to do so without Melchizedek.

The link inside me that bridged my heart and my intellect exploded in dismay. Quite literally. Two days after returning home from the retreat, without Melchizedek's support, my dural membrane split open at my brain stem right where the Fifth Gateway narrowed down at my neck. After Melchizedek disappeared right at the end of the retreat, the Prana or internal energy I had been experiencing was very strong but unable to flow freely through my neck because the area was tensed up through trying to force my way back to Melchizedek again. After returning home from retreat at the end of January, while eating lunch with two friends in the beautiful gardens at my workplace, feeling distracted, disconnected and irritable, I become vaguely nauseous, with a dull, throbbing headache spreading from my occiput all the way through my brain to my eyes. Initially, I had no idea what had happened to my neck. I only knew that I was experiencing an unbearable headache and that Melchizedek was gone. It was not a migraine. If anything, I felt very badly dehydrated. Three hours later, stuck in evening traffic on the way to a family gathering, it increased to an intensity that was overwhelming and had me whimpering in pain. Arriving at my stepmother's house, I rushed to the bathroom and vomited from the pain before greeting anyone, and then promptly disappeared to bed. Melchizedek was nowhere to be seen or felt or heard, and under the blanket I was miserable. Hiding under the pillow, tears of self-pity poured out of me and soaked the bed. The next day, the presumed diagnosis was tick-bite fever contracted while meditating in the mountains, and I, who shunned antibiotics, took a hefty course of doxycycline for six days that didn't make the slightest difference to the headaches since the tick-bite diagnosis was incorrect. Lifting my head higher than my body was intensely painful, so I stayed prone and crawled to the bathroom. Nix, my son, came to stay and looked after me with huge care for two weeks. I was grateful and expressed it by whinging, weeping and sleeping. He had a ticket booked for Australia, however, and life had to go on. A few weeks later, in mid-March, I had clients whom I could no longer postpone and training courses to run that had already been rescheduled once. In between, I hid in my bedroom and slept.

Melchizedek was not there to guide me through this, so I turned every which way for answers. It took a couple of months to find them. Fairly early on, Anne, a superb kinesiologist, had told me that it was not tick-bite fever, but fluid leaking from my skull. The doctors told

179

me that was impossible. Anne's diagnosis eventually turned out to be perfectly correct, and in due course an MRI identified that I had had a cerebrospinal fluid (CSF) build-up in my brain, which, when the pressure grew too great, tore the dural membrane and created a spontaneous CSF leakage at the point where my spine met my brain-stem. My brain was hanging un-cushioned and dryly shrivelled off my membranes, and I was in a literal desert, not just a metaphorical one. By mid-April, I had been to the neurologist, had a couple more MRIs, and the leak was eventually sewn up by a neurosurgeon who left an impressively long scar on my shaved occiput. The headaches continued for about a year, but the operation reduced their intensity greatly.

I had to learn not only to deal with the headaches, but I had to do it without the guidance and the calm cloak of energy that was Melchizedek. It was all a bit overwhelming. Sitting in meditation was okay, though, because I had learned to be present to whatever was arising during meditation, which helped me let go of resistance more easily. I kept returning there and then slowly started listening to my inner voice and writing down what felt authentic. Somehow the Gateway of Truth required an individuation process where I found my inner truth without Melchizedek. Gradually, a feeling that I can only describe as Melchizedek-me began to emerge.

I had scheduled a three-week training course in Soul Integration for facilitators a few days after the operation. I taught it lying down on the couch in my office, and it was a turning point for me. My body was exhausted; my soul felt flat, but from somewhere deep inside, the stillness and truth that I had been feeling through the meditations emerged into this teaching space. It was a calm abiding that belonged to me alone and not to Melchizedek. The three weeks were nurturing, fun, and filled with love. We took things slowly, which meant that we felt our way into the soul connections at a deeper level.

A week after the Soul Integration course ended, I ran a nine-day training for birth facilitators. This one was really daunting for me because I needed to access a whole lot of left-brain clarity and structure for it, and my brain was still a shrivelled mess, with brain waves that were like a choppy sea instead of being long and resonant. I had no choice but to teach it like the Soul Integration course, slowly and very quietly, all of us inching our way forward through it. Although I was still exhausted, once again it was a beautiful and nourishing time for us all. I recognized that this slow, patient feeling of my way forward moment by moment was the only appropriate way to progress. I began to explore the truth of what I was doing on Earth. It felt like I was in integrity, and that 'grit' was holding me there. It took will, self- determination, and courage to teach those classes, but it was a will that was aligned with the natural flow of life unfolding in all its mysterious ways, which included leaking cerebrospinal fluid and horrible headaches. And it required faith for me to trust in that when Melchizedek was not there to guide me.

Finally, in the last week of May, I had a reading with Norma, another of my teachers who was a transparently clear channel of the Ascended Masters and particularly useful in this Melchizedek-empty wasteland. Through her, Melchizedek assured me that I had had to go through that experience to learn to find my own light within. It was a stage on the journey to wholeness, where they withdrew their assistance so that I could enter the void space. I needed to traverse this dark wasteland on my own, so that I could recognize that Melchizedek without was none other than my own light within. As I heard those words filter through me, my depleted energy started refuelling. Understanding that this had been a profound and important stage on my journey rather than an off-road I got lost on made me stronger than before. My neck, the bridge between my head and heart, was less contracted and defensive by the end of this period. I could express myself from this strength in a way that was healthy and firm. I could survive saying 'No,' even though it was still a challenge to me. The headaches were subsiding more each day. I was grateful for this journey, and I was happy to be home.

Part of moving through the Fifth Gateway of Truth meant embracing all my imperfections. Imperfection became my new rock 'n' roll. If I was rolling around at rock-bottom, I also had huge potential for expansion. The further back into my limited self I was drawn, like an arrow on a bow string, the further potential I had to shoot into expanded states of consciousness.

I gazed backwards at the Fifth Gateway. It didn't feel as though I had emerged from it triumphantly, with trumpets blaring and victorious flags flying high, but I was through, and I was committed to aligning my free will to the Will of God. I wondered how aligning myself with the Will of God could help with my moving forward to enter the Sixth Gateway?

THE SIXTH GATEWAY:
CLARITY AND WISDOM

The obstacles: Ignorance, delusion, dullness and disbelief.

Question to ask: Can I imagine a more wholesome world into being by becoming it?

Manifestation required that I envisaged the outcomes in vivid detail, then gave them away to a higher power and trusted that it would take care of it.

I was swept into the busyness of important stuff to do without engaging with the next Gateway for ages. At first, it seemed burdensome and worrying that I never had enough time to complete endless lists of tasks that I had set myself. The Compassionate Birth Project was requiring an enormous amount of logistical and analytical attention; clients needed sessions, I was training doulas, pregnant parents, and sometimes medical students. And the task of investigating the Seven Gateways and writing about them, without Melchizedek's constant presence, seemed cumbersome and ungainly.

I was also feeling overwhelmed by the level of unconsciousness that surrounded me; it sucked me back into ignorance, like some kind of sludge machine.

I watched souls being pulped by the mechanization of birth, when the caregivers were not present enough to even notice the arrival of the soul into the infant's body. And I remembered when I had been involved in hospice work in Botswana, how institutions would often drug dying people and their families up to the gills to suppress their own fear surrounding death. Interventions at birth and death sometimes invaded the sacred moment of coming into or leaving this body.

Even though they could often be gratifyingly life-saving, institutions often unconsciously mangled the people they were processing through their machinery, which was deeply invested in saving lives and making money instead of simultaneously making sturdy, supportive bridges for the souls crossing over the threshold of birth or death.

We were living in an age of quarrel and strife; the world was dark and depressing, and other people who often experienced a similar sense of hopelessness surrounded me. We felt it as a separated sense of loneliness that extended beyond ourselves to our partners, our children, and the world. These very constricted feelings bled the colour out of our lives.

Without Melchizedek's guidance answering questions about how to get through the state of confusion, I had to ask myself some questions. Previously, when I was feeling confused or indecisive, I could turn to the felt sense of Melchizedek and know that the resolutions that arose in that place were more reliable than those coming from my everyday awareness. At this stage, despite not fully grasping it yet, I was just beginning to trust that I had that knowing within myself. It took a long time to settle into me.

The journey, I realized, was one of remembering and forgetting, of dismembering and of piecing together. It was a little like birth, which, as a midwife, was familiar territory for me. During labour, the baby usually moves a little way down the birth canal, and then retreats, over and over again, in a slow, sometimes painful, often tentative journey out into the world. Like that, I ventured forth into moments of clarity and peace, and then scuttled back once more into the security of the familiar and the outworn.

Remembering Melchizedek's advice from the earliest Gateway, I decided to start with reconnecting to Presence. I would need to meditate a while until my mind became quieter.

I lit some incense to set up a feeling of calmness, brushed some of the morning's breakfast crumbs off my meditation mat and rearranged my meditation cushion. I sat, breathed deeply, and half-closed my eyes. My attention settled and sank lower in my body. A calm, peaceful weightiness connected me to the mat beneath me, to the floor and the earth beneath that. Oh, but I loved meditation. Why did I not maintain this quality of awareness all the time? It was so easy to do if only I put my mind to it. And yet my mind still wandered constantly. It was as if my will was not quite strong enough to keep me constantly in alignment with this quiet, easy, present-moment focus.

I breathed easily and waited. I realised that no matter how tidy I made it, it wasn't my mind that needed to do the sleuthing to find out how to attain clarity and wisdom; I would just have to sit and wait in the calm solidity of Presence until the sleuthing came to me.

A PRAYER OF GRATITUDE

I might have been beginning to find pockets of stillness that were truth-fully me, but I still longed to find Melchizedek's expansive luminosity within myself, and the only way I was going to do that was to take myself through the Sixth Gateway. I figured out that if I was moving upwards through the chakras on the same route my *kundalini* energy had taken, then the logical next stop would be centred in my third eye. And since the third eye was traditionally believed to be the inner eye of insightful perception, this would be the Gateway of Clarity and Wisdom. As these qualities had always been Melchizedek's trademark, I decided that if I could find them within myself, then the gaping hole left by his departure might disappear.

I waited in a trusting space of Presence as I began to figure out a route that would lead me through this Gateway. I was trusting myself enough to sit more comfortably in my separate left-brain, logical self, and the Fifth Gateway had helped me to find more balance between the right and left sides of my brain.

I made a list of what I considered to be the attributes of a person whose third eye was open and clear. Then I made another list of the kind of obstacles I might encounter there, which had kept my third eye closed.

> *List number One—Sixth Gateway attributes:*
- Imagination
- Manifestation and co-creating with God
- Pure, clear light luminosity and wisdom
> *List Number Two—Sixth Gateway Obstacles:*
- Murky, clouded mind

This was as far as I got because overall my mind was still feeling quite murky and clouded.

How could the Sixth Gateway help me find the answers when they were hidden deep in my unconscious mind, I wondered. A light bulb went on. It was my lack of consciousness that was the problem. Not only did I choose to turn a blind eye to my own hurt and pain, I also sometimes chose to close my heart to the plight of the planet and its people. I ignored global warming, genocide, corruption, sexual abuse, and planetary destruction because to care was just too hard. The hurt and pain that babies experienced when, as a midwife, I was not aware of the huge journey their magnificent souls were making by entering their tiny, helpless bodies, was something I might have chosen to remain unconscious to, perhaps because I didn't want to be reminded how hard it was for me during my own birth.

If I wanted to replace the gap left by Melchizedek's disappearance, I was going to have to recognise where I was being unconscious and move into the vulnerability of being open to whatever revealed itself. Once again, I was being led back to needing to see my own mind from within my mind, which was like seeing my own face from within my head without a mirror. There was something real and trustworthy about this. In my bones, I knew that even though I might be far away from real clarity, this was the right direction towards Melchizedek-me. I breathed deeply and calmed down into my belly.

I decided then to focus on the attributes of the Sixth Gateway first, in the hope that they would bring some light to the murkiness. Thereafter, I would bring my attention back to the obstacle of unconsciousness. And having cleared that up, I hoped to gain some of the clear-seeing, present-moment wisdom that belonged both to the Sixth Gateway and to Melchizedek.

Or that was my plan at least.

I started with a prayer of gratitude. 'Thank you, God, the Universe, Melchizedek, wherever you are, Mother Mary with your quiet presence and all the angels for guiding me through the murkiness even when I don't know you're there.'

I felt through the gratitude into the internal spaciousness of Melchizedek-me. And in the spaciousness, I noticed that my gratitude was fed through the language of my imagination.

I imagined feeling grateful, and as I did so I felt the soft, warm hug of appreciation for my guides, for myself and for the wind in the trees outside. My imagination took my internal thoughts and translated them into feelings in my body, which changed how I related to myself and my world. Imagination belonged to this Gateway of the mind's eye as well. And through my everyday work of conducting Soul Integration sessions, I already had a good deal of experience with imagination. Could I use my imagination to lead me past the befuddlement and into the clear light of wisdom?

I had a look at how the obstacle of ignorance obscured my vision. I pictured the way Robyn related to her world.

Firstly, she knew there was the Soul-Self, unhindered by the ways of the world. Secondly, within the Soul-Self, she had learned to understand something of the matrix or blueprint that laid out the guidelines for who Robyn thought she was. This matrix was created out of her experiences, both past and present. It caused Robyn to react in certain ways. It set up patterns of expectations and behaviour. Thirdly, there was Robyn who thought she was a separate entity, living a three-dimensional life in a three-dimensional world that was sometimes out to get her.

And finally, there was Robyn's belief that this everyday world, plus the Liminal Lands of her dreams, plus the experiences she expected to have when she left her body at death, were real, when in fact from the perspective of Melchizedek-me, all three of them were as inconsistent and mercurial as a five-year-old with attention disorder.

The biggest obstacle barring my way to the clear light of wisdom was my ignorance about the nature of the Soul-Self. I remembered back to the Buddhist injunction that the three hindrances to enlightenment were Aversion (which I had discovered in the Third Gateway of Power), Clinging (which I had found in the Fourth Gateway of Love), and now here the last and apparently most intractable hindrance, Ignorance. In my imagination, ignorance looked like a poisonous taproot buried deep in the unconscious. From there it polluted the tree of the collective consciousness by feeding it toxins, prejudices, rancour, dullness, and disbelief, which then spread as a global contagion out into the leaves, flowers, and fruits of the manifested world.

Ignorance caught me in the web of illusion that this world was real when deep down I knew that this world was as ephemeral as the Liminal Lands of my dreams.

I considered what all the other Gateways offered me as tools for uncovering ignorance:

The First Gateway of simplicity and Presence moved me into a place of stillness where the muddiness of my mind and the turbulence of my emotions could settle.

The Second Gateway of letting go of constriction allowed the fiery *kundalini* power of sexuality to flow freely through my body, releasing tension and connecting me with the Universal life force within me and around me. There was a wisdom in this life force that was entirely intuitive; it was a natural wisdom that knew the truth of what was right or wrong as compared to choices made by my intellect, which, although equally valuable, were based on the laws of morality and other peoples' judgements rather than my own inner knowing.

The Third Gateway allowed me to become quieter and less judgemental. It taught me the wisdom of a power that was humble and gracious. It helped me to let go of the emotional conflict created by resentment and aversion.

The Fourth Gateway helped me to let go of angst, fear and clinging.

The Fifth Gateway aligned me with the Will of God and taught me the value of speaking my Truth with clear boundaries and an ability to say 'No.' Boundaries focused my direction and created a clearer pathway through my misconceptions.

Each one had aided in the gradual process of letting go of the obstacles obscuring the underlying clarity of my mind. But despite all the previous Gateways, I could feel that I was still caught in delusions that I believed were true. I had bought into them from my family history, from my birth, from the experiences in my life that had caused me to constrict in fear or pain or anger, and from our collective consciousness that had become blinkered by our shared and painful past. Our collective ignorance was also caught in the deception that our thoughts didn't affect our reality, or that where we placed our attention was irrelevant in the grander scheme of things.

Only a few days previously, I had watched a group of kids playing a gruesome video game, which was as realistic as an interactive 3D movie. They were the criminals. I watched as they enacted hijacking cars, racing them, tyres squealing, over extremely lifelike policemen who had been gunned down in the road, then smashing into buildings on two wheels while they lobbed hand grenades out of their car windows. The kids were utterly engrossed in killing one another and the cops, and it wasn't a big leap for me to imagine them gunning down school kids in a real-life enactment of their virtual reality world. Apparently, this violent, hyper-lifelike game was the fifth most popular game of all time, and according to the Internet, 'the most popular title among male gamers, with 42% having played it in the last six months.' It had sold more than eighty-five million units and shattered seven Guinness World Records. Reading those statistics, my feelings of optimism or any hope for humanity had taken a serious dive, and Melchizedek wasn't available for comment.

Why didn't those kids question the wisdom of being sucked into alternate realities that were so brutal and grisly? It made me question myself too. Where was I caught in thoughtlessness that was equally unconscious?

I thought of the children who had withdrawn into themselves because they had no conventional barriers to defend themselves against the onslaught of twenty-first-century life. I considered the millions of youngsters who were sexually abused, the pubescent girls who were being raped and impregnated, bearing children before they had had a chance to finish childhood themselves. I thought of the eight-year-olds growing up in slums where they headed the households. What would it take for the machinery of all our systems to quiet down enough to be able to listen to these silently screaming children?

If I was to move beyond my unconscious reactions to my environment, I needed to trust in the possibility of uncovering Melchizedek's wisdom within myself. I remembered Ajahn Cha's words, 'If it wasn't meant to be this way, it wouldn't be this way.' I wasn't the mother or father of the video-game playing children, who were still responsible for helping them make decisions, so although it was probably okay to engage them in conversation, I needed to trust that the kids would wake up in their own sweet time.

Did I know an appropriate response to the damage that, on a gut level, I felt imaginary games in virtual reality were inflicting on the world? No, I didn't. And Melchizedek wasn't there to guide me. However, by feeling deeply into the stillness to retrieve my direction, perhaps I could detect how I could relate to this ultra-violent external world we all lived in. I began speaking to Melchizedek-me within myself. The replies were something that filtered out of me in a clear but tiny stream initially. The Melchizedek-me portion of my energy field spoke to Robyn as if she were waiting for guidance. It figured out this much:

Infuse your senses with the lightness of the Heavenly realms, then ground it into the Earth as one uniform, seamless whole. Soften and dissolve into your soul and merge with your spiritual knowing. Let the longing for a peaceful, healthy, joyous world sing through the cells of your body and release this hope to the winds of change. Allow the wisdom of your Higher Self to create it on your behalf. Holding onto nothing, everything becomes possible. Clinging to the smallest outcome places the possibility for change back into your small and insignificant hands.

It wasn't much because it was all a repeat of things I knew already, but it felt true, and it felt like this method of tapping into his wisdom as part of myself was worth investigating further.

Melchizedek-me could still figure out a way forward, it seemed, and the fact that the feeling of Melchizedek-me was as far removed from the virtual reality of video games as it was possible for my mind to go filled me with a slight relief.

I continued my search for something more real beneath the unconsciously created drama of twenty-first-century life. My second grandson is named Benicio, which means 'Benediction', the bringer of blessings. He was living up to his name before he even received it. The day after his birth, my son Rory, daughter-in-law Pame, and Benicio's four-year-old brother, Caetano, sat down to lunch together, while I curled up with Beni on my chest for an hour in the bedroom. Initially he was awake, rooting and squirming a little, finding his way into his unfamiliar and as yet uncomfortable body. And then we dissolved into a shared resonant space: his newborn heart wide open, soft and vulnerable, and my granny heart melting at the enormous sensitivity and beauty of the soul essence that still shone through him. I was so grateful to his family for giving me this time with him and for loving his soul wisdom.

The hour was liminal, the two of us bridging worlds. We were both here in our human forms and expanded way beyond them into a spaciousness where we were merged in love. It felt like this was how we were always meant to be, and it felt like a stark contrast to the harsh reality of the world beyond the bedroom windows.

Benicio could teach me to reconnect to the sensitivity and perception of a pre-verbal state of being, to the liminal consciousness of my true nature. His quiet way of absorbing me as if I was him was so different to the way people in institutions—medical, educational, financial— sometimes didn't really see me or anyone else as a valuable being with a complicated and sensitive emotional field.

The next example I had of this state was taught to me by Kate-Louise, who gave me a craniosacral therapy session. Her hands were listening intently and very quietly to the stories held in my body. Her hands showed her where my life-force was flowing freely and where she needed to guide my body to release its restrictions.

My body felt so grateful. 'Aah', it sighed in relief, 'here is someone who speaks the language of an expansive perception of consciousness.' Kate-Louise's hands were an expression of a consciousness revolution that I had noticed was occurring globally, like spores being released into the wind to infiltrate the collective consciousness. Kate Louise's hands couldn't have listened into the unconscious stories in my body if she hadn't connected to them directly through her open heart, and if her heart wasn't tuned into her intuition and her wisdom. She was not only attentively present, aware of the physical layers of tension in my body and the emotional baggage that caused the tension, she listened deeper still, to the subtle flow of life itself that belonged not only to me but to our interaction and to the air between us and beyond. Kate-Louise reminded me that the dissolution of ignorance comes not solely from the expansion of information but from expanding beyond the limitations of our present level of consciousness.

Yet another understanding of this subtler level of awareness came through Thanissara, who is helping to change the world for the better, not because she writes as a spiritual activist, but because she writes with a vulnerable, open heart that does not close down in the face of the suffering she engages with fully on a daily basis, and her words weep for the world.

She is a strong leader with a fiery integrity that stands up for the oppressed. I'm not sure how she managed for twelve years in a Buddhist monastery, where women were mightily down-trodden. I imagine that when she was a nun, she would have bent the rules that didn't make sense to her. In these times of massive global ignorance, she writes books and articles about our need to stand up and speak out.

Thanissara wrote that, 'It is an act of resistance to love in the face of hate. It is an act of hope to say we remember another way, we know, we will live, we will work, sing, dance, vote, hope, laugh, embody another way—the way of ethics, rule of just law, the abiding by fair and full democracy, the fearlessness of speaking out with open hearts, clear minds, and embodied connection. It is an act of love to not generate divisive consciousness.'

My heart was touched not by Thanissara's words in themselves, but by the quality of astute attention that lay beneath them; it woke me up from my unconscious judgements.

The entrance to the Sixth Gateway of Clarity and Wisdom seemed to require trusting in a sensitive exploration of unknown, liminal spaces.

I could trust in the liminal worlds as Benicio did; I could feel my way through to them as Kate-Louise did; I could refuse to shut my heart to the suffering as Thanissara did; or I could use my training in working in the worlds of imagination as an entrance into these lands.

IMAGINATION

A few years back, Melchizedek had discussed imagination with me. I searched through my journals and until I found this excerpt:

> *Don't discredit your imagination as unworthy, Beloved, as it can travel beyond the furthest galaxy and into the deepest recesses of your mind. It is the language of your soul. It holds the wisdom of the collective consciousness and your inner matrix. It contains the wisdom of all those who have passed before you. It is the method by which your true knowing communicates itself to you. It belongs to you alone and is authentic and rich with symbolism. You shape your images by who you think you are. Treasure your imagination for the gifts it brings you. Your imagination is the language with which you receive our communications and can interpret them in worldly form. Imagination can change the matrix of who an individual perceives him or herself to be.*

Having worked in the Liminal Lands of imagination and interior spaces for years, I understood Melchizedek's instruction about my imagination

191

being authentic and rich with symbolism.

The Soul Integration work I had trained in under Mother Mary's watchful eyes in Amsterdam in the early 1990s had taught me how to use active imagination to develop more clarity in my life. I might have needed a bicycle to clear my head after the intensity of the sessions, but they offered a powerful method for letting go of emotional gunk and for developing insight. Symbolic consciousness operated on many different levels. Years ago, I might have thought of imagination as rather unimportant and childish. Yet my imagination could be the bridge between my waking consciousness and the blueprint I'd created and stored in my unconscious mind that informed my perceptions, attitudes, and even experiences. When I learned the language of my imagination and how to interpret its symbols, I created a new level of awareness that shifted me more fully into my ability to co-create my reality, and I managed this alongside the other influences that I couldn't control, like karma, God, my genetic inheritance, destiny, world events, and so on. When I was imaginative enough to see the symbolism in every aspect of my life, from flat tyres to a praying mantis at my front door, I noticed that my external life was mirroring my internal experience in subtle and obvious ways. Everything in my world seemed to be speaking to me and teaching me; some of these lessons were synchronistic and awe-inspiring, some were challenging.

Imagination, I already knew, was a language that resonated at different frequencies, so by using the language of imagination I could lift myself up into higher frequencies of love and light, or I could drop deeply into my shadowy underworld of pain and suffering. This imaginative replaying of the same old tired stories was, I realised, the unconscious pattern of ignorance that I was trying to move beyond.

Imagination could therefore either help me move me out of ignorance or it could hinder my clarity through keeping me caught in repetitive stories of judgement and despair. I could use my imagination unconsciously, and this would tie me up in ignorance, or I could use my imagination consciously. The more conscious I was, the more I could direct my life experience through my imagination. I thought of the time when I was caught in the delusion of feeling fat in my twenties. My imagination played so many tricks on me to keep me stuck in that role of judgement and self-doubt. For years I looped the same dreary stories through my imagination without even knowing that I had a choice to step away from that spiel and choose a different way of seeing. I could either consciously use my mind to clear my mind, or I could unconsciously let my mind keep muddying itself.

Sometimes I needed a Soul Integration facilitator to help me identify the unconscious patterns looping through the stories of my imagination. I could see other people's shadows much more clearly than I could see my own.

The images that arose in sessions were as unique to me as they were unique to each client that I worked with. During sessions, I had experienced being a dirty, snotty orphan; a hard-hearted shaman who used magic to become more powerful; a dragon; an exhausted baker, who made beautiful loaves of bread that were filled with her resentment; a kind mother; an angry mother, and many types of angelic beings. I had hundreds of sessions where I envisioned archetypes representing aspects of myself that either needed clearing or imprinting, depending on whether they were positive or negative. They illustrated the underlying causes of my behaviour or my lot in life. They taught me to forgive, let go, and expand into a spaciousness that extended beyond the story-lines of either the sessions or of my own little life.

My clients' imaginations spoke to them in the languages that they resonated with and understood best. Jim was a scientist and an atheist who didn't believe that there was a 'higher reality' other than this three-dimensional physical one. He did a session for connecting to his unborn baby because he loved his wife, and she wanted him to develop this connection. He didn't think he would be able to find his Higher Self, though, because he didn't believe he had a Higher Self. And he needed one in the session because our Higher Selves resonate at a similar frequency as the incoming babies and can help us to communicate with them on a soul level. In the session though, Jim easily recognized his Higher Self, which took the form of a fractal. This symbol of his Higher Self was one that he understood as a scientist; it spoke a language he trusted, and to his surprise, it knew exactly how to communicate with the soul of his unborn child. He cried when his 'baby on a soul level' touched him in the session because she opened his heart in a way that he had never remembered experiencing before that time.

Babies understand the language of imagination well. They give us a very clear sense of their needs during Soul Integration sessions when their parents come into alignment with their imagery. If the parents send their baby a visual image that symbolises love when he or she is sleeping, accompanied with the felt sense of it, often the baby will respond with a visible softening, a smile or a sigh of relaxation.

Babies learn about who they are and how they fit into the world by 'tuning in' to the overtones and undertones in the atmosphere created by their parents and caregivers. They are already registering these finely nuanced feelings and signals when they are in the womb. Babies are enormously perceptive, more so than we are as adults because we have shut ourselves down to the subtle cues as a defence against the harshness of life. Babies are also interactive and able to communicate their feelings and needs with us through images and non-verbal signals.

Babies and toddlers live in liminal space. They have not yet entirely left the world of dreams and cosmic consciousness behind, and simultaneously they are fully immersed in the fascinating exploration of living in a tiny, rather uncooperative body. Their liminal perspective is contagious.

My son Rory would drop into this liminal space when he played with Caetano as a toddler. Rory's face softened; he became enchanted and captivated when he saw the world through Caetano's eyes where even cracks in the dusty Lima pavement could be fascinating areas for investigation. The communication of pre-verbal babies reminds me of the fine art of imagination.

MANIFESTING

From my Soul Integration work, I already trusted that imagination was the driver for co-creating our three-dimensional experience. Manifestation, or the art of co-creation, happened either consciously or unconsciously. Using imagination to co-create my external reality didn't eliminate ignorance, but it was nevertheless useful.

I remember teaching antenatal classes to a group of parents-to-be. We were talking about using visualisation as a powerful technique to manage the intensity of labour. One of the men present spoke about how he had been given an exercise for developing his imagination when he was a drama student at university. The students were all told to imagine drinking a cup of coffee every morning for six weeks. He reported that by the end of the six weeks, his imagined cup of coffee smelled stronger, tasted better, and gave him more pleasure than his actual coffee, which was sometimes slightly bitter or not quite warm enough.

In my own daily life, using my imagination could help me move beyond the dragging, tedious monotony of traffic jams, bank queues, disgruntled shop assistants, depressing news reports, medical students who weren't coping with the stress of fourth-year clinical practice, or my own emotional fall-out. My imagination created my state of mind, which changed my felt sense and influenced all those experiences. I could choose, through my imagination, to anchor vibrational states of love and joy into my body in response to events I had previously disliked. This was not a process of disconnecting from the traffic jams and bank queues. It was one of being fully present, while simultaneously using my imagination to expand my consciousness beyond the constrictions of my less healthy emotions that the unpleasant experiences tended to incite. Simply put, if I imagined being more loving, and felt it as strongly as the drama student had imagined his cup of coffee, so that all my senses awakened to how that actually felt, then the shop assistant was likely to melt out of her disgruntled state and the traffic jams were likely to clear faster. This was weird but true.

I could use my imagination to change how I behaved because I could change how I felt about myself. As an analogy, my brain was like a car—gears, driveshaft, door-handles, wheel bearings, air filters, ABS breaks, nuts and bolts, all efficiently synchronized to get me where I was headed, although occasionally it broke down. As the driver, when I woke, I habitually climbed into the car I identified as mine. Mine was speedy, and a metallic powder-blue, not a flashy Porsche, more like a mini with a high-speed engine under the bonnet. It cornered well, and was adaptable to different road conditions, but when the wheels fell off, it crashed at high speed. All I could do then was crawl out of bed, aching, bruised and heart-sore, wondering why I hadn't chosen instead to drive a sturdy tractor with magnificent endurance and a slow, steady pace.

I had discovered that I could choose which vehicle to drive each day.

It was like the Universe had opened a rent-a-car in my head. Initially it took some getting used to, as my brain was accustomed to the powder-blue mini; it knew where the gear shift was and on which side of the steering wheel the indicators were positioned. My brain could intuit how it would respond to conditions on the road. But sometimes I needed a four-wheel drive or a vehicle with higher clearance. Sometimes I wanted to have a blast in an open-topped Maserati, Angelique Kidjo blasting from the speakers, all guts and power and showmanship. Sometimes it would have been fun to be on a scrambler bike or a sand-bike, or a kite-surfer or a snowboard.

And my brain, that 90 percent of it that I never use, had all these other options, like Avatars or skins from a video game, which I could choose to adopt for the day.

So if I needed to get my book-keeping done, there was no use my climbing into the powder-blue mini that represented the part of me that disliked book-keeping or being cooped up in front of ledgers and calculators and the constriction of tidy handwriting and pristine columns of figures. Much better to let the mini have a day off and choose the Organiser instead. I imagined the Organiser as a steel-grey vehicle, the colour of the tar road, with a quiet air-conditioner and refined jazz streaming through the Bose sound system. Even though it had been so long ignored, it was free of dust, and it purred with an almost inaudible hum as it manoeuvred its way efficiently through my untidy piles of disregarded paperwork. It was even discreetly excited about sorting out the mess!

All I needed to do was to tap into my God-self who managed the car dealership in my brain, breathe deeply to become centred, spacious, and still, and ask for guidance to find the right mode of transport for my needs at each moment. And, bingo, there it was. Once I became used to the quiet feel of it, and the scent of new leather and the immaculate sound system, I signed the Organiser out of the dealership by asking my God-self to keep a watch over me since I was operating outside of my habitual unconscious tendencies, and then I could drive off into the day.

Even though I hadn't made the connection at the time, learning to stand in my truth and to let go of control had provided me with an unexpected bonus; in the process of losing Melchizedek and finding Melchizedek-me, my organisational skill switch had been activated. I had cleared out my filing cabinet and stacked the piles of paper. I had trawled through my computer and deleted duplicate, triplicate and sex-tuplicate files, and I had arranged the remainders in neat folders. I had caught up with two years of tax returns. And I did it all cheerfully and with genuine enjoyment. When I considered this change in my attitude towards admin, I guessed that learning to stand up for myself, and be my unique individual self, cleared out the sludgy critic in my left brain that had kept me stuck for years.

Having acquired this new skill, I sat back while watching the Organiser whip through my tax returns. *Ha*, I thought, *watch out super-ego, judge of whether Robyn is efficient enough or spiritual enough or amusing enough or well-behaved enough or confident enough—here comes rent-a-car-Robyn. Once she has returned the Organizer to its parking place after sorting out her admin, she is going to rent a bicycle and head to the beach to watch the sunset and play.*

I had used active imagination in sessions for years to uncover the underlying root cause of my negative patterns of behaviour and to assist clients to do the same with theirs. I wondered if I could help to integrate a new level of consciousness into the world simply by imagining that it was possible. I wasn't convinced that individually imagining a better world would create one. But the worst thing I could lose through exploring the idea was my credibility, and in my own mind that had already taken a dive when I started chatting to imaginary figures of light.

Most of me loved this work, but much as I loved being among like-minded soul travellers who were comfortable with the Liminal Lands, much of my time had been spent interacting with medical institutions, both as a midwife and as a teacher of compassionate care to medical staff. I didn't expect a lot of support for my visions of Melchizedek and Mother Mary in those circles, and I had learned to phrase the concepts they were teaching me into more scientific language that could stand up to some rational analysis. It wasn't easy, and I often felt quite out of my depth in attempting it, but part of my liminal experience was in learning how to bridge these two worlds.

To find the language that was best understood by the people I was talking to, I imagined raising my consciousness to a level where I was resonating with joy, peace, love, wisdom, serenity, and compassion. From there the appropriate words emerged more fluently. Through appropriate use of language, I could bring more people on board with Melchizedek and Mother Mary's ideas. Speaking to fairly cynical, highly rational medical students about Melchizedek and Mother Mary as figures of light whom I spoke to inside my head might have made for a very short-term contract with the Department of Obstetrics. But I could engage with them on the topic of compassion, because it was something that many of them felt was deeply lacking in their worlds.

A NEW AWARENESS

If a relatively small number of individuals learns or integrates a new behaviour or belief, it becomes commonly available to the entire species. This is known as morphic resonance. When enough people are merged with their inner stillness, the calm peacefulness that is created has the possibility of breaking through into our collective awareness. Malcolm Gladwell described a 'Tipping Point' when changes in attitude reach a point that the entire culture moves into a different state.[21] We need a certain number of conscious individuals to shift the collective awareness into a new way of being in the world.

Melchizedek had shown me in the past that the more we individually accessed the archetypes of divinity through imagining them, the more solidly they settled as archetypes in the collective consciousness of all humanity. It could either take one person's huge vision or many people's smaller visions to change our collective perceptions. As I wrote this, my iTunes was playing a Joni Mitchell track from Woodstock. The lyrics were a reminder to me of days long gone:

> We are stardust
> We are golden
> And we've got to get ourselves
> Back to the garden
> By the time we got to Woodstock
> We were half a million strong

21 *The Tipping Point: How little Things Can Make a Big Difference* by Malcolm Gladwell. Abacis, 2002.

And everywhere there was song and celebration
And I dreamed I saw the bombers
Riding shotgun in the sky
And they were turning into butterflies
Above our nation.

I reflected on the synchronicity of hearing these lyrics. Woodstock had caused vast numbers of people worldwide to start questioning the validity of the Vietnam War. I was reminded of a similar shift in consciousness that occurred through the Occupy Wall Street protest movement in New York's financial district in 2011. Protestors camped out for weeks on end and created worldwide awareness of economic inequality, greed, corruption, the undue influence of corporations on governments, and the whole culture of sub-prime mortgages, which had created a false economic boom and subsequent market collapse.

I looked at our more recent, growing awareness. A few large corporations were placing a high value on becoming green. The Internet was spreading new ideas like wildfire. Avaaz had forty-four million members at the time I wrote this. It was a movement with vast political clout. Its petitions and non-violent Internet protests had grown into a powerful agency that governments worldwide were forced to reckon with. Even while governments seemed to be cracking down on freedom and instituting laws that were bigoted, parochial and deeply ignorant of the plight of the earth, movements like 'Black Lives Matter', youths standing up against gun control, and the 'Dakota Access Pipeline Resistance' movement which managed to stand up to the fossil fuel industry were small examples of the shift that was beginning to crack open a new level of awareness in our collective consciousness.

VISUALISING A DESIRE

Manifestation also had practical day-to-day uses that were far more personal than changing the collective consciousness or creating a more harmonious world. The trick to any kind of manifestation was to move out of the ego-self into a place of inner stillness, where I was not directing the show but was rather flowing with life as it unfolded around me. Then I visualized the outcome I would have preferred to manifest. And finally, I gave it up to God or the Universe, or the parking fairy if I was looking

199

for a parking place. I had to let go of trying to control the outcome if anything higher than my little self was going to take care of it for me. And sometimes God or the Universe or the parking fairy took care of it exactly as I requested but not exactly as I imagined or would have preferred. Manifestation works best when my ego is not involved, and I'm focusing on the highest frequency of love and light. But sometimes I've used the technique for more mundane stuff.

One of the most disruptive and uncomfortable places I ever lived in was a house I manifested as a result of deciding that I wanted to live on powerful ley lines. I can't remember why that appealed to me, but I suppose that I imagined it would make me more intuitive. The house had a huge mountain to the side of it, with great rivers pouring off it in the rainy season. The rivers flooded past the house and then veered sharply in front of it, at a juncture where they met the highway. The highway running parallel to the new direction of the river had a prominent traffic light right opposite my house, where another large road, running towards my house, intersected it at a T-junction. I had water and traffic and the sirens of police cars and ambulances and fire engines running the red light, and hectic energy rushing past me all day and night. These, I discovered, were ley lines of sorts, channels for energy, and the house reflected the unease of all that frantic energy.

I decided to change that reality. I imagined and then made a list of the kind of house I wanted to live in next. I wanted it to be on the slopes of a mountain, with one bedroom, but with space for my kids if they came to stay. It had to have a good view of nature, be peaceful, have no hectic ley lines, etc. I created a long list of minor details such as Internet access. Then I burned the paper and forgot about it. This was before Melchizedek's disappearance. He woke me up early one Sunday morning and instructed me to *Drive up to Constantia Neck and turn right.* It didn't sound like a directive but more like a thought in my head. I didn't want to live in Hout Bay, which is down that road, but I was ready to move on from the disruptive place, so after breakfast, I climbed into my car and did as I was told. Less than a kilometre after Constantia Neck, way before Hout Bay, I drove past a small gravel road leading to Orange Kloof Nature Reserve and then I did a U-turn and drove down it. It had never occurred to me that I could live in a semi-rural area inside of the city. It was beautiful. Two days later on Gumtree, the website for classified advertisements, goods for sale, etcetera, there was an advert for a bedsit in Orangekloof. I would never have gone to look at it because I wanted a one-bedroom place, not a bedsit. I only followed up on the advert because it seemed so weird that it was overlooking Orangekloof, which comprised only about ten houses in total at that time. I went to look at it, and it did, in fact, have a separate bedroom. It was not only ideal for me, it also perfectly reflected the other requirements that I had specified in my list. I lived there very happily for quite a few years.

My cottage on the Helshoogte Mountains also arrived with ease and grace. My soul longed to live further outside the city, ideally among the mountains where I felt more at home. It took me less than an hour to find it. I drove out to the mountains beyond Stellenbosch, having phoned a friend to tell her what I was looking for. And there it was, waiting patiently for me to move into; no estate agent, no contract, and no hassle, just my cottage.

I was also a champion at creating what I didn't desire, using the same process of focusing intently on it, unconsciously rather than consciously, with enough emotional strength to cause my deeper levels of consciousness to manifest it for me. I could easily manifest a sore tummy, or a cough, or brake failure, or a flat tyre on my car that synchronistically reflected my emotional states back to me. It was so easy, I didn't even know I was doing it most of the time.

Manifestation is an interesting indication of how powerful we are when we drop into the zone of effortless effort. My friend Cha's son Tobin reminded me of how he, his brother Justin and my son Maf worked with manifestation through imagination. He said to me:

'When you were recording your demo movie clip that was explaining about active imagination, you spoke about a guy on the Tube in London who imagined bouncing red and blue balls to children across the aisle when he was bored on his way home from work. He told you that the kids would often follow the balls with their eyes as if they could see them clearly. Once, the man told you, he was playing the game with a toddler, and he eventually lost interest in it. A few minutes later when he refocused on the toddler, she was still watching his imaginary ball bounce up and down and following it intently with her eyes.

'So a day later we were at the farm, me, Justin, and Maf. In the evening, we were playing guitar and drumming on empty buckets,

and we started speaking about our favourite animals. Maf said the rooikat (otherwise known as a desert lynx or caracal) was his favourite animal but that he'd never seen one in the wild because they are so elusive. In fact, Kapokie, who'd worked on the farm for sixteen years, had only ever seen one once, even though the rooikats occasionally took chickens or ducks. We were talking about active imagination and decided to imagine what would draw a rooikat to us. We imagined dead chicken carcasses, etcetera.

'We went for a walk up the farm the following morning with the dogs. We started speaking again about manifestation through active imagination. About five minutes later, we were walking across an open field. Less than twenty metres in front of us, a rooikat emerged from the bush on the one side and ran across our route towards the dam on the other side. It had amazing black tufts from its ears and was such a beautiful russet colour. We were so ecstatic; we hugged each other and yelled with joy. It was a complete celebration!'

Manifestation becomes exponentially more powerful if we approach it from a place that is free of ego-manipulation. Truly enlightened people can manifest global change. Groups of people working collectively can also have a powerful effect on the world, as evidenced by Transcendental Meditation groups organising peace meditations in cities and producing measurable outcomes in reduced crime rates.

The most powerful and valuable form of manifestation might go completely unnoticed by others. It is the manifestation of the Soul-Self expressing through the body when we release our obstacles and drop into the very centre of the stillness within.

This type of manifestation brings us back into harmony and balance with the natural world. Coming back into balance with nature is something that shamans and rainmakers know how to use to manifest rain in a way that seems magical to me.

It didn't occur to me that Geshe La might be a rainmaker. We didn't discuss the appalling drought we were experiencing in Botswana when he came to stay for ten days. I had read that rainmakers from different traditions worldwide meditated or prayed or held rain dances, and that they did so until they resonated with the land. Then when the rainmaker and the land had come into harmony and balance, the rain came naturally.

Geshe La had escaped from Tibet in the late 1950s. He was a recognised reincarnation of a previous enlightened lama; he stayed in a place of centred stillness at all times and mostly he sat in his room whenever he was not teaching and meditated—all day long and, for all I knew, all night long as well.

One evening we drove to the city, twenty kilometres away, for him to give a talk, even though his accent was so thick that it was difficult to understand him. I didn't mind; I just liked sitting near him.

For the first time since the drought began nine months previously, there was a tiny bubble of a cloud had formed in the sky above us as we drove. It looked like a cartoon cloud. Then it moved directly overhead and started drizzling down on us. This weird little cloud that didn't look like it could possibly store any rain followed us to town, raining on us all the way. Those were the first raindrops of the year, and it was already autumn, so the land was desperately thirsty, and the cattle were ribs-and-sinew thin. I looked out of my side windows and it was dry. Ahead of me, the road was dry. Behind me, dry. But the rain sprinkled on us for twenty kilometres and stopped only as we arrived at our destination.

That night, great, heavy clouds gathered, huge banks of them, and the rain started in earnest. It poured down. It was the best rain we had had for seven years. The earth, the people, the cattle all sighed with relief, and the next morning at breakfast I thanked Geshe La for the rain, half expecting him to refuse responsibility for creating it. He didn't though. "Ah." He bobbed his head quietly, always smiling, no big deal. "Relieb plants suppering," he said in his thick Tibetan accent as he spooned scrambled egg on toast into his mouth.

MOTHER MARY'S NECTAR

It was my imagination that linked me to Melchizedek and Mother Mary, and it was my imagination that dispelled my disbelief in our potential to move into a more expanded form of consciousness on Earth. It was my imagination that had Melchizedek and Mother Mary appear, and it was even my imagination that on some deep level made Melchizedek eventually disappear. It was the language through which they and the deeper levels of my consciousness communicated with me. My imagination, which communicated to me not only though visual images but also through thoughts, feelings, emotions, colours, scents, sounds, and sensations of higher levels of consciousness became a source of nourishment that filled me with joy. Equally, when I focused it on creating images built out of my anxieties, my resentments or my rage, it would keep me caught in loops of frustration or fear for days. It was entirely my choice where I focused my imagination. After I met Melchizedek, I began a practice of centring on either his energy or on Mother Mary's every day. They taught me through my imagination, through experiences that were not happening in the physical world. They showed me through examples how to be more than my little self. They guided me towards the Soul-Self by showing me first through images of them and then through dissolving into a quality in the very air I breathed how to navigate towards something less illusory than Robyn. I had thought that my physical form was real, and my imagination was illusory, only to experience through my imagination that they are both illusory. However, my imagination was one step closer to being real in that it was the language that linked me to the Soul-Self. My imagination's limit was that it couldn't take me beyond my sensory experience; it could get me to the doorway of the Soul-Self and then it too, like Melchizedek, would have to drop away.

In the meantime, in my imagination, Mother Mary was seated in a field in the sunshine. She hadn't entirely disappeared with Melchizedek. It looked like she was meditating, she was so still. I could hear crickets, small finches chirping and the breeze rustling through the grass seeds. My feet were bare, and the grass felt slightly damp, as if it had been raining earlier in the day. A few tiny white butterflies were clinging to the grass, and as I walked towards Mother Mary, they lifted off and circled me, exposing violet-blue-grey upper wings. The place had a timeless feel, as ancient as the earth beneath my feet. Mother Mary smiled at me as if she had been there forever too—as if being there forever was some kind of secret. She gestured for me to sit down in front of her. There were bees flying around her head, gathering pollen or nectar from the aura of gold surrounding her. She closed her eyes, and I sank down and relaxed into her soft, feminine presence. Time slowed to a near stop. It felt like my atoms had slowed their spinning, as if there was no need to breathe here, and I could see the space between the particles of my cellular networks. A fluid substance of love, both magical and rosy, flowed into the spaces. I felt the cells of my body plumping with contentment. The nectar she exuded nourished my molecular structure. I wanted to stay there with her, to always feel this much at home. "You too can be like me in this lifetime,' she said with her eyes rather than her mouth. I heard her words with my heart rather than with my ears. In this eternal valley I could see that even though this message was coming to me, she clearly meant "you" as a plural. 'Your humanity in the twenty-first century can be like me in this lifetime'. The liminal lands had expanded my perception of what each of us was capable of creating. Mother Mary showed me through the felt experience of her within my body that it was possible for us to mirror her energy. Likewise, I became aware that we could choose where to place our intention. Liminal awareness had expanded the vastness of the potential available to each of us in each moment. I realised that I, along with everybody else, had a choice about whether we wanted to either resonate at a frequency that was light and expanded or to remain as contracted, limited beings.

Even though people in every era in history presumably felt that they were special in some way, the difference today is the surge in computer-driven information which has opened up our collective consciousness to new ways of thinking. This is compounded by the fragile state of our planet, which is demanding that we find new solutions in order to survive. The opportunity to shift belongs to this liminal space between worlds, this land of the imagination. The opportunity is like a Gateway that has only recently opened to more than just the few mystics and psychotics who had played or gone mad in these fields before.

BEYOND ILLUSION

The potential to be like Mother Mary in this lifetime was magnificent yet slightly misleading from the level of my Soul-Self. I knew that my imagination was illusory; my everyday life was illusory; my dreams were illusory, and the Liminal Lands and the Bardo that I might perhaps move into after I left my body were all part of a dream that I had created. From the perspective of Absolute Truth, I was neither Mother Mary, my dreams nor my everyday sense of Robyn as a separate being. However, the path of letting go of Robyn's sometimes constricted and judgemental perspectives of her reality, was assisted through expanding my awareness through Mother Mary's wisdom or the wisdom of my dreams. They were like pointers along the way towards Truth. So I followed the guidance I was given with gratitude. And the easiest way for me to intercept this guidance was to resonate with her wisdom by feeling her energy inside me. This felt like breathing in her compassionate heart, having it expand my own heart so that I became the dappled sunlight through the leaves, or the river meandering past me as I sat on its banks. When I dropped into an experience of becoming her and becoming the natural world around me, there was a strong link between the stillness and spaciousness of the clear light and the great noble heart of Mother Mary. They came together in a way that dissolved some of the ignorance and expanded my own sense of self towards something truer and more trustworthy. And in that truth, I recognised that I was responsible for my world. It became abundantly clear that the way I perceived the world influenced the way I experienced it.

I remembered being infuriated by the man who nicked my handbag as I was climbing into my car in a parking lot in Gaborone in Botswana. I felt personally invaded and ran after him in the parking lot, yelling after him, to no avail. And yet in comparison, I was utterly filled with peace when two silent robbers, clothed in black balaclavas, black gloves, and black tracksuits broke into my cottage at three in the morning in Cape Town, where break-ins can be extremely violent. Those guys pushed me around a bit, took whatever valuables they could find, and then left ten minutes later. I wasn't sure why I had had such different experiences, as the two encounters were similar in terms of material dispossession. Although the break-in was more intense and potentially more life-threatening, this was not how I experienced it. I felt as calm and peaceful as Mother Mary herself. I slept like a baby after they left, fixed my jimmied door lock the following day and then carried on with life.

There seemed to be two ways to address the illusory quality of everything that had always seemed real to me. The one was to use imagination to create an illusion that was more expansive and integrated than the one I was currently experiencing. This use of imagination could govern whether I chose to relate to the robbers with fear or peacefulness, and it could help me to become Mother Mary and the slow, rhythmic pulse of the Earth. The other was to move beyond the illusion of my worlds altogether, into the clear luminosity of the *prajna paramita* or the mystery beyond the knowing of my mind and perceptions. I felt like I might understand this better once I had arrived at the Seventh Gateway at the crown of my head, as I didn't feel I had a proper grip on the experience of *prajna paramita* yet. Mostly though, I felt that being like Mother Mary full-time was an impossible ideal.

 Not at all' she said with a smile, *all you need to do is to let go of whatever is stopping you from being like me. Begin by listening to your own pain. Listen to your pleasures and your ability to play, listen to the story of your own life.'*

I breathed deeply into that advice. I remembered how Kate-Louise listened, not with her ears but with her hands, and how when I listened deeply, I used not only my outer ears, but also my inner ones. To listen as deeply as Mother Mary suggested, I had to become the rock or tree I was listening to, or the story a client was telling me about their experience of sexual abuse or become Mother Mary in all her extraordinary grace.

And then I turned to face the Seventh Gateway so that I could move beyond imagination towards the mystery that was free of identifying as Robyn and her separate self.

THE SEVENTH GATEWAY:
AWAKENING THE SOUL-SELF

The obstacle: Identification as the separate self

Questions to ask: What is my little self resisting? Who am I? Where are the obstacles to being true in my life? Can I take responsibility for it all? What am I grateful for? What do I need to do to learn how to play?

In many mystical traditions, there is a description of a void-like state, or a falling away of the known and moving into the unknowable, which happens before one can experience any kind of Awakening. My first tiny taste of touching the unknown happened in an unravelling. In the early 1990s, I was driving home after picking up the kids at school. They were still quite small, and I was feeling as wobbly and unsure of myself as Alice did when she fell through the rabbit hole. I didn't know what was happening to my world; all I knew was that my solid, reliable sense of being Robyn driving a solid and reliable car along a very sturdy tarmac road was dissolving. It left me shaky and vulnerable, and that night at supper, I had to leave the table in tears to phone Kittisaro. He was my go-to person for spiritual breakdowns, as Thanissara was for mental and emotional ones. 'I feel like the bottom is falling out of my world,' I gulped. The ground beneath my feet literally felt like it was giving way. The earth was not solid; it was unreliable. And having the solid ground beneath me morph into something pliant and ill-defined made me feel as if I was on some kind of bad drug trip. Kittisaro said my experience was a good sign and perfectly ordinary. Once I was reassured, the world slowly stabilized again. I was never absolutely convinced if the world stabilizing was a good thing because if my material world had entirely given way, it would have allowed me no choice but to surrender into an experience of being so much more than Robyn as a separate self; however, I, Robyn, was terrified of that and was immensely grateful to retain my sense of a separate self at the time.

With my experience of my reliable and down-to-earth life as a mother of three kids who ran a craft centre in Botswana venturing into unfamiliar territory, my definitions of life had to rapidly expand beyond my limited concept of them. I was used to time marching steadily forward from one day to the next. I expected space to be dependable, and the ground to be solid. But over the years since that first time of unravelling, bit by bit, my time had become more elastic, and my spatial perception was turned inside out. When I moved to Stellenbosch many years later, I experienced being the early morning birdsong, or on a different day I might not know whether the fires raging in the skies above my home with their smoke that caught and constricted my throat were inside or outside me. I knew that the arsonists from the informal settlements were having a wild time because the southeaster had been pumping up to gale force that past summer. South Africa sometimes feels like a keg of gunpowder waiting for a match to ignite it, and the arsonists, for reasons ranging from political activism to anarchists on crystal meth looking for distractions, hold some of the matches. From my perception as Robyn, the fires and the smoke added extra carbon to the air and extra heat to the ground. It was January, so of course it was hot, but Stellenbosch was hotter than usual, perhaps because of the drought, and in the meantime, the sun was sucking the dams drier daily. The fires matched the simmering anger burbling in the hearts of so many residents. Their patience had burned as dry as their homes made of wire and bits of wood and garbage bags that flapped and tore apart in the incessant wind. For hundreds of years, poverty and the daily grind had forced the rage under wraps, but the fires sparked by the angry few were waking up a dormant shadow in the townships that was becoming hard to contain. It was more frightening for those in whose hearts it was smouldering than it was for me watching from the mountainside, but part of me wasn't just watching from the mountainside anymore. In the heart of the communities, the flames were fierce, hot, and frighteningly angry and somehow, I couldn't separate myself from them as easily as I had in the past. This was paradoxically both easier and more difficult to deal with. More difficult because I could no longer simply pretend it didn't exist and easier because I was not as emotionally entangled as I would have once been. As I became aware that I was intricately interwoven and energetically dispersed into the life force essence that permeated every one of us, so I also expanded beyond the constricted expressions of anger, fear, and repressed emotions. I could feel them, but I was also beyond them. They had less of a direct personal impact on me.

MERGED WITH MELCHIZEDEK-ME

I felt the Soul-Self through every tree, fence post, or person that I passed because my experience was of being absolutely still within, whilst outside everything moved towards me to meet me. It felt like being in a movie where the camera is in the car and it seems that the scenery is flowing past the car rather than the other way around. It was a dance of pure Presence where the trees, the fence-posts, and I became the movement flowing together, choreographed by a Divine creator who directed the movement within which Robyn was merely an integral part.

Melchizedek as a trustworthy aspect of Grace and Divine Wisdom had already dissolved into me. This internal manifestation of Grace changed my perception. The Grace was none other than the Oneness that belonged to us all in our deepest nature. It was indivisible, incomprehensible, unconditionally loving, and changeless—always there because it was beyond time and space and beyond form. Melchizedek was no longer speaking to me, but Melchizedek-me was becoming stronger daily. My internal compass produced this guidance for my pathway forward:

 As you stand connected between Shambhala and Earth, the light of Shambhala and the love of Earth join to create a glow within you. It becomes apparent that the Earth's mystery and ancient knowing are nothing but a reflection of your own self. You and the Mother are One.
As one being, you are no longer willing or able to hurt her. The love she feels for you, her daughters and her sons, is the love she feels for herself, and it is the love you feel for yourself. There is no difference. Come home through this Gateway of Awakening, see who you truly are, and recall that your journey through separation is part of a cycle of merging individuation and Oneness.

Integrating your individuated self with the power of Oneness shifts your level of consciousness to a place where you can work on a collective level. In your world, you influence one another and blindly carry one another's collective beliefs. Yet you also have the individual power to shape those beliefs on a collective level.

As you trust your inter-connection, your perspective adjusts to a point where you no longer choose to harm the collective. In this place of integrating the individual, the collective and Oneness, all the pain of humanity is felt. A broader perspective can hold it all simultaneously with love and care.

Melchizedek had felt like my special secret. He was unique to me; he had felt like my own creation of all that was pure and sacred, like my highest potential. Yet from the perspective of Melchizedek-me, he was very clearly the same highest potential that existed and was readily available to everyone. He was present in his different unique way to my friend Justine, who was the Best Listener in the World and who flowed into her highest potential by simply being present to other people's stories in other people's-lives. When Justine did that she glowed with a trust-worthy gentleness, and her smile reassured me that everything was okay. He was present in Peterson, the security guard at the gate of the farm, who bounced beaming out of his *hokkie* every time I drove in or out of the farm. Every day he taught me a new word in Xhosa, which I forgot within sixty seconds of turning into the traffic. Peterson bounced out to greet me even in the weeks after his brother was killed in a gang fight.

Besides Justine and Peterson, Melchizedek was the gold that flowed through the veins of every person on the planet, even the man who killed Peterson's brother, although some people's gold might be very deeply hidden and mining for it would take some heavy machinery. Nevertheless, the gold was always there, even in these times when we were tumbling into chaos, when presidents were building walls to separate us, and nu-clear armaments hung over our heads; in these dark times, paradoxically, the veils were getting thinner. Viktor Frankl, Nazi concentration camp survivor, spoke of how the horrors of the Holocaust also brought out the best in some people. At work, when guiding someone through a Soul Integration session to connect to their highest potential, what twenty years ago took someone twelve hours now took most people choosing to do the work only two or three.

Melchizedek-me was getting more fluent, almost chatty, and had this to say as a more practical guide to integration:

Do not imprison your soul by suppressing it into a bottle of depression. Do not entangle your soul by expressing it in the wild and thorny excitement of excess. Release your soul to expand into the reality of its own true nature where it can dissolve into Oneness. You are not seven billion people living in one world. You are living in seven billion separate worlds, which are all a magnificent expression of the Soul-Self experiencing itself, where each of you is nothing and everything at the same time.

LIGHTENING UP

I as Robyn could recognise the concept of Oneness intellectually. I knew that I was made up of atoms and quarks and even the Higgs boson particles of God, and that these were the same atoms and quarks and God particles that were in leaves and plants and earth and other beings. I recognised that there were vast dimensions of being beyond this earthly one. I recognised that this existence was as illusory as my dreams and that I created it. I recognised that life after death was not an automatic wake up from the illusion.

And I also recognised that the single thing that was keeping me caught in this 'dream', that was keeping me from realising my Soul-Self, was my identification with Robyn as a separate self, with feelings, a physical body and an intellect. The problem wasn't Robyn herself, or her body or feelings or thoughts; it was my identification with them to the exclusion of everything I had understood as 'not me', that was the problem. Robyn was a beautiful vehicle for experiencing this wonderful journey of life, but I was so much more than Robyn. It was as if Robyn was simply a channel through which life flowed. She flavoured life with particular tastes, smells, nuances and ideas, but I had never been Robyn. I was the life force that flowed through her. And there was no difference between this life force and the life force of the Universe. If I tried to capture and contain this life force by separating it out into Robyn and not Robyn, I became tight, dense, and hardened.

I was acutely aware of the value of being simultaneously both the flavour of Robyn with all her beautiful imperfections and the essence of Robyn, which could not be separated from life itself.

There were so many layers to this understanding, however, and I didn't understand them all. I might feel myself dissolving in meditation through the *kundalini* energy into the *prana* that belonged to it all. I might feel this energy as an infinite capacity of awareness that included all the hearts of every sentient being on the planet, but although Robyn might have disappeared, the energy was still being perceived. I knew that there were states beyond perception and that those would have to go into the next book, perhaps written in another life, if at all. For now, I focused on touch-tapping the flavour of the Soul-Self, and then integrating that into the unreal dream world of Robyn as a separate self.

212

I drove down to Llandudno beach in Cape Town and sat on one of the massive boulders jutting out into the ocean. They spoke to me quietly as I watched the sun go down over the sea:

Return your life to the Radiance pinning you to the boulder as the sea froths and crashes the question, 'Who Am I when I no longer exist?' The seaweed churns and heaves its reply, and the rock glistens crazy, salted wisdom.

I sat back and looked at the whole story of Robyn that I had created, just as we all create our stories. It was as impermanent as history, which was nothing more than His Story, as ephemeral as the Mystery that was expressed through My Story. In creating the story of my life, I had to be careful what I wished for. In my creation, there was nothing more worthwhile than becoming One with the Soul-Self, but for that to happen, everything had to go. It was unconditional. I couldn't say, "I will become One with the Soul-Self, but will take along my toothbrush, or take along the dream of a fantastic job or lover that I long for or take along my resentment at my ex-best friend that I'm just not ready to relinquish quite yet." All of it had to go.

Open-hearted, tender, raw, move beneath the pain into deep belly life. Sink deeply into form, arrive at emptiness. Sink into emptiness, become the form.

Melchizedek-me continued with an explanation:

Trust your divinity. The Unknowable is within the 'ten thousand things'. God manifests through your refractions as you filter the Unknowable. Each of your limitations is exposed so you can perceive the denseness or lightness of your filters.

However, despite being home, I had a vague, nagging feeling that there was more to Melchizedek's disappearance than simply finding my own light within. I had a hazy recollection of something he had once said about everything having to go. I had a look back through my journals where I had written down his messages and found the place where he was talking about looking at the world through the eyes of an infant. He had said: *In letting go of everything, you can have anything.*

Now he had left me to find my own way to the Soul-Self. Since the Soul-Self is everything and nothing, I could take nothing along. Even he had had to go.

I looked at what I might still be holding onto or resisting strongly and dropped them into a fire that was burning in the centre of my body and streaming out into infinite space. It was the fire that Melchizedek had become. I threw my relationships with my children into this internal fire. They were grown by now, all in their thirties, but it was one of the hardest things I had ever done. I surrendered to the Soul-Self any longing I had for them to be one way or another, or for me to protect them and keep them safe from themselves or the world. I surrendered them with the trust that they knew what was best for themselves. I surrendered them the way Melchizedek surrendered me when he merged with the Soul-Self—with absolute love. I was not sure if I could have done this if they were still children, even though I knew that there would still be a Robyn person doing human things and taking care of the mundane necessities as long as there was a Robyn body.

I threw into the fire my dreams and aspirations: for this book, for my training programmes, for the projects I was involved in. With those went the sense of myself as a professional, as a colleague, as a teacher, a mother, and a grandmother, as a member of society.

I threw self-judgement and judgement of others into the fire. I tossed my concerns about what other people might think of me into the fire. They kept popping out, and I had to keep on throwing them back in again.

For the next few weeks, I continued throwing things into the fire. I cast in my feelings of inadequacy and triteness. Sometimes I tried to grab them out again.

I threw my judgements of others into this vast fire. I threw my judgement of humanity for messing up our beautiful Earth, my judgement of murderers and paedophiles and, most especially, people who hurt others simply because they were unconscious of their actions. This was not as difficult as I expected it to be. I already knew intuitively that every action had karmic repercussions, so I wasn't letting them off the hook entirely. But I understood that it wasn't necessary for Robyn to act as the judge. They were perfectly capable of judging themselves as the Universe reflected their actions back to them one way or another. This didn't mean I shouldn't speak out from a place of truth, or that I shouldn't take appropriate action where necessary. It was the critical and condemnatory aspect of myself that I threw into the fire that day.

PLAY

I had a vague, tingling knowing in my marrow that play was the highest form of spirituality available to me. Other people might express their highest forms of consciousness in different ways, but this was mine.

I loved the direction this tingling could point me towards. Initially I thought play was conventional play, which I expressed best through dance, so I signed myself up for an energetic weekend-long dance workshop and tore an intercostal muscle between the ribs that were protecting my heart. It hurt to breathe and to move, and a deep, sore sadness welled up through the torn space. My whole life felt tearful, and play felt like something forced and unnatural. I eventually fell through the cloak of soft, velvety sadness into a place where the torn muscle linked itself around my rib cage to a place beneath my shoulder blade. It opened up old, rigid patterns that were filled with an ancient rage beneath the sadness. I felt like I had inherited this dark vortex of rage from a long, ancestral line of Scottish women who had borne their lot in life with forbearance and a lack of protest. These women did not play. Rage unwound itself from beneath my shoulder blade and exited through tense shoulder muscles and a spasm in my jaw. Underneath this hidden aspect of myself that had tried so hard to be perfect, play showed up as life itself. It wasn't about dance, or about sexuality, or about relationships, I realised, although play was about all those things too. Play was soft and tentative, like a baby. Years ago, Melchizedek had described this to me:

Can you listen with the sensitivity of a baby who attends to the sounds of the world at ease? he had said. *Can you feel with the sensitivity of a child who has not yet closed her heart to the demands and the gifts of the world? Can you taste a banana with the fascination of an infant, who can still smell its rich warmth, sunshine and moisture, who can*

215

squish its softness between pudgy fingers, who can lick its
tiny seeds and salivate over its velvet smoothness?

Play was a way of being. Play was an expression of the Mystery and the Soul-Self in individuated form. I had learned that as I became more still internally, I was able to weather the harshness of the world differently. The stillness was simpler, and I was less rigid. I met the world more fluidly, and like seaweed swaying to allow the currents to flow past harmlessly, I became more open to embracing what was before me.

Play sounded so delightful, like flowing through soft glades on fairy wings swept aloft by Tinkerbell's tinkling bell anklets and Peter Pan's giggles. Melchizedek had told me early on that my task in this lifetime was to learn how to play. However, one of the problems was how little I really knew about this. I had been okay at playing when it involved partying and drinking too much, but once I gave that up, I became overly serious. Learning to play was by far the most difficult thing I almost never did. Mostly I continued to work very hard: attending births, seeing clients, writing a book about birth, implementing the Compassionate Birth Project, until finally, twelve years after his suggestion, I took the need to play seriously.

I seldom saw play in the international grown-up world of busyness and business as usual. But I had seen it elsewhere. Many Tibetan lamas I had met had an irrepressible gaiety about them that was infectious and inspiring, especially since their playfulness had survived the tremendous hardships many of them had experienced escaping over the Himalayas from occupied Tibet.

And when I lived on the farm in the Kalahari Desert in Botswana in the early 1980s, the Bushmen who came and went on the farm had a very similar ability to play. They were employed to work on the farm, but they sometimes dissolved back into the desert, sometimes even on the day before payday, because it called them, and they were still hunter-gatherers in their souls.

Unless they were confronted with a life and death situation, almost every circumstance was amusing to the Bushmen in one way or another. When the going got tough, their giggles got louder. When farmers berated them, they mimicked them among peals of laughter. When two men, during a massive argument, threw one another's purchases off the back of the farm truck that was driving the two hours back home from the local village, everyone found it hilarious, and the following morning that particular fight had been resolved because they had both walked back together through most of the night to retrieve their slightly banged-about goods. They found their own imperfections amusing and had the same tolerance for one another.

Stuff, material stuff, belonged to everyone equally, and play seemed to arise out of this sense of sharing. The community on the farm shared everything. The dress that I gifted to Bau was an example. It was a pretty dress, three-quarter-length on me, but ankle-length on her—an early 1980s, straight-out-of-art-school, pretty hippie dress. Bau loved it and had a party that night to celebrate her prettiness. We could hear the singing and dancing carrying on until pre-dawn. The following day she looked shredded and worn out, and the dress had moved on to her friend. Every day it was passed from pretty woman to pretty woman. It became a pretty tatty dress and in less than two weeks, having worn out all its temporary owners, it was itself worn out and shredded. And then it passed out of the community on the farm, perhaps beyond the farms out into the wild expanse of the Central Kalahari to go hunter-gathering, or perhaps into a new incarnation in a new community as cloths for headbands or for carrying babies.

Another aspect of play among the Bushmen was the warmth, friendship and love they mostly shared with their small families of seldom more than two children per couple. Their lives were tough; they could carry what they owned on their backs, alcoholism was a problem, poverty was rife in the larger community and members of the group sometimes bickered or fought with one another, but the children were carried close and everybody sang, danced, shared stories together and belly laughed more than any group of people I've been among before or since that long-ago time.

Their playful attitude towards life seemed to emerge from a close connection to their gods, and from being so attuned to nature that they could intuit animal movements and weather patterns. Play was about being in tune. It was about *wu wei* or effortless effort. Most of the Bushmen on the farm could hear vehicles from twenty-five to thirty kilometres away (which took forty minutes to arrive on those sandy, desert roads), and they would know who was coming to visit by the sound of the trucks. They would play games to see who was correct, and Charlie and I once took the sand bike out into the bush and hid behind an anthill for ninety minutes because they had recognised the approaching truck as one belonging to the boring *dominee*[22] from Namibia, coming to see if he could save our souls. Undeterred, the *dominee* proceeded to settle his uninvited self into our cottage for the night, and eventually we had to go home to have our souls saved because we were hungry.

Another thing I discovered about play was that if I wanted to learn how to do it, I had to invoke the Mystery, which was more palpable when I allowed Mother Mary's energy to infuse mine.

When I tapped into the Mystery of Play, I felt more tender towards life, and life felt softer, although it was me in fact that was softer. Mystery initially seemed like it would be difficult to access because it was unknown and difficult to define. But it was utterly simple. It took me back to Presence, and to the settled, harmonious quality of Melchizedek and Mother Mary. Mystery in its earthly expression was tangible through the senses, but it had to be sensed with the silent, immensely intuitive attunement of the San hunter-gatherers in the Kalahari. I recognised that if I knew it all, the experimentation would fall away, and the Mystery would be lost. Not knowing it all was the most wonderful gift.

When I felt anxious or concerned, I could turn my attention back to the Mystery, and the anxiety would dissolve into a playful puddle of sometimes muddy, sometimes crystal clear, splish-splashing delight where nothing had changed except my attitude.

The difference was particularly tangible to me as a facilitator at training courses for pregnant parents, medical students, midwives, or student doulas. When I was anxious about my teaching style, it immediately reflected back to me from everyone in the room. However, when I tuned into the Mystery and allowed it to teach through me, the training courses were fun. Dirk would have far preferred to spend his weekend tinkering with his motorbike and going on a breakfast run with his buddies than attending an antenatal course with his pregnant wife, particularly because in the course I practised meditation with the attendees and encouraged them to look into their feelings and focus on how they could create sacred spaces for supporting their children through birth. I felt daunted by

22 Preacher in Afrikaans

his resistance, and then I let it go and instead breathed quietly into the Mystery, whereupon interacting with Dirk became a real pleasure, and I could resonate with his lack of enthusiasm. After all, motorbikes were way more interesting to him than a foetus in a womb that didn't belong to him, or a woo-woo group of people playing the kind of light and love games that he and his buddies probably joked about over their beers.

I'm not sure what happened, but I think it was the eye-gazing exercise he did with his partner that finally captured his attention and turned his resistance into genuine enquiry and interest. It turned out that Dirk was an amazing guy, refreshingly honest, perceptive, and highly intelligent. And he really got the concept of the Mystery. He described how he experienced it when biking at exceptionally high speeds, preferably with a couple of beers under his belt so that the world flowed by effortlessly. Despite the recklessness of that, I could feel how the experience was as thrilling as an extreme sport for him, which is really just another way of getting close to God.

And then there was play as play, like playing with my food or playing with my friends, all of which became lighter when the Mystery interwove it. There was also playing with expanding into the Liminal Lands, tapping into the mystery there and feeling it anchoring subtly into a collective consciousness. When I was aligned with this level of consciousness, my responses were more appropriate in every situation.

Surrender into playfulness didn't have to be an esoteric, other-dimensional experience. One day, I recognized that familiar uneasy, anxious feeling going on in my solar plexus and belly, and I knew I had been grinding my teeth the previous night. The moment I let go into the soft play of energy beneath it all, the anxiety disappeared, except for a vague residue of sadness that I didn't stay consciously aware of my God-self all the time. Then I focused on Mother Mary, and she indicated that I needed to garden, and then rest and then go play with friends. I felt that I needed to do my admin, get back on my computer, answer all those emails, see what was happening in the world, and worry about it in case it helped.

I decided to follow Mother Mary's advice. A good few hours later, and I had dug a garden bed in soil that was soft after the rains. I had planted seeds of spinach, Chinese cabbage and a white ground-cover called Alyssum. I had noticed that most of my worry was not even about me, which must have energetically created some heavy baggage for the person I had been worrying about. By the time I had finished gardening, the mellow winter sun had disappeared behind my mountain, leaving golden rays trailing behind it, the lemons were glowing, the dogs were sleeping on the small patch of lawn, and one of the pigs was determinedly slurping up my newly planted beds. There was no arguing with Mephista the pig, as she was at least double my weight and had double my determination. In a sensibly uncontested argument, she would be the winner. Since getting out into the garden to play, I felt centered again, and it was easy for me to surrender into a peaceful response to Mephista's view that these were not garden beds created as womb homes for spinach and cabbage, they were exceptionally comfortable, smoothed over and caringly tended beds for her. I let go of any last vestige of frustration at Mephista and figured that in time it'd be a great idea to create a Mephista barricade around my next attempt at veggie gardening. I turned back towards Mother Mary, with a long outbreath of relief at the release of resistance that came through simply playing.

Mother Mary was pure presence. But she was no longer as I expected her to be either. Merged with Mother Mary, I expected to be soft and flexible, flowing with the currents of life, without resistance. But instead, I was only fluid on the outside. My boundaries were more fluid, my responses were more fluid, yet my core was as strong and unyielding as a great rock the size of Uluru, the massive sandstone monolith in Australia: It was paradoxically strong and unyielding because it was also as still, soft and as sweet as Mother Mary. This core strength didn't want to get up and do battle with Mephista. It was a strength that emerged from becoming bigger than my narrow perspective, which usually wanted things to go the way that suited Robyn best.

The mud and confusion settled when I looked out at my surroundings through Mother Mary's eyes. The luminosity was an experience, not a concept. I became the dappled sunlight through the leaves and the breeze gently stirring in my hair. The breeze whispered to me in breeze language.

WINGS

I was visiting Warsaw last year, a place where Mother Mary was very present. After a long day of seeing clients, my host had taken two of us out for a 'surprise gift'. The gift was Johanna, who sang to us in her tiny Warsaw apartment for half an hour in a voice so powerful it blew me apart. As we came to the end of our own personal *a capella* concert, she decided to gift us one last song. It was the 'Ave Maria', and it hit my heart so hard that I burst into tears. I was not quite sure what had happened that day. However, Melchizedek-me interpreted the feeling:

 Let the denseness of your material world dissolve into a connection between heart and spirit. Symbolically, this reflection grows wings on your back. These wings connect your beating heart beneath your shoulder blades to your Spirit that is your own individualised God form. Let them grow large and powerful. They protect you. They connect you. They bind Heaven to Earth. Do not underestimate your magnificence. You become the Gateway through which other beings may pass.

I looked for the wings on my back and realised that the impact with her during the 'Ave Maria' had punched them all the way through my shoulder blades into a wide-open extension as if I had been a butterfly emerging from a chrysalis. It wasn't that unusual or special; all of us have wings. But in the collision with her, she knocked me into recollecting that we all had them. We were all intimately connected to a more profound reality, and the wings symbolised the bridge from here to beyond, beneath, between. All we had to do was remove the limitations that blindfolded us and kept our wings furled tight.

I used tenderness to keep my wings open. As someone who was still imperfectly trundling through lifetimes, I needed wings and a higher perspective to anchor wisdom and love into my earthly existence. In doing so I became a bridge between Heaven and Earth and I could walk through the Gateways to Shambhala.

I then realised that we are also sometimes Gateways for one another and I remembered when I had assisted in opening a Gateway for my dad, who was terminally ill with cancer. He had been bedridden for a few months, at home with amazing hospice nurses who came and went at intervals.

Early in the morning, I was walking past his bedroom to brush my teeth in the bathroom when I heard this weird death rattle coming out of his throat. I rushed to his bedside. He was panting like he was running a marathon. His tongue was sticking out of his mouth, and his eyes were darting back and forth between two upper corners of the opposite wall, although whatever he was seeing was invisible to me. He looked extremely agitated. I had never seen him frightened before; he had always been the embodiment of 'calm in a crisis'. It scared me.

I observed my brain click through a very definite series of thoughts. One by one. Almost in slow motion.

'Dad's dying'.

'Get help; he mustn't die'.

'But he's been suffering for so long with the cancer, and he's been in so much pain'.

'Find Bob' (my step-mum).

'No, stay with him; he needs you.'

This last thought penetrated my midwife instincts, and I reached forward, my hand on his dry, papery arm. 'You can do this, Dad. I'm with you. You can let go. It's okay. You can do this.' It was like being with a woman in labour. My own breathing became sure and calm, although I could still feel my heart pumping wildly. I had two people in one body: Melchizedek-me's calm presence and Robyn-me's primal, fearful one.

Mother Mary was also present. She is the one who sits at the end of the bed of those who are leaving their bodies. She looks over the shoulders of those who are heaving and labouring to bring new souls into being. She whispers to those who listen deeply enough; she tells us that we who journey to embrace the travails and dark passions of life on Earth are the Brave Hearts.

It only took a few moments. Dad turned to me, looked directly into my eyes, although he was still very far away, and relaxed in a slump. He sank back into the bed in surrender. Peace pervaded the room. His breathing slowed to a whisper.

I breathed with him, breathed in this peace he had created, awestruck by his beauty. Then I got up and went next door to find Bob to tell her he was dying. I waited outside the room for five minutes as she said goodbye, then I came back in again, and the three of us sat together quietly for another five minutes while he slipped away, breath by imperceptible breath.

There was nothing to mourn when Dad died, and I never missed him, although I expected to for months afterwards. I had grieved for my mum for years, but there was something so complete in Dad's passing that when he let go, I let go with him. I had to surrender my clinging to help him yield to the transition of death, and when I did so, he healed me and completed our relationship in the most profound way.

It had become a seamless whole; my interior world and my everyday life had blended into a larger reality where, as I was walking down the path, I felt that that Melchizedek was the walker and Mother Mary blew the cool mountain air stirring in my hair right through my heart. This heart was her heart. The cool air blew it open enough so that moment by moment, no matter what happened in the world, it had the capacity to be present with great tenderness and compassion. Back home, I expanded beyond the limited everyday world of traffic and telephones, emails and diesel fumes, so that the sound of the neighbour's parrot outside my window, squawking an imitation of my landlady instructing her children to get in the car right now, became an integral part of the experience.

LETTING GO OF IDENTIFICATION
AS THE SEPARATE SELF

Before early morning meditation on a retreat in Groot Marico near the Botswana border, I wandered up the hill to a place that had been designated for a temple sometime in the future.

The bushes and pale grasses moved past me, breathing in and out to the slow rhythm of the Earth. From a rock on the top of the hill, I looked over rolling vistas turned white-green from the recent rains, the colour of fresh sage in the early morning air. Acacia scrub and low trees dotted the landscape; low, gentle clouds floated above me; soft rays of sunlight broke through them from the east, and a small gap in the clouds above the western horizon revealed a milky blue sky. The colours were all pastel, nothing like the radiant golds of the Heavenly realms.

And yet it was clear that searching for Shambhala in the Heavenly realms was not the answer. Melchizedek had advised me at the beginning of this journey to start and end with finding myself. I looked, and there was nothing there. The Soul-Self was beyond me, within me, without me; it incorporated the perfume of the Heavenly realms and the ever-present flies. Shambhala, through the Soul-Self, was nothing more than the details of my everyday life.

223

I wandered back down the hill. In meditation that morning, the pathway to dissolving the obstacles in all of the Gateways developed a luminous clarity. I sat unmoving for an hour and a half because I was watching the experience. After about an hour, my tailbone felt bruised and sore from the long period of contact with my meditation cushion. Having been on retreat before where I had experienced that kind of discomfort building into a screaming monster that mimicked the pain of childbirth in its intensity, I observed the pain to see how it related to the obstacles in each of the Gateways.

I looked first at the obstacle of distraction and simply stayed with the pain. I welcomed it with focused awareness, and slowly my sense of Presence grew large enough to contain it.

I looked at the obstacle of contracting my body away from the pain, and I welcomed that too by opening my metaphorical arms to embrace it. The Prana or internal energy began flowing easily through my body as waves of warmth.

I looked at my aversion to the pain and at the conflict it was creating within me. I welcomed even the resistance and fighting of the pain. My sense of self was growing to make space for all these obstacles. I experienced a sense of the power that was humble, quiet, and calm.

I looked at the obstacle of fear that the pain would be here till the end of the meditation and that I had no idea how long that would be. I recognised a very definite fear around the length of time in front of me, and I melted into that. Love for the whole experience arose as the fear dissolved. I could feel myself becoming one with the cushion, the floor, the people sitting in front of me and to my sides.

I looked at the obstacle of untruth and dissolved any stories I wanted to create to make this better. A sense of integrity and wholeness began to arise.

I looked for obstacles of ignorance where I might have been projecting veils of illusion onto the direct experience of my painful bum on the cushion, and by this stage, I was also experiencing similar aches in my shoulders and my right knee. I expected to experience it as tremendous pain, but strangely it wasn't pain any longer, just intense experience held in a very spacious, open awareness.

I looked for the obstacle of separation, where I might have been trying to disconnect, to be anywhere but here. It, too, dissolved into the spaciousness that felt like Melchizedek's powerful light, and like Mother Mary's patient listening to a pain that by now had quite simply disappeared.

Aah, but this was bliss. If I had tried to stay with this bliss, it might have created another type of suffering arising from clinging to wonderful experiences. But it felt like easy come, easy go. It amused me to recognise that Shambhala was nothing more than a pain in the bum.

I turned to the powerful light energy and felt how it expanded into infinite space. My eyes were open, but there was no sense of belonging to the body of Robyn that was experiencing the sensations of bliss. The other bodies in the room were equally part of the spaciousness. The energy of the spaciousness was as present in the centre of the earth as it was in the room, or on the other side of the planet. This was a Truer Self. It was easy for enough humans to tap into this energy to create a hundredth-monkey shift in the collective consciousness.

The tiny butterfly that was Robyn flapped its tiny butterfly wings, and without a shadow of a doubt there was a thunderclap on the other side of the ocean.

The Seven Gateways were all facets of one Gateway, with Presence as its foundation.

Free-flow of *prana* no longer belonged to this body. It was as wide as the atmosphere, as deep as the earth's core, and the perception of a spine for *prana* to knock through had dissolved into oceanic awareness.

True power did not belong to Robyn. The heart of Oneness belonged to multiple hearts, each connecting every sentient being in a great web of heart healing around the globe. One heart and many hearts dissolved into an empty spaciousness that still retained awareness of the Great Heart.

Will aligned with God was not constricting. It was simply *wu wei* or effortless effort.

Great luminous clarity was not only the awareness of the creaking roof and croaking frogs, but it was without form while it was within form. The clarity beneath and beyond and within form was the clarity of the stillness of the heart.

And in the clarity of the Great Heart, what was there to be separate from? Not the suffering, not the bliss, not physical discomfort. They were simply ephemeral manifestations of this dream that was me.

This awareness was the unchanging, infinite Universe of the Soul-Self. I had come home to myself.

Robyn might change her mind about this when the flies became bothersome, or if she got ill, angry or caught in the longing to keep her kids safe, but she could recognise the illusion and return to the spaciousness and simplicity of the Still Point. Gazing backward from this point of no constriction, it initially seemed as if the Gateways had merged to become one, but there were, in fact, no Gateways. They, too, were part of the illusion of this great cosmic movie show, designed to delight, frustrate and fascinate us as we played out the drama of consciousness's contraction and expansion.

Arriving home after the retreat, I sat on the *stoep*, looking at the mountain cliffs towering above me. The flies swirled lazily around. In the shantytown in the valley, there was an outbreak of gastroenteritis. Lots of children were sick. There were biting midges in the grass; I kept my feet tucked under me in the camping chair. The colours were a blend of all shades of green from pale to olive to bottle green; the rocks were orange-brown and a whitish grey. There were a few pink roses left on the bushes and one nasturtium flower.

Melchizedek and Mother Mary were both me: The vast, spacious clarity of Melchizedek, my once-upon-a-time lover, spiritual friend, guide, and Mother Mary, the soft and gentle being who listened to the sound of the world with gracious ease, offered me the potential to surrender to their wisdom in this lifetime.

Mother Mary-Melchizedek-me had a final message:

Do not reject your form altogether. The reflection of sunlight off leaves and clouds and dewdrops is rich and beautiful— it enlivens the 'ten thousand things'. Allow the light of God to reflect off you into the world of duality through participating fully in it. Embrace your body, thoughts, feelings, and perceptions. Stand on the earth without resistance to the experience. This will bring Heaven to Earth. You are here to reflect God, Beloved. This is the Return.

POSTSCRIPT

Two months later, I recognise how every experience that brought me closer to the Soul-Self was an experience of letting go of the illusion of Robyn. When I attuned to Zhoma, I lost my sense of being in charge. As a child, I became the apple-blossom and then the Henry Moore sculptures and the rock. I empathized with Rory as a colicky baby so deeply that my heart grew big and strong. I aligned with Mother Mary on a cellular level. I merged with Melchizedek.

Robyn didn't write much of this book. She had to get out of the way and let it be written through her. It was both easy and difficult; easy to surrender into the beauty of the experience of walking down the road and becoming the road flowing past me but difficult to let go of the distraction and constriction of my self, the conflict in my body heart and mind, the fear, the untruth, the ignorance of my deluded mind, and the identification as a separate self that powered up the illusion of Robyn.

The Universe is none other than each and every one of us, if only we have the sense to bow down in gratitude and allow it to flow through us.

Having arrived at the end of writing this book expecting that it should have brought me to a happily-ever-after, like good books sometimes do, I find that, in fact, I do not know it all, and within the Soul-Self, the little Robyn still gets distracted, is unknowingly ignorant and plays power games. I had always secretly longed to be the very best Know-It-All. It was a role I had attempted with some minor success in the past. And yet, I've now come full circle to discover that here I am, back at the first obstacle of distraction. I'm not any kind of spiritual guru and, in fact, it seems to me that I know less than when I started the journey. This satisfying cosmic joke fills me with a vaguely ironical delight. The little me knows only this: when life flows through her, her most appropriate response is to surrender to the flow with humility, humour, love and as much truthfulness as she can muster.

I am sitting in the sandpit with my grandson Benicio, who is dribbling sand through his fingertips into my sneakers. I need to remember to mention to Rory and Pame that the sand seems to smell very faintly of cat pee. The sun warms my back; a gecko blinks on the vibracrete wall; Abi, the Border collie, nuzzles us both. Melchizedek-Mother Mary-Me whispers quietly, 'just this much.' And the final resolution becomes perfectly clear: 'just this much' is enough.

MEDITATION
GUIDE

MY SHORT INTRODUCTION TO MEDITATION

What follows is my take on a few meditation techniques that I have used over the years. It is not necessary, nor wise, to want to excel at all of them. Different techniques suit different personalities. Choose one or two that you are drawn to, and preferably find a teacher close by, who can guide you further in that technique.

Do not be put off by my biases; I have the greatest respect for people who count their breaths, even though my own brain doesn't have a natural inclination towards breath counting.

Meditation is often seen as synonymous with mindfulness these days. Mindfulness is the practice of being present to what is occurring in each moment of our lives with openness, curiosity and a willingness to be present without resistance. I have seen it used with excellent results, both for individuals who are seeking more awareness, and also in institutions like schools, hospitals, prisons, and corporations.

However, the real purpose of meditation is more powerful than that. The Dalai Lama describes its purpose as seeing your "natural state of your consciousness". The root purpose of meditation in all the different traditions is to clear the way to a deeper understanding of the Soul-Self. Different as they are in other aspects, no matter whether the schools of meditation are Buddhist, Christian, Islamic or secular, they all seem to understand and practice similar paths of progression for meditation techniques, from focused meditation to calm abiding meditation, in order to finally develop the wisdom that arises when we let go of the limitations of our constricted and disconnected perspectives.

Samadhi meditation within the Buddhist tradition, is a practice of focused attention. The intention is to develop concentration, as practised through mindfulness and staying in the present moment or by counting the breaths, among other techniques.

Shamatha meditation practice develops stillness and a calm abiding, which arises after the obstacles of mental distraction have been dissolved. The purpose is to tune into the natural wisdom that reveals itself within that calmer state. This is rather like trying to find clarity in a deep, still pool of water once the mud has settled, compared to looking for clarity within murky water. This still point is the point of it all, and it only

231

became truly valuable when I found it in the middle of my daily life.

There are many meditation techniques that focus on the attainment of Samadhi, although it has the potential to be misinterpreted as a way to escape from our lives into some bliss-filled haven of peace. But that is not its purpose. When I began meditating, I spent years using the techniques of Samadhi to remove myself from the chaos of my life, from my wounded, painful self, and from taking responsibility for any of it. It was very tempting to use spirituality to bypass the difficulties of my life or the chaos of the world.

In Thailand, there's a name for elderly monks who have reached a certain level of attainment and sit happily in that still place without engaging in the world and without any real spiritual focus or direction. Sort of vegetating there. They are called 'Little old apples'. While I can relate to the attraction of that, it is a very definite cul-de-sac.

Vipassana means 'insight meditation'. The intention is to discover insights into the true nature of being. Insights occur more readily from a calm abiding state of perception because it is generally wiser than ordinary, everyday consciousness.

Buddhists describe the subtlest of these insights as *prajna paramita*—*pra* means 'before', and *jna* means 'knowing' or 'gnosis', and joined together, they mean profound knowledge or the root of knowledge that comes before intellectual knowing. *Paramita* means 'gone beyond'. Therefore *prajna paramita* means using direct experiential understanding or knowing to discover that which is beyond our knowing. This sounds like a paradox—a bit like using my mind to understand the mind or seeing my head from inside my head.

DEVELOPING CONCENTRATION OR SAMADHI

Presence: Meditation techniques for developing Presence can either focus on an object like the breath or can be more open-ended. A powerful example of the open, non-focused meditation technique is called *Shikantaza* in the Japanese Soto tradition. It literally means 'nothing but (*shikan*) precisely (*da*) sitting (*za*)'. In other words, simply sitting without the 'support' of something particular to focus on, which makes it quite a slippery technique to master. More commonly, meditation focuses on a particular object, such as the breath, or sounds, or sensations.

Watching or counting the breath: This method requires focusing on the nostrils or lungs or belly and watching the flow of breath as it enters, circulates, and exits the body. The technique includes noticing each time the mind wanders and then returning over and over, in a non-judgemental way, to the breath. It sometimes includes counting the breaths from one to ten and returning to one every time the mind wanders or returning to one at the end of a cycle. Most people seldom get past three or four counts unless they are so distracted that they are unaware of how unaware they have become. I seldom got past two. The technique seems to appeal to organised people who like structure. To many people, it can be the fast track to enlightenment. To me, although counting my breath never got much beyond a boring pathway to hell, it was a teacher of discipline and the value of staying with a process.

Mindful awareness: The word 'mindfulness' is a translation of the Pali word sati, which is defined as an active form of non-judgemental, non-discursive attention. This very popular technique becomes powerful when we apply mindful awareness to everyday life, all the time, and not just to times of meditation.

Thich Nhat Hanh, a Vietnamese Buddhist monk living in France and the US, teaches beautiful mindfulness retreats, which are focused more on daily activity like walking, talking, eating, and playing rather than on extensive periods of sitting meditation. As Jon Kabat Zinn, founder of the mindfulness movement, said in his book of the same name, 'Wherever you go, there you are.' Mindfulness techniques use one-pointed focus to develop awareness, after which they encourage practitioners to use this awareness in every moment, not only during periods of meditation. I find mindfulness to be the best practice for integrating meditation into my everyday life.

DEVELOPING SHAMATTA OR EQUANIMITY

These techniques work more effectively after developing a degree of one-pointed focus. It took me many years to learn that Shamatta was an experience on the path, not a goal. When I used Shamatta as an endpoint, I was usually trying to escape from my earthy, mucky, sometimes traumatic, sometimes delicious, sometimes boring daily life.

Deep-breathing meditation: One of the easiest ways to release tension is to breath all the way down into the belly. When I was relaxed and at peace, my internal rhythm slowed, and my breathing became deep, slow, and even. I began to resonate with the more profound pulse of my soul-self. When I breathed deeply, my diaphragm relaxed, and my solar plexus area shed pent-up tension.

Allowing my breath to deepen and slow was simple because my breathing was always there. It was a tool I could pick up in the traffic, in a meeting or a supermarket queue. When that bored, irritated voice came to visit (the one that said, 'Argh, I've got such an important, busy life, when is this ridiculous traffic light going to change?' or 'Why won't that stupid woman get off her phone and pay the teller so that this queue can move forward already'), coming back to deep breathing in my belly calmed me down in the way that meeting an old, easy-going friend might have done.

Breathing more deeply as a practice tricked my body into thinking it was relaxed, and as a result, I did settle quite naturally into that calmer place where insights and grace had the opportunity to visit. In later years, coming back to my breath was a sure way to tune into Melchizedek's energy, and when I did that, my whole body softened.

Focusing on sensations in the body: This technique combines emotional, physical and energetic awareness within the body. It is useful when there are strong areas of physical and emotional discomfort that are too distracting unless they become the point of focus for the meditation. All emotions are experienced in the body; therefore, we can use body awareness to notice our emotional states and then stay with them as sensations in our bodies, no matter how distressing they are. I found it useful, when my body and mind were quiet enough, to notice the flow of my life force as a sensation or a tingling, electrical charge. I learned that it was possible to focus on sensations in my body and through that to develop an awareness of the deeper streams of energy that belonged to the flow of my life force. My body was the way I connected best with this life force.

Focusing the body sensations on the heart: The heart is a soft and often painfully constricted centre in the body, so this technique centres awareness on how we are feeling in our heart centres, on noticing what emotions are held there and then staying with those. I found the technique was softer, more delicious and therefore easier for me to maintain as a practice than watching my breath. Watching my breath sometimes required will to pull it off effectively, whereas focusing on my heart brought up emotions that were more interesting to me. But I was also more easily distracted. Working with my heart opened me up to the shadows hidden in the darkest corners.

Metta or 'Loving Kindness' meditation involves sending love, first to oneself, then to those close to you, thereafter to people who are more challenging, and finally outwards into the world at large.

Bhakti yoga, or the devotional practice of loving God, belongs to heart-focused meditation. After I began working with him, my adoration of Melchizedek was devotional, and so devotional practice was a big focus of my meditations.

Focusing on a mantra: Sound is a powerful tool for centring attention. We can use it to combine listening with the vibrational resonance of the sound and then to connect those to the meaning or intention of the mantra or chant. A mantra is a word or phrase or poem that is repeated as a chant or song until it induces a sense of calm, present-moment awareness. Mantras are used in Buddhist, Christian, Islamic, and Judaic traditions and in many indigenous spiritual or religious practises. The mantras can be powerful in their language of origin even if we don't know their exact meaning.

Singing and chanting created a resonating chamber in my belly. It was through singing that I learned to eventually speak my truth and become less afraid of the power of my voice. Two of my meditation teachers, Thanissara and Kittisaro, sing beautifully, and chanting precedes and completes many of their meditation sessions, encasing each in a space of settling and reverence for what is here and now. At Thich Nhat Hanh retreats I attended, the monastics and retreat participants sang at intervals through the day. The singing was very pure, and it opened my heart to a reassuring hopefulness. Hare Krishna devotees singing *kirtan*, born-again

Christians singing Gospel songs, or monks chanting in deep booming voices seemed to mostly be quite happy groups of people getting high on spiritual song.

When I lived in the Central Kalahari semi-desert in Botswana for three years, we were sometimes invited to Bushman trance dances. We would all sit around the fire in a circle, clapping and chanting, while the dancers formed an inner circle between us and the fire, where they fell into deep meditation, clapping, stomping, and singing. They moved in a mesmerising rhythm that included the depth of the night sky, the vivid desert stars, the gods, and their tribe's animal totems, which they brought to life through enacting them in their trance states.

Visualisation of deities: In my work I know that active imagination is the language of the soul. Through visualising powerful beings that held wisdom beyond the usual limited capacity of my daily interactions, I learned to tap into a deeper level of compassion or wisdom within myself. There are many powerful Tibetan techniques that work with visualisation of many different deities; both fierce and loving ones. For my own practice, I used the technique of visualisation, combined with heart-centred meditation, to develop a stronger sense of connection to Mother Mary and to Melchizedek after they arrived in my life.

The devotional practice of having an imagined deity figure to whom I prayed, and whom I integrated into the felt sense in my body, increased my trust in my potential enormously. Deities, or imagined figures of Divinity, acted as intermediaries for me to experience Oneness. They were visual enough for me to trust. They gave me a reliable image to soften into, so I could let go of some of my armouring. I could imagine deity figures, angels, or gurus and feel their energy in my heart. Thereafter, I could take difficult and trying experiences and surrender them to the deity to take care of. It was a wonderful method for helping me to let go because I could only let go if I trusted enough. It could seem counter-intuitive to trust in something that I had made up, but it was not. These deity figures had to be experienced through my imagination. Through this process, I gradually experienced them as a felt sense that was solid and trustworthy.

INSIGHT OR VIPASSANA
Insight techniques include the following:

Koans are paradoxical questions that can't be answered through logic or the intellect, such as 'What is the sound of one hand clapping?' or 'If a tree falls in a forest and no one hears it, has it fallen?' Their purpose is to take the practitioner beyond the mind. The only way to crack or solve a koan is to understand it viscerally as an experience, instead of as a concept. Even though a question might seem abstruse, it points us to engaging with our own lives as we do the koan; we question the life that we are living. Koan work uses the mind to move beyond the mind, which I found was a bit like pulling myself up by the bootlaces. It was fun, it was challenging, and it broke down many of my preconceived notions.

Who Am I? This powerful technique involves stripping away everything that isn't 'me' in order to discover the Absolute beneath all the masks. I know people who used this technique to move directly to advanced states of awakening, beyond my understanding of it. I am not my body, my mind, my feelings, my thoughts, my soul or spirit. If anything about 'Who I Am' is subject to change, then it isn't 'Who I Am' at its core. Therefore, 'I Am' is indefinable because if I can pin it down by describing it, it would have an opposite that it is not; it would be subject to change, and it wouldn't be the Absolute.

I can highly recommend this type of meditation, but since it is so direct, it doesn't come with allowances for scenic routes, which has often been the path I have taken, but is obviously not the speediest one.

Walking meditation: This is nothing more than sitting meditation in action. I can use any of the Samadhi or Shamatta techniques and apply them to walking (and by extension to eating, driving, typing on the computer....). One walking technique similar to counting breaths is to move so very slowly. That. I. Lift. Each. Foot. While. Noting. It. Lifting. It. Moving. It. Placing. It. Until. My. Head. Explodes. From. Boredom. Which no doubt removes some ego preconceptions. Or I can walk in an immersion of dissolving Robyn into the landscape and becoming the grasses.

ACKNOWLEDGEMENTS
Without the guidance of the archetypal beings guiding me home to my Soul Self, there would be no story that is worth my while to tell. My search for truth has been guided by a wisdom that leaves me awe-struck, with head bowed, whispering 'Thank you' as the only meaningful prayer.

Thanks must also go to my spiritual teachers in human form. There have been many of them, but those to whom I am most grateful are Kittisaro, Thanissara, Thich Nhat Hanh, Kaira Jewel Lingo, Norma Milanovich, and Donal Creedon.

I thank Margaret Diehl for the extraordinary care and insight she brought to editing the manuscript, and Maurice Sweeney for his clarity and perception in further editing, for his encouragement and for the long hours he spent doing all the work it takes to get a book from manuscript form to you, the reader.

I owe much gratitude to both Anne Hoefinghoff for all the time she so generously spent on the cover design, and to Peter Van Straten for the beautiful painting that drapes itself around the book.

I appreciate my friends Justine Evans, Rose Meran and Susan Schuurmans for their insightful feedback and for holding my back. Ben Wise and Marina Evans also gave me valuable input during the years I spent writing the book.

Lastly, I'd like to thank Rorx, Maf, Nix, Pame, Cano and Beni for requiring that I get down-to-earth-real about practising what I preach, which is a whole lot harder, messier and more entertaining than writing about spiritual insights.

Disclaimer
While many of the concepts expressed in this book came from time-honoured lineages, often Buddhist and occasionally from Christian, Islamic and Taoist mystical traditions, they were filtered through my own experiences into the thought-forms expressed herein. These were my personal reflections on what I experienced to be the truth as one more practitioner on the path.

22955252R00154

Printed in Great Britain
by Amazon